Criminology, Conflict Resolution and Restorative Justice

Criminology, Conflict Resolution and Restorative Justice

Edited by

Kieran McEvoy
Professor of Law and Transitional Justice, Queen's University, Belfast

and

Tim Newburn
Professor of Social Policy, London School of Economics, UK

First published 2003 by
PALGRAVE MACMILLAN
Houndmills, Basingstoke, Hampshire RG21 6XS and
175 Fifth Avenue, New York, N.Y. 10010
Companies and representatives throughout the world

PALGRAVE MACMILLAN is the global academic imprint of the Palgrave
Macmillan division of St. Martin's Press, LLC and of Palgrave Macmillan Ltd.
Macmillan® is a registered trademark in the United States, United Kingdom
and other countries. Palgrave is a registered trademark in the European
Union and other countries.

ISBN 0–333–76145–6

This book is printed on paper suitable for recycling and made from fully
managed and sustained forest sources.

A catalogue record for this book is available from the British Library.

Library of Congress Cataloging-in-Publication Data
Criminology, conflict resolution and restorative justice/edited by Kieran
McEvoy and Tim Newburn.
      p. cm.
      Includes bibliographical references and index.
      ISBN 0–333–76145–6
      1. Restorative justice. 2. Conflict management. 3. Criminology. I. McEvoy,
Kieran. II. Newburn, Tim.

HV8688.C75 2003
345'.001–dc21   2002044813

10   9   8   7   6   5   4   3   2   1
12 11 10 09 08 07 06 05 04 03

Printed and bound in Great Britain by
Antony Rowe Ltd, Chippenham and Eastbourne

This book is dedicated to Alice Plunkett, a true unsung hero, and to the memory of Beryl Moorhouse

Contents

List of Contributors   x

Acknowledgements   xi

1 Criminology, Conflict Resolution and Restorative Justice   1
Kieran McEvoy and Tim Newburn

  Criminology and the relevance of conflict
    resolution literature   5
  The collection   10

2 Criminological Ideas and the South African Transition   21
Dirk van Zyl Smit

  Introduction   21
  Criminology in the time of crisis   22
  From resistance to proactive intervention   25
  Criminological ideas and the new South African state   31
  Constraints on change   34
  Prognoses   36
  Conclusion   40

3 Criminological Discourses in Northern Ireland:
   Conflict and Conflict Resolution   45
Kieran McEvoy and Graham Ellison

  Introduction   45
  Positivism and the Northern Ireland conflict   46
  Critical criminology and the Northern Ireland conflict   50
  Criminology and conflict resolution: lessons
    from Northern Ireland   57
  Conclusion: criminology, transition and memory   65

4 Conflict Prevention and the Human Rights
   Framework in Africa   83
Rachel Murray

  Introduction   83
  Human rights within the context of conflicts:
    the approach of the OAU   85

A conflict mechanism	86
Recent developments	87
The African Commission on Human and Peoples' Rights: conflict in the context of human rights?	88
An early warning mechanism for Africa?	89
Conclusion	92

5 Critiquing the Critics of Peacemaking Criminology: Some Rather Ambivalent Reflections on the Theory of 'Being Nice' 101
Jim Thomas, Julie Capps, James Carr, Tammie Evans, Wendy Lewin-Gladney, Deborah Jacobson, Chris Maier, Scott Moran and Sean Thompson

Introduction	101
What is peacemaking criminology?	103
Addressing the critics	106
The Marxian/radical syndrome	107
The functionalist syndrome	108
The conservative syndrome	109
The chaotic syndrome	110
The (in)credibility syndrome	114
Responding to critics	115
The Marxian/radical syndrome (redux)	117
The Enlightenment background	118
Transcendent values	118
Human nature	119
The functionalist syndrome (redux)	122
The (in)credibility syndrome (redux)	123
Peacemaking as criminal justice praxis	125
Peacemaking as metaphor	129
Conclusion	130

6 A Restorative Framework for Community Justice Practice 135
Harry Mika and Howard Zehr

Restorative justice: a somewhat worrisome road	135
The devil is in the details: defining restorative justice	138
Principles of restorative justice	141
Crime is fundamentally a violation of people and interpersonal relationships	143
Violations create obligations and liabilities	143

Restorative justice seeks to heal and put right
   the wrongs   144
Restorative justice: signposts and the road ahead   145

**7 Cross-cultural Issues in Informal Juvenile Processes:
   Applying Urban Models to Rural Alaska Native Villages   153**
Lisa Rieger

Introduction   153
Teen, youth or peer courts   153
Theoretical perspectives on youth courts   154
Restorative justice in youth courts?   157
Who volunteers to be part of youth court?   157
Teen courts and recidivism   158
State and federal promotion of teen courts in Alaska   158
The Alaskan context   159
Traditional social control in Native villages   160
Options promoted by state government   161
Seeking a viable bush justice   165
Conclusion   167

**8 The Prospects for Restorative Youth Justice in
   England and Wales: A Tale of Two Acts   171**
Adam Crawford

Introduction   171
Background to the reforms   172
The legislation   176
Potential unintended consequences of referral orders   187
Potentially confused roles and responsibilities   192
Principal dynamics and future questions   194
Conclusion   201

**9 'I can't name any names but what's-his-face up the road
   will sort it out': Communities and Conflict Resolution   208**
Sandra Walklate

Introduction   208
Conflict resolution: some observations   209
Conflict resolution as making amends: the formal response   211
Conflict resolution as making amends: informal responses   212
Conclusion: trust, making amends and conflict resolution   219

Index   223

List of Contributors

Julie Capps, Northern Illinois University, USA

James Carr, Northern Illinois University, USA

Adam Crawford, Professor of Criminology and Criminal Justice, Centre for Criminal Justice Studies, University of Leeds, UK

Graham Ellison, Lecturer in Criminology, School of Law, Queen's University, Belfast, UK

Tammie Evans, Northern Illinois University, USA

Deborah Jacobson, Northern Illinois University, USA

Wendy Lewin-Gladney, Northern Illinois University, USA

Chris Maier, Northern Illinois University, USA

Kieran McEvoy, Professor of Law and Transitional Justice, Queen's University, Belfast, UK

Harry Mika, Visiting Professor of Sociology, School of Law, Queen's University, Belfast, UK

Scott Moran, Northern Illinois University, USA

Rachel Murray, Lecturer in Law, School of Law, Birkbeck, University of London, UK

Tim Newburn, Professor of Social Policy, London School of Economics, UK

Lisa Rieger, Associate Professor, Justice Center, University of Alaska, Anchorage, USA

Jim Thomas, Professor of Sociology, Northern Illinois University, USA

Sean Thompson, Northern Illinois University, USA

Dirk Van Zyl Smit, Professor, Institute of Criminology, University of Cape Town, South Africa and Professor of Comparative and International Penal Law, School of Law, University of Nottingham, UK

Sandra Walklate, Professor of Sociology, Manchester Metropolitan University, UK

Howard Zehr, Professor of Sociology and Restorative Justice, Eastern Mennonite University, Harrisonburg, Virginia, USA

Acknowledgements

We owe a considerable debt to a range of people who have assisted us along the way in putting this collection together. First we would like to thank our contributors to this volume for their patience with the long period which it has taken us to bring the project to fruition. We hope it has been worth the wait. Kieran McEvoy would also like to acknowledge the friendship and scholarly encouragement which he received from Henry Steiner, Peter Rosenblum and Eitan Felner while a Visting Fellow at Harvard Law School Human Rights Program (where his input to the book was finished), John Feerich at Fordham Law School, and Jim Jacobs and David Garland at New York University, where he conducted earlier research while a visiting scholar in the summer of 2001. He would also like to acknowledge the financial support of the British Academy, the Fulbright Commission and the Arts and Humanities Research Board, which funded various aspects of his research in the area. Ruth Jamieson, Brian Gormally, Stephen Livingstone, John Morison and Gordon Anthony also offered useful encouragement. As ever, Lesley's patience was formidable. Tim Newburn would like to acknowledge the friendship and support of erstwhile colleagues at Goldsmiths' College, London – particularly Frances Heidensohn, Geoff Pearson and Carole Keegan – and to current colleagues at the London School of Economics.

KIERAN McEVOY AND TIM NEWBURN
April 2003

1
Criminology, Conflict Resolution and Restorative Justice

Kieran McEvoy and Tim Newburn

As with many such projects, this book began in a series of conference conversations conducted over a number of years bemoaning our discipline's failure to address a common preoccupation. Its particular genesis was in discussions concerning what we perceived to be criminology's lack of substantive engagement with the processes of conflict resolution. Although, as is discussed below, our focus soon broadened – to include conflict resolution not just at the political level within states but also micro-conflict resolution between indigenous and metropolitan cultures, within and between justice systems, and within neighbourhoods – our deliberations began with the role of criminology in peace processes such as those pursued in South Africa and Northern Ireland.

In all such processes, the standard issues of criminology (policing, prisons, the criminal justice system, the treatment of victims and so forth) clearly remained central both during the respective conflicts and in the subsequent eras of conflict resolution and transition. Criminologists working in such jurisdictions were obviously engaged in research on such matters. However, we felt that greater effort was needed in attempting to link this criminological enterprise in a more systemic and theoretical fashion to the contours of conflict and the process of conflict resolution. If, as Gouldner (1973) suggested, *The New Criminology* succeeded in making criminology intellectually respectable by linking it to wider concerns of social theory, then to us it appeared that these events were too important (and too clearly within the disciplinary remit) for criminology not to have something more to say.

Paul Walton has argued that 'from a small marginal discipline in faculties of law and social science, criminology has emerged as an important and politically crucial discipline ... ' (Walton, 1998:4). We agree with that assertion. Yet central to the intellectual development and maturation of a legal/social science discipline is its willingness to encompass the analysis of phenomena which are themselves politically crucial. Writing in the wake of the terrorist attacks on the USA on 11 September 2001, it is all the clearer how important is the study and analysis of political conflict. Criminology, if it wishes to continue to be taken seriously, must contribute to such central debates in the new millennium. Indeed, as both Van Zyl Smit (with regard to South Africa) and McEvoy and Ellison in particular argue (with regard to Northern Ireland), the analytical frameworks and epistemological strengths of criminology offer a particularly grounded vantage point for the analysis of 'terrorism' and how to deal with it.

At the other end of the scale criminologists have, in recent years, shown increasing interest in the resolution of smaller-scale conflicts and what such techniques and processes might have to tell us about our formal systems of justice (both their limitations and how they might be reformed). Despite the relatively recent revival of interest, according to its major proponents 'restorative justice has been the dominant model of criminal justice throughout most of human history for all the world's peoples' (Braithwaite, 1998:323). It appears, to take one example, that during the time of the Roman Empire victims could select between civil and criminal proceedings. Non-judicial forms of dispute resolution took precedence over state-centred remedies. The shift towards state punishment (Lacey, 1988) was a gradual one, moving away from restorative approaches towards retributive models in which crime was treated as a matter of fealty to and felony against the monarch occurring simultaneously with the decline of feudalism (McAnany, 1978; Braithwaite, 2002). Reflecting on this trend in a now famous essay, Nils Christie (1977) commented on the way in which conflict had been appropriated. Criminal conflicts, he argued, have progressively either become other people's property, usually lawyers', or have been defined away by those in whose interest it is valuable to do so.

Christie suggested that criminology itself was complicit in this process and that 'maybe we should not have any criminology' (1977:1). The latter point, it should by now be clear, is not one with which we agree (and nor in practice, it appears, did Christie). Christie's starting-point was that conflicts are important and that industrialized societies, far from having too much conflict, actually have too little. In this he was following John Burton's rather more colourful analogy that conflict is like sex. It is pervasive, should be enjoyed and should occur with reasonable frequency. After it is over, people should feel better as a consequence (Burton, 1972). In this manner, Christie argued that 'conflicts ought to be used, not only left in erosion. And they ought to be used, and become useful, for those originally involved in the conflict' (1977:1). His view was that conflicts are scarcer than property and are immensely more valuable. They are valuable because they provide an opportunity for participation, an opportunity for the clarification of values and principles, and in the criminal justice setting, an opportunity for victims to gain a better grasp of their experience and reduce their anxiety through contact with the offender. In the current system 'the offender has lost the opportunity for participation in a personal confrontation of a very serious nature. He [*sic*] has lost the opportunity to receive a type of blame that it would be very difficult to neutralise' (1977:9).

Since the publication of Christie's essay a number of authors have sought both to develop more fully theorized versions of non-retributive forms of justice and to promote practical experiments. One of the authors in this volume, Howard Zehr, was among the first to develop an 'alternative justice paradigm' in which it was proposed that victims should play a much more central role and offenders should assume greater responsibility for their actions and for repairing the harm caused (Zehr, 1985, 1990). Zehr's early work placed great emphasis on victim–offender mediation, and such ideas were particularly influential in the UK from the late 1980s onwards (Marshall and Merry, 1990; Wright, 1991; Umbreit, 1994). Criminal-justice-focused forms of mediation and conflict resolution have developed in numerous other directions since then, encompassing both theoretical developments such as 'reintegrative shaming' (Braithwaite, 1989) and 'responsive regulation' (Braithwaite, 2002), as well as practical advances such as 'family group conferencing' (Morris, Maxwell and Robertson, 1993; Morris and Maxwell, 2000), 'sentencing circles', and 'community justice' (Karp, 1998), and advances in business regulation (Ahmed et al., 2001).

It is at this point that work on large-scale conflict resolution and that on alternative justice begin to come together as restorative justice theorists have turned their attention to broader matters than the operation of the criminal justice system. For example, the South African Truth and Reconciliation Commission made specific reference to the concept of restorative justice and the related African notion of *ubuntu* (Truth and Reconciliation Commission, 1998).[1] Villa-Vicenzio (1999), one of the report's authors, has explicitly seen the 'amnesty' process under the TRC (whereby human rights violators were granted immunity from prosecution in return for truth telling) as an expression of the practical applicability of restorative values in a transitional context. Such an approach to restorative justice and conflict resolution has not been without its critics (e.g. see Leebaw, 2001). None the less, restorative justice has been linked with a wide variety of conflict resolution settings, including discussions concerning post-conflict 'truth' processes in the former Yugoslavia (Nikolic-Ristanovic, 2001) and East Timor (United Nations, 2001), the Gachacha arbitration hearings established in the wake of the massacres in Rwanda (ICRC, 2000), the setting up of the international criminal court (Popovski, 2000) and ongoing attempts at finding alternatives to paramilitary punishment violence in Northern Ireland (McEvoy and Mika, 2002).

At both the macro and the micro level, restorative justice theory and practice offer a template for addressing harms which fits broadly within the increasingly accepted requirements of transition from conflict (Teitel, 2000). A focus on reparation and healing of victims as opposed to retribution visited upon wrongdoers, hearings which are directed towards truth finding rather than adversarial contests, processes which emphasize community involvement and ownership rather than exclusive 'professional' stewardship – these and other features of restorative justice have become increasingly important as ways in which societies seek to emerge from violent and divisive political conflicts.

In perhaps the most far-reaching linkage of restorative justice to conflict resolution, Braithwaite has suggested that the restorative justice paradigm (when linked with work on responsive regulation) is useful 'for reconfiguring how to struggle for world peace' (2002:169). Entering a terrain normally reserved for political scientists and international relations theorists, Braithwaite argues that in light of the end of the cold war, wealthy, economically interdependent states tend to avoid going to war to resolve their differences with each other but rather engage in what he terms 'restorative diplomacy'. Drawing directly from the literature on business dispute regulation and resolution (discussed further below), he argues that they settle disputes through established techniques such as conciliation, mediation, conferences and summits. As developing nations become similarly economically integrated through the process of globalization, Braithwaite (2002:172–4) contends that this creates a more organized sense of 'an international civil society', a process which is directly analogous to the conditions necessary for effective restorative justice at the micro level. Braithwaite goes on to suggest that what he regards as the failings of traditional 'elite' diplomacy (e.g. President Carter's mediation between President Sadat and Prime Minister Begin at Camp David) can be met by 'the democratised peacemaking that is restorative justice'. Modern peacemaking, he argues, must go beyond the notion of top-down deals cut at the negotiating tables to 'restorative' processes where pragmatic accommodations are stretched to 'shame' violence, move away from retribution, promote the protection of human rights, engender greater communal ownership of the settlement and ensure that all is framed in the generous language of idealism, peace and justice rather than humiliation or victory for any of the protagonists.

While even some restorative justice advocates would balk at the scale of Braithwaite's ambitions, his attempt to draw out the theoretical and practical links between what has traditionally been viewed as the preserve of criminology and the broader process of resolving conflict is formidable. We admire and support that objective. For us, where criminology, conflict resolution and restorative justice meet offers a challenge to the traditional boundaries of the criminal justice process and to conventional, criminological definitions of conflict. The approaches outlined above seek a more holistic understanding of justice which attempts to overcome the long-standing separation of bureaucratic approaches on the one hand and those that place greater emphasis on emotions on the other. As Bazemore (1998:337) puts it, 'this focus implies a vision of justice as "transformative" as well as ameliorative or restorative'. The bottom line in such an approach is that it must involve meaningful forms of participation not only in 'justice' but, at least as importantly, in solving problems, resolving conflicts and rebuilding damaged relationships.

Criminology and the relevance of conflict resolution literature

While conflict resolution has been defined both broadly and narrowly, we have found the definition offered by Ho-Won Jeong most useful for our purposes.[2] As criminologists, our primary focus in this book is the intersection between law, criminal justice and social regulation on the one hand and the process of resolving conflict on the other. While not the only meeting point (see the chapters below on peacemaking criminology), restorative justice is one of the key criminological arenas in which such ideas coalesce. Bearing in mind that our gaze is primarily limited to matters criminological, we have chosen at this juncture to draw out particular elements of the conflict resolution literature which are relevant for our current purposes. As an academic discipline, conflict resolution has its origins within at least three distinct arenas: international relations and peace studies; alternative dispute resolution; and organizational development and management science

(Tidwell, 1998) – each of which can be directly linked to central criminological problematics.

It is within the field of international relations and peace studies that the phrase conflict resolution is perhaps most often encountered (Burton, 1986, 1987, 1997; Jeong, 1999). It emerged as a distinct discipline within the social sciences in the late 1950s in tandem with the growing realization that war, long seen as a staple form of relations between states, had become 'in a very real sense a threat to the survival of humanity' (Rapoport, 1999:vii). By the 1990s, with the demise of the cold war, the focus of the discipline had broadened considerably as scholars and activists recognized that the nature of conflicts had changed. For example, Wallensteen and Sollenberg (1997) note that of a total of 101 armed conflicts between 1989 and 1996, only six were inter-state conflicts. The vast majority were between different identity groups defined by racial, religious, ethnic, cultural, political or ideological terms (often a combination), and most such conflicts had a long history.

As the particular configurations of conflicts studied within international relations and peace studies have broadened, so too has the range of conceptual devices used to analyse both conflict and the processes required for its resolution. At least three key features may be drawn from this literature which are of particular relevance to the study of criminology and conflict resolution.

First, the notion of 'structural violence' (Galtung, 1975) in particular broadened the focus to an understanding of issues such as poverty and the denial of human rights as forms of violence often as harmful as physical violence itself. Thus, as Murray argues in her chapter below (Chapter 4) with regard to the prevention of political, social or ethnic conflict in Africa, conflict prevention cannot be divorced from the protection of basic human freedoms. More critical variations of this school (particularly those that focus upon gender, race and power relations) often offered the most sustained critiques of forms of conflict resolution such as mediation. These they saw as promoting a manipulative ideology of harmony, one which inevitably favours the dominant class or order (Lederach, 1989). While not all conflict resolution commentators would share that degree of cynicism, a critical attention to social structure has become a key element in more grounded conflict resolution theory (e.g. Dukes, 1996, 1999). Such a focus resonates strongly with a number of criminological intersections with conflict. For example, the chapter below on 'peacemaking criminology' by Thomas and colleagues (Chapter 5) is located firmly within this paradigm, arguing in essence that no honest attempts at peacemaking can be made which neglect to address the pernicious influence of a retribution-obsessed criminal justice complex.

Second, the concept of 'ripeness' in the conflict resolution literature appears to us to be of considerable academic usefulness (Aggestam, 1995; Mitchell, 1995; Lieberfeld, 1999). Simply put, this is a view that *timing* is all in resolving conflict, perhaps best summed up by the poet Seamus Heaney (with regard to the Irish peace process) as a juncture when 'hope and history rhyme'.[3] Conflicts may be ripe for conflict resolution at a particular time because of a complex interaction of political, ideological, social, cultural, individual personalities and other factors. A diminution in the legitimacy of the established order and a willingness realistically to address legitimacy deficiencies, pressures for resolution from outside and inside the parameter of the conflict, a viable alternative to armed struggle, individual political leaders willing to take risks and lead their constituencies – these and other factors have all played varying roles in the (apparently) more successful peace processes of recent times. Conversely, conflicts may be *unripe* for resolution, particularly when in the absence of the collapse of an (arguably) viable state system, those seeking to resolve conflict are hamstrung by 'political realities'.[4] 'Premature resolution' will tend to result in only temporary success (Deutsch, 1987). Both the chapters by McEvoy and Ellison (regarding Northern Ireland – Chapter 3) and Van Zyl Smit (South Africa – Chapter 2) are premised on the notion that these were conflicts which had 'ripened' to a greater or lesser extent at the political level. In addition, the process of conflict ripening in both jurisdictions meant that criminological actors and criminological discourses (on issues such as prisoner release, police and criminal justice reform etc.) were moved centre stage in respect of the overall conflict resolution process.

Third, the forms of conflict resolution themselves reflect important underlying tensions, in particular with regard to the role and legitimacy of the state. Rubinstein (1999) has characterized this will by suggesting that those seeking to resolve conflict fall into two broad camps, *technocratic* and *political*. *Technocrats* tend to accept as 'givens' existing legal, conflict management and other arrangements of the state infrastructure. Within such a framework, conflicting parties are assigned to negotiate their differences in state-sanctioned forums. *Politicals* on the other hand consider such dispute resolution as system maintenance. Theirs is a more ambitious project, not only to resolve individual disputes but also to assist in the creation of a political will designed to make structural changes possible. Thus, for example, a *technocratic* approach to the mechanisms of informal dispute resolution employed by high-crime communities described below by Sandra Walklate (Chapter 9) would fail to take full account of the centrality of local communities' lack of trust or faith in the state's capacity to 'deliver'. A *political* approach to such problems would not assume state legitimacy as axiomatic but would instead grasp that confidence in state mechanisms must be earned and informed by a much more realistic appraisal of the personal, organizational and community networks where trust and power actually lie in many such communities.

The overlapping sub-discipline of *alternative dispute resolution* (ADR) emerged in the USA in particular from the 1970s onwards in response to increased dissatisfaction with the capacity of the formal justice system to deal effectively with a range of conflicts (Goldberg, Frank and Rogers, 1992). Under the broad ADR umbrella, community mediation centres such as the San Francisco Community Boards (established in 1976), mechanisms for dealing with environmental disputes, family dispute resolution and mediation centres (some of which are centrally linked to the courts) have developed in the USA, Australia, New Zealand and elsewhere over the past three decades (Carpenter and Kennedy, 1988; Astor and Chinkin, 1992). As Mika and Zehr suggest below (Chapter 6), the current prominence of a range of contemporary restorative justice techniques can be traced in part to the ADR movement in the USA, and these are considered at some length below by Rieger and Crawford in their respective chapters on justice practices in Alaska Native villages and the British youth justice system (Chapters 7 and 8).

The final variant of conflict resolution literature is that drawn from management and business literature. Within management science, conflict was originally viewed as inefficiency, an unfortunate by-product of the workplace to be overcome by more efficient management strategies (Mouzellis, 1981). However, later, conflict came to be viewed not necessarily as a totally negative force within organizations but rather something that could be harnessed and directed through 'problem solving', thus improving overall organizational health (Blake and Mouton, 1964; Pascale, 1990; Scimecca, 1991). Most management theorists now view conflict resolution or problem solving as an intrinsic element of the managerial *process*. As Tidwell (1998) argues, many of the conceptual tools and practices currently utilized when discussing social or structural conflicts (such as mediation or arbitration) were mainstreamed by their promotion in labour relations contexts, albeit focused primarily on making conflict less costly and more efficient.

As noted above, Braithwaite (2002) has argued strongly that such practical techniques may be borrowed directly from the business and management world in order to underpin the application of 'restorative diplomacy' to the resolution of conflict. At the conceptual level, the centrality of a *processual* approach to conflict (a key characteristic of the managerial literature on the topic) is equally significant. Such an approach has led some commentators to refer to *conflict transformation* rather than *conflict resolution* when referring to protracted social or political conflicts (e.g. Rupensinghe, 1995). Transformation is inherently process-focused, a more open-ended and holistic approach to conflict. As Lederach (1995) has argued, conflict resolution connotes a bias towards 'ending a given crisis', whereas conflict transformation allows for a deeper and longer-term analysis of the ways in which conflict changes things both constructively and destructively. A focus on transformation concerns 'broader social structures, change and moving towards a social space open for cooperation, for more just relationships and for non-violent mechanisms for handling conflict' (Lederach, 1995:202).

For criminologists and lawyers who work on conflict, this process orientated attention to the nature of transformative or transitional justice has become a key concern (Osiel, 1997; Hayner, 2001; Mika, 2002). As McEvoy and Ellison argue in their chapter below (Chapter 3), the contours of post-conflict legal order with regard to decisions on whether or not to prosecute previous human rights abusers, instigate truth commissions, or release political prisoners; all of these issues both shape and are shaped by the nature of transition. This notion of a *process* of conflict transformation (rather than a definitive deal after which a conflict may be said to be resolved) more accurately captures the depth and complexity of change which follows intense social or political conflict. As Teitel has suggested, transitions may be conceptualized along a transformative continuum during which

> law is caught between the past and the future, between backward looking and forward looking, between retrospective and prospective, between the individual and the collective... Accordingly in transition, the ordinary intuitions and predicates about law do not apply. In dynamic periods of political flux, legal responses generate a sui generis paradigm of transformative law.
>
> (Teitel, 2000:6)

To recap, the conflict resolution literature echoes a number of central concerns and themes within the discipline of criminology. Our contributors do not (in the main) use the same language as conflict resolution specialists. This is hardly surprising, given that most see themselves as *criminologists* and *lawyers* rather than experts in *conflict resolution*. None the less we are struggling with very similar themes.

From the conflict resolution of international relations and peace studies we have drawn particular attention to the notions of structural violence, the centrality of the idea of timing or *ripeness* and the distinction between technocratic and political conflict resolution. All of these notions are centred around the key problematic of the state accepting its role and responsibility to resolve conflict as the defining characteristic of what a state *does*. The traditional Weberian notion of the state defined primarily by its monopoly on the use of force (Weber, 1966) – in effect to engage in *conflict making* – is matched here by an articulation of a parallel responsibility to accept its responsibility to engage in *conflict resolving*. Alternative dispute resolution (ADR) places the community at the front and centre in the process of dealing with conflict and is an important source for discussions concerning the utilization of restorative justice theory and practice in dealing with conflict. Business and management science, in particular with its emphasis on the processual nature of conflict resolution/transformation, resonates strongly with contemporary criminological discourses on transitional justice. While within our respective spheres conflict resolution specialists and criminologists have been talking about many of the same issues, we have often done so by speaking in different tongues.

The collection

Van Zyl Smit's chapter (Chapter 2) charts the complex patterns of criminology in the South African conflict and transition to democracy. He draws out the three central tenets of South African criminology. Afrikaner nationalist criminology provided an intellectual justificatory framework for the apartheid regime. Such criminology fed the state paranoia concerning the communist-inspired onslaught against South Africa and suggested, for example, that the wholesale exclusion of black communities might be justified on the grounds that their 'simpler' natures were better suited to a life removed from urban temptations. Legal reformist criminology, which had both conservative and liberal wings and was dominated by lawyers, focused largely on trying to make the system more humane and more effective. Dominated by a largely technicist framework, these lawyers, judges and civil servants produced research which focused largely upon the formal equality provided by the South African criminal law while at the same time protecting, or at least not undermining, the socio-political status quo of apartheid. The third tradition identified by Van Zyl Smit is critical criminology within South Africa, a broad church which exposed the legitimacy deficiencies of the criminal justice system and its structural links to the apartheid form of governance, and was committed to democratic change and criminological praxis at local community levels. Van Zyl Smit concludes by acknowledging that while much critical criminological thought has been mainstreamed by the transition to democracy, he remains sceptical as to whether its communitarian ideals will survive the demands of a society where high crime rates persist and an agreement remains to be reached on the values which must underpin the respective roles of the state and local communitarian initiatives.

McEvoy and Ellison (Chapter 3) take up the theme of criminology and political conflict resolution in the Northern Ireland context. Their discussion of criminological research during that conflict focuses on the two broad traditions of positivism and critical criminology, with legal reformism (sometimes uncomfortably) straddling both. They describe as positivistic those who engaged in the study of political violence as a largely security-driven endeavour designed better to understand and therefore either better manage or *defeat* the terrorists. Similarly they argue that other variants of criminology which focused on ordinary crime (which either *blamed* paramilitaries for a perceived breakdown in social order, argued that order was *retained* despite the men of violence or focused on ordinary crime while wilfully ignoring the effects of the conflict – a 'don't mention the war' criminology) may all be accurately described as positivist. They then consider a number of variants of critical criminology, including the response to the institutional sectarianism of the Stormont era and the mobilization of the civil rights campaign, the response to the government attempts at the criminalization of political violence from the mid-1970s onwards and the mainstreaming of critical criminological discourses (arguably to a lesser extent than in South Africa) in the period since the ceasefires. Drawing in particular from the critical criminological tradition, they argue that there are at least four major themes drawn from the criminology of conflict resolution that may be of relevance to the discipline more broadly. These are: criminology as a political project; criminology as a moral project; criminology as an international and comparative project; and finally, the interrelationship between criminology, human rights and conflict resolution. They conclude with some reflections on criminology, transition and the creation of public memory in a post-conflict society.

Rachel Murray (Chapter 4) continues the theme of exploring the relationship between conflict resolution and human rights discourses and frameworks. She argues that there is a dialectical relationship between human rights abuses and conflict whereby the former often lead to political, ethnic or social conflict whose outbreak often in turn leads to further human rights abuses. However, despite this clear interconnection, Murray argues that often the institutions established to monitor or prevent conflict are institutionally separated from those concerned with human rights violations. By way of example, she considers the respective roles of the Organization of African Unity (which has a specific mechanism designed to 'prevent, manage and resolve' conflict) and the African Commission on Human and Peoples' Rights which is tasked with enforcing the African Charter on Human and Peoples' Rights. She shows how, while both institutions have been engaged in the development of mechanisms to forewarn about events such as occurred in Rwanda in the 1990s, and have recognized the need for greater collaboration, the two frameworks remain quite distinct and are still some distance from the required *holistic* approach to conflict prevention.

In putting together this collection, we were conscious that an important sub-school within the discipline had for some time been wrestling with an approach to crime and criminal justice which was rooted firmly within a conflict framework, that is, peacemaking criminology. Jim Thomas and his colleagues (Chapter 5) offer a sympathetic but critically insightful reflection on the developments within peacemaking criminology over the past two decades or so. Tracing its origins to the criminological work which recognized crime as but one form of violence among many (including war, social and political structures, and other factors that suppress human potential), peacemaking criminology is described as an approach to crime and justice which focuses on universal social justice in order to eliminate other forms of interpersonal violence and harm. Thomas and colleagues address head on some of the criticisms levelled against peacemaking criminology, including the overarching charge that it is really a disparate body of thought focused on the theory that 'it's nice to be nice!'. More specifically, they organize these critiques into five broad thematic categories. These include the charges that peacemaking criminology: is incompatible with Marxist/radical theories; is theoretically akin to functionalism; is inherently conservative; reflects overwhelming intellectual chaos; and lacks intellectual or empirical credibility. Returning to the difficulties of definition, Thomas et al. suggest that peacemaking is perhaps best understood as a metaphor, a lens through which it is possible to reframe and suggest alternatives to existing responses to social offending and control.

Perhaps the best-known theoretical and practical development to emerge from the broad church of peacemaking criminology over the past ten to 15 years has been that within the field of restorative justice. Variants on the theme of restorative justice as conflict resolution take up our next three chapters in this collection.

Harry Mika and Howard Zehr's chapter (Chapter 6) offers an outline of restorative justice as a framework for community justice and conflict resolution at the local community level. As they discuss, while there is some debate as to whether restorative justice may be accurately described as a social movement, or a convergence of different progressive social and political movements, its current predominance as the 'flavour of the month' critique of conventional justice approaches is indisputable. Mika and Zehr caution that unless restorative justice is grounded in a series of properly articulated values and principles, there are real dangers that its potential will be subverted, in particular by its close working relationship with and (at least in some cases) dependence upon the conventional justice system. They suggest that there is a continuum of programme types which operate currently under the umbrella of a restorative framework, from the fully restorative to those that are incompatible with the theory and practice of restorative justice. In articulating their definition of restorative justice values and principles, Mika and Zehr suggest that all should be drawn from the two fundamental understandings, that is, that restorative justice is harm-focused, and that it promotes the engagement of an enlarged set of stakeholders. Their definition is composed of three major headings which include: the notion that crime as a violation of people and interpersonal relations; the idea that such violations impose obligations upon offenders and liabilities upon communities; and the view that justice practice within a restorative framework must be focused upon healing and putting right the wrongs created by the violation. Mika and Zehr go on to suggest that a restorative approach to conflict must not treat it as the product of the mistakes or weakness of individuals, but rather as a phenomenon which is social and relational in nature, extending the gaze to the role of community and the state and beyond the limited venue of crime and delinquency.

Lisa Rieger (Chapter 7) highlights the particular conflict which may be generated by the uneasy application of western models of youth justice to Alaskan Native villages in the area of juvenile justice. Rieger charts the attempts at introducing peer justice models developed in urban American settings (based upon restorative principles) to divert juveniles from the more formal juvenile court system. There is federal pressure to

extend these models to geographically remote villages where many justice services are unavailable. However, as Rieger cautions, the dissemination of a successful mechanism from one venue to another raises
significant questions of cultural appropriateness as well as political and
structural questions regarding the federal and state government's dicta-
tion of solutions and priorities for local communities. She argues that
this purported variation of 'restorative justice', using a western blueprint
for Native communities, presents an unusual twist where restorative
justice is often viewed as attempting to use indigenous peoples' conflict
resolution techniques transposed to a western context. Rieger's chapter
explores these questions in the context of the shifting boundaries of
legal culture in Alaskan Native communities and the difficult relationships between these communities and state and federal government,
which in turn highlight the more general conflicts between localized,
culturally sensitive justice and the state or national systems within
which they operate.

Adam Crawford (Chapter 8) explores similar restorative-justice-related
conflicts concerning the operation of the youth justice system in
England and Wales. He examines in particular the impact of two important youth justice reforms (the Crime and Disorder Act 1998 and the
Youth Justice and Criminal Evidence Act 1999) which he argues reflect
an eclectic approach by government to the integration of restorative justice into the youth justice system. He focuses on the introduction of
referral orders and youth offender panels, by the 1999 Act, which appear
to offer the most striking development in restorative justice in England
and Wales. Crawford suggests a number of tensions which may appear
within the justice system as a result of referral orders, including the
swamping of youth offending teams with overwork, resistance amongst
magistrates to the curtailment of sentencing discretion leading to
greater use of custody, the diminution in the participation of victims
and the risk of youth offender panels being overrun by lawyers and
becoming overly formalistic. He also points to the inherent strains
between the normative objectives of restorative justice (i.e. that it is
focused on the individuals, relational, reintegrative etc.) and managerial
(e.g. that it is efficient, cost-effective and produces measurable benefits).
Crawford goes on to criticize the potential for the Crime and Disorder
Act to widen the net through the criminalization of 'anti-social behaviour' and points to central concerns regarding the assumed homogene-
ity of the moral community encompassing authoritarian notions of
appropriate parenting and acceptable youthfulness. He concludes by
suggesting that the conflict in the application of restorative justice

provisions to the UK youth justice system reflects a broader tension concerning the respective responsibilities of the modern state regarding its crime control functions in an era when the limitations of the traditional criminal justice system are increasingly acknowledged.

The final chapter, by Sandra Walklate (Chapter 9), focuses on the resolution of conflict at a local neighbourhood level through community self-policing in high-crime areas in the United Kingdom. Based upon a two-and-a-half-year study, Walklate draws on the development of local community norms, values and practices which contribute to the process of dispute resolution in two distinct communities. In one, normative strictures against 'grassing', criminal gangs deemed an integral part of the community, a powerful but unnamed 'Mr Big' who will sort things out, public shaming through graffiti, physical violence – all of these intersect to create an informal hierarchy of making amends and contribute to a highly localized sense of justice. In the other community under examination, the absence of organized gangs actually contributed to a greater sense of insecurity (particularly among the elderly) where there were no working formal or informal means to allow for public making amends. Walklate goes on to argue that the sense of well-being which individuals construct in high-crime areas concerning the resolution of conflict is defined by a square of trust. The square of trust is made up of the state, the level of organization or disorganization of local crime, the level of organization or disorganization of the local community and the mechanisms for sociability within it. In one community, trust in the state (e.g. evidenced by grassing) was foresworn in favour of a reliance on more organized criminal gangs or better inter-community relations which could sort things out, thus creating better social solidarity. In the other, the lack of a parallel organized gang or community infrastructure led to a general trust in state officials to resolve conflict, but with little expectation that this might actually happen. Walklate concludes that if conflict resolution policies are to work, they need to be more realistically rooted in the localized mechanisms which sustain or threaten social regularity and in understanding the processes associated with the manifestation of trust at interpersonal, community and organizational levels.

Many themes link the contributions to this volume. Perhaps the most powerful is the positive approach taken by all the authors. This is not a subject that is held back by a sense of failure or, worse still, an attitude that 'nothing works'. The contributions stand in contrast, therefore, with the doom-laden pessimism of much criminology and the nihilistic impossibilism of the worst forms of postmodern theorizing. It is also an approach, or set of approaches, that combines criminology and a political project. This project implies something more complex than determining 'whose side are we on?' (Becker, 1967). The 'sociology of the underdog' is by no means entirely absent here, for it is clear from the essays that a key linking theme is the recovery of conflicts from the monopolistic clutches of the state and their return, at least in part, to their key actors. None the less, a broader normative concern with the nature and direction of social change, and the future of participation and democracy, is also evident. And yet, ironically, in some respects some of the barriers to such a project seem more powerful than ever. This is the paradox of late modernity. Though the gap between 'rich' and 'poor' is ever-widening, there appears to be little political will to mitigate, let alone reverse, such processes. Moreover, as several commentators have noted (*inter alia* Hirst and Thompson, 1999; Harvey, 2000), what now sets us apart is not simply the absence of such a project, but the appearance that such a project is impossible. In Roberto Unger's phrase, we appear currently to be 'torn between dreams that seem unrealizable and prospects that hardly seem to matter' (1987:331). What should our response be? At least part of the answer lies within the following quotation from Bauman (1999:8):

> We tend to be proud of what we perhaps should be ashamed of, of living in the 'post-ideological' or 'post-utopian' age, of not concerning ourselves with any coherent vision of the good society and of having traded off the worry about the public good for the freedom to pursue private satisfaction. And yet if we pause to think why that pursuit of happiness fails more often than not to bring about the results we hoped for, and why the bitter taste of insecurity makes the bliss less sweet than we had been told it would be – we won't get far without bringing back from exile ideas such as the public good, the good society, equity, justice and so on.

Bauman's view has important implications for the conduct of everyday life in general, and for politics in particular. It also has implications for how, for example, we 'do' criminology. His argument resonates with one recently offered by John Braithwaite (2000:87), who suggests that criminology is a 'dangerous discipline' because its disciples slide back and forth between legal positivism and critical moral relativism. His argument, it seems to us, is especially apt in relation to those contemporary analyses of crime control policy where criminology has come to be dominated by 'explanatory theory' (how the world is) at the expense of 'normative theory' (how the world should be). His argument is that what is required is a theorization of our current situation which integrates both the explanatory and the normative. It is incumbent upon us not only to attempt to explain how it is that we come to be where we are, but also to render explicit where we believe we should be. This is not a plea for the investigation of 'policy alternatives', important though they may be, but for a fuller, considered exploration of what we might still think of as the 'good society'. As Braithwaite (2000:88) puts it: 'without a broader social and political agenda, it is hard to see how to build a society with less crime and what place, if any, criminal law has in such a project'. It is within this context that the following chapters are best understood.

Notes

1. For a detailed discussion of the notion of *umbunto* and its link to restorative justice see Skelton (2002).
2. 'Conflict can be described as a contentious process of interpersonal or intergroup interactions that takes place within a larger social context. As sources of grievances are often associated with structural injustice, most serious conflicts encompass various types of social problems reflected in intergroup relations. Thus intergroup conflict is often imbedded in a political framework, and its meaning can be socially interpreted and constructed. ... Resolution of serious social conflicts means more than finding solutions to contentious issues. Enduring and mutually assured outcomes will not be attained without taking into account power imbalances and equitable social and economic relations. Self esteem and identity as well as physical well being are key elements to be considered in conflict resolution and peace building. The nature of relations between adversaries needs to be examined in terms of looking for transformative possibilities. In rebuilding communal relations, long term hostile relationships have to be overcome to prevent future occurrences of violent conflict' (Jeong, 1999:3).
3. History says, Don't hope
   On this side of the grave.
   But then, once in a lifetime
   The longed-for tidal wave
   Of justice can rise up,
   And hope and history rhyme.
   (S. Heaney, Excerpt from *The Cure at Troy*)
4. For example, in the generic criminological context, political realities such as the pervasiveness of retributive and actuarial responses to crime may appear to mitigate more progressive views being put forward by the political elites because the climate is not right (Taylor, 1999; Young, 1999; Garland, 2001).

References

Aggestam, K. (1995) 'Reframing International Conflicts: "Ripeness" in International Mediation', *Paradigms* 9 (2), 86–106.

Ahmed, E., J. Braithwaite, V. Braithwaite and N. Harris (2001) *Shame Management Through Reintegration*. Cambridge: Cambridge University Press.

Astor, H. and C. Chinkin (1992) *Dispute Resolution in Australia*. Sydney: Butterworths.

Bauman, Z. (1999) *In Search of Politics*. Cambridge: Polity.

Bazemore, G. (1998) 'The "Community" in Community Justice: Issues, Themes and Questions for the New Neighbourhood Sanctioning Models', in D.R. Karp (ed.) *Community Justice: An Emerging Field*. Lanham, MD: Rowman and Littlefield.

Becker, H. (1967) 'Whose side are we on?', *Social Problems* XIV, 239–47.

Blake, R. and J. Mouton (1964) *The Managerial Grid*. Houston, TX: Gulf Publishing.

Braithwaite, J. (1989) *Crime Shame and Reintegration*. Cambridge: Cambridge University Press.

Braithwaite, J. (1998) 'Restorative justice', in M. Tonry (ed.) *The Handbook of Crime and Punishment*. New York: Oxford University Press.

Braithwaite, J. (2000) 'Republican Theory and Crime Control', in S. Karstedt and K.-D. Bussmann (eds) *Social Dynamics of Crime and Control: New Theories for a World in Transition*. Oxford: Hart Publishing.

Braithwaite, J. (2002) *Restorative Justice and Responsive Regulation*. Oxford: Oxford University Press.

Burton, J. (1972) *World Society*. Cambridge: Cambridge University Press.

Burton, J. (1986) 'History of Conflict Resolution', in L. Paudlin (ed.) *World Encyclopedia of Peace*, Vol. 1. Oxford: Oxford University Press.

Burton, J. (1987) *Resolving Deep Rooted Conflict: A Handbook*. Lanham MD: University Press of America.

Burton, J. (1997) *Violence Explained: The Sources of Conflict, Violence and Crime and Their Prevention*. Manchester: Manchester University Press.

Carpenter, S. and W. Kennedy (1988) *Managing Public Disputes*. San Francisco: Jossey-Bass.

Christie, N. (1977) 'Conflicts as Property', *British Journal of Criminology* 17 (1), 1–15.

Deutsch, M. (1987) 'A Theoretical Perspective on Conflict and Conflict Resolution', in D.J.D. Sandole and I. Sandole-Staroste (eds) *Conflict Management and Problem-Solving*. London: Frances Pinter.

Dukes, E. (1996) *Resolving Public Conflict: Transforming Community and Governance*. Manchester: Manchester University Press.

Dukes, E. (1999) 'Structural Forces in Conflict and Conflict Resolution in Democratic Societies', in H. Jeong (ed.) *Conflict Resolution: Dynamics, Process and Structure*. Aldershot: Ashgate.

Galtung, J. (1975) *Essays in Peace Research*. Copenhagen: Cristian Ejlers.

Garland, D. (2001) *The Culture of Control: Crime and Social Order in Contemporary Society*. Oxford: Oxford University Press.

Goldberg, S., E. Frank and N. Rogers (1992) *Dispute Resolution*. Boston, MD: Little Brown and Co.

Gouldner, A. (1973) 'Foreword' in I. Taylor, P. Walton and J. Young (eds) *The New Criminology*. London: Routledge and Kegan Paul.

Harvey, D. (2000) *Spaces of Hope*. Edinburgh: Edinburgh University Press.

Hayner, P. (2001) *Unspeakable Truths: Confronting State Terror and Atrocity*. London: Routledge.

Heaney, S. (1991) *The Cure at Troy: A Version of Sophocles' Philoctetes*. New York: Noonday Press.

Hirst, P. and G. Thompson (1999) *Globalization in Question*. Cambridge: Polity Press.

ICRC (International Commission of the Red Cross) (2000) *Annual Report of the International Red Cross*. Geneva: ICRC.

Jeong, H. (ed.) (1999) *Conflict Resolution: Dynamics, Process and Structure*. Aldershot: Ashgate.

Karp, D.R. (ed.) (1998) *Community Justice: An Emerging Field*. Lanham, MD: Rowman and Littlefield.

Lacey, N. (1988) *State Punishment: Political Principles and Community Values*. London: Routledge.

Lederach, J.P. (1989) 'In Pursuit of Dialogue', *Conciliation Quarterly* 8 (3), 12–14.

Lederach, J.P. (1995) 'Conflict Transformation in Protracted Internal Conflicts: The Case for a Comprehensive Network', in K. Rupensinghe (ed.) *Conflict Transformation*. New York: St Martin's Press – now Palgrave Macmillan.

Leebaw, B. (2001) 'Restorative Justice for Political Transitions: Lessons from the South African Truth and Reconciliation Commission', *Contemporary Justice Review* 4 (3–4), 267–91.

Lieberfeld, D. (1999) 'Conflict "Ripeness" Revisited: The South African and Israel/Palestine Cases', *Negotiation Journal* 15 (1), 63–82.

Marshall, T. and S. Merry (1990) *Crime and Accountability: Victim/Offender Mediation in Practice*. London: HMSO.

McAnany, P. (1978) 'Restitution as Idea and Practice: The Retributive Prospect', in J. Hudson and B. Galaway (eds) *Offender Restitution in Theory and Action*. Lexington, MA: Lexington Books.

McEvoy, K. and H. Mika (2002) 'Restorative Justice and the Critique of Informalism in Northern Ireland', *British Journal of Criminology* 42 (3), 534–62.

Mika, H. (2002) 'Approaching Evaluation', in J.P. Lederach and J. Jenner (eds), *Into the Hurricane: A Handbook For International Peacebuilding*. San Francisco: Jossey-Bass.

Mitchell, C. (1995) 'The Right Moment: Notes on Four Models of "Ripeness"', *Paradigms* 9 (2), 38–52.

Morris, A. and G. Maxwell (2000) 'The Practice of Family Group Conferences in New Zealand: Assessing the Place, Potential and Pitfalls of Restorative Justice', in A. Crawford and J.S. Goodey (eds) *Integrating a Victim Perspective Within Criminal Justice*, Aldershot: Ashgate, 207–25.

Morris, A., G. Maxwell and J.P. Robertson (1993) 'Giving Victims a Voice: A New Zealand Experiment', *Howard Journal* 32 (4), 304–21.

Mouzellis, N. (1981) *Organisation and Bureaucracy*. London: Routledge and Kegan Paul.

Nikolic-Ristanovic, V. (2001) 'Possibilities for Restorative Justice in Serbia', paper presented at the International Conference 'Positioning Restorative Justice', Leuven.

Osiel, M. (1997) *Mass Atrocity, Collective Memory and the Law*. New Brunswick, NJ: Transaction Publishers.

Pascale, R. (1990) *Managing on the Edge*. New York: Touchstone Books.

Popovski, V. (2000) 'The International Criminal Court: A Synthesis of Retributive and Restorative Justice', *International Relations* XV (3), 1–10.

Rapoport, A. (1999) 'Foreword' in H. Jeong (ed.) *Conflict Resolution: Dynamics, Processes and Structure*. Aldershot: Ashgate.

Rubinstein, R. (1999) 'Conflict Resolution and Structural Sources of Conflict', in H. Jeong (ed.) *Conflict Resolution: Dynamics, Process and Structure*. Aldershot: Ashgate.

Rupensinghe, K. (ed.) (1995) *Conflict Transformation*. New York: St Martin's Press – now Palgrave Macmillan.

Scimecca, J. (1991) 'Conflict Resolution in the United States: The Emergence of a Profession?', in K. Avruch, P. Black and J. Scimecca (eds) *Conflict Resolution: Cross Cultural Perspectives*. New York: Greenwood.

Skelton, A. (2002) 'Restorative Justice as a Framework for Juvenile Justice Reform: A South African Perspective', *British Journal of Criminology* 42 (3), 496–513.

Taylor, I. (1999) *Crime in Context: A Critical Criminology of Market Societies*. Boulder, CO: Westview Press.

Teitel, R. (2000) *Transitional Justice*. Oxford: Oxford University Press.

Tidwell, A. (1998) *Conflict Resolved? A Critical Assessment of Conflict Resolution*. London: Pinter.

Truth and Reconciliation Commission (1998) *Truth and Reconciliation Commission of South Africa Report*. Cape Town: Juta and Co. Ltd.

Umbreit, M. (1994) *Victim Meets Offender*. Monsey, NY: Criminal Justice Press.

Unger, R. (1987) *False Necessity: Anti-necessitarian Social Theory in the Service of Radical Democracy*. Cambridge: Cambridge University Press.

United Nations (2001) Regulation No. 2001/10 – *On the Establishment of A Commission for Reception, Truth and Reconciliation in East Timor*. New York: United Nations.

Villa-Vicenzio, C. (1999) 'A Different Kind of Justice: The South African Truth and Reconciliation Commission', *Contemporary Justice Review* 1, 407–29.

Wallensteen, P. and M. Sollenberg (1997) 'Armed Conflicts, Conflict Termination and Peace Agreements 1989–1996', *Journal of Peace Research* 34 (3), 345–60.

Walton, P. (1998) 'Big Science, Dystopia and Utopia: Establishment and New Criminology Revisited', in P. Walton and J. Young (eds) *The New Criminology Revisited*. Basingstoke: Macmillan – now Palgrave Macmillan.

Weber, M. (1966) *Max Weber on Law in Economy and Society*. Cambridge, MA: Harvard University Press.

Wright, M. (1991) *Justice for Victims and Offenders*. Milton Keynes: Open University Press.

Young, J. (1999) *The Exclusive Society: Social Exclusion, Crime and Difference in Late Modernity*. London: Sage.

Zehr, H. (1985) *Retributive Justice, Restorative Justice*. Elkhart, Indiana: Mennonite Central Committee, US Office of Criminal Justice.

Zehr, H. (1990) *Changing Lenses: A New Focus for Crime and Justice*. Scottsdale, PA: Herald Press.

2
Criminological Ideas and the South African Transition*

Dirk van Zyl Smit

Introduction

The year 1989 was not one in which the prospects for peaceful social change in South Africa seemed particularly promising. In May the Institute of Criminology at the University of Cape Town held a conference with the theme, 'Towards Justice? Crime and State Control in South Africa'. Mr Dullah Omar (later to become Minister of Justice but then an advocate at the Cape Bar and a well-known community activist recently released from detention without trial) gave the keynote lecture. He analysed state lawlessness in a society that was still in crisis. An academic critic of the government had been assassinated the previous week. One could not yet speak of a society in transition (Omar, 1990).

Mr Omar's overview paper listed the ways in which during the past century the state had used the mechanisms of the legal system to control and exploit the majority of the population of South Africa. Other papers provided the legal and criminological detail (Hansson and Van Zyl Smit, 1990). On the legal side, there were critiques of the continued widespread use of corporal punishment and of how the doctrine of common purpose had been applied to gain convictions and to justify the imposition of capital punishment. More explicitly criminological were accounts not only of police brutality, but also of how communities had organized to deal with it. In addition, the collection included reflexive accounts of how social scientific knowledge could be used in courts of law to explain forms of resistance, which were being criminalized by the state.

In order to set the context for these papers I sought to identify the primary intellectual currents then prevalent in South African criminology. I identified three such currents which I described (with the usual academic qualifications about the ideal-typical nature of such categorization) as Afrikaner nationalist criminology, legal reformist criminology and a third that I declined to label but called, somewhat optimistically for the time, 'a criminology for a democratic South Africa' to which the papers read at the conference broadly belonged (Van Zyl Smit, 1990).[1] Even in 1989 these categories were not original contributions to the sociology of knowledge. They had come to correspond closely to the tripartite conservative, liberal and radical streams in criminological thought that had been identified in many other societies. What was of particular interest was how these categories had emerged in South Africa, how the ideas underlying them had been shaped and had interacted with each other in a very different social environment, and how they were used either to protect or change the status quo.[2]

The emergent meaning of these categories and particularly their impact in the extended crisis that the apartheid state faced during the 1980s provide my points of departure for understanding the impact of criminological ideas in the more recent South African history. I propose to trace the development of the intellectual trends in the period leading up to the first democratic elections and then to focus on the role that they have played in the subsequent reformation of the South African criminal justice system. I then give my prognosis of what I think their future role will be. In the conclusion, I briefly consider the desirability of these intellectual trends for the further development of the South African criminal justice system and society generally. It may well be that other deeply divided societies in transition to democracy will react similarly to the nostrums that idealists of the different categories would prescribe.

Criminology in the time of crisis

By 1989 Afrikaner nationalist criminology in its pure form was something of a spent force. In its heyday of the late 1930s and 1940s it had been an articulated intellectual movement which had provided a critique of individualistic theories of crime and justice by emphasizing the socially determined nature of crime amongst white Afrikaner victims of imperialist and capitalist exploitation and by stressing the oft-overlooked significance of nationalism as a social force. Unfortunately, as in Germany and elsewhere in Europe, nationalism and socialism, combined with the widespread, scientifically sanctioned racism of the 1920s and 1930s (Channock, 1995), provided an all too heady brew for young Afrikaner nationalist intellectuals. Some of them succumbed to the dubious charms of Nazi theory and used it in a specifically criminological discourse to develop and justify the ideology of grand apartheid as a solution to the problems of urban crime in particular. Blacks were to be excluded from the cities and allowed to live in their own areas where their simpler natures would not be corrupted and criminalized by urban temptations (Van Zyl Smit, 1989). In 1989 the intellectual children and grandchildren of these pioneers still held positions of institutional prominence in South African criminology but as theorists they were a spent force. Their empirical research too was very limited, and concentrated on subjects that would not challenge the authority of the state in any way. Their primary preoccupation had long been the defence of the status quo. In its most extreme form this was expressed in the sub-specialization of military criminology with the specific objective of resisting the 'total onslaught' against the Republic of South Africa (Stevens, 1988:22).

In contrast to Afrikaner nationalist criminology, which was an intellectual movement with an identifiable doctrine and trajectory – a rapid rise and a long decline disguised by its continued political influence – legal reformist criminology was much more diffuse. As the name suggests, it was less of an intellectual movement but was dominated by lawyers, both judges and civil servants, who sought to make the existing system work more humanely but also more efficiently. To this end they sought to use the findings of 'value-free' empirical research and the intervention of professional social workers. From the beginning of the century onwards, they had laboured to develop a criminal justice system which recognized formal equality before the criminal law while at the same time protecting, or at least not undermining, the socio-political status quo, which allowed whites to maintain effective authority over blacks. Legal reformism had both liberal and conservative wings. Over time the distinction between the two wings became more marked. The conservative wing continued to work through the framework of government commissions of inquiry, which largely avoided considering the wider implications of the implementation of the stated policy of formal equality before the law and limited themselves to technical reforms (Van Zyl Smit, 1990). On the other hand, not all lawyers denied the manifest inequalities of South African society. At least from the late 1950s onwards there had been committed lawyers who were prepared to defend persons charged with crimes against the state, but with individual exceptions they had continued to operate within the existing framework. The 1980s saw the emergence of a group of lawyers, both academics and practitioners, many of whom were employed by newly founded public interest law organizations, who not only were involved in defence work but who began to challenge the legal positivism which underpinned much of the legal system and with it the wider societal status quo (Abel, 1995). Some of their thinking was reflected at the 1989 conference, but although theirs was a general concern with human rights, it was not yet underpinned by a developed vision of an alternative to the current legal order.

Unlike legal reformism, the criminology for a new democratic South Africa sought to break with the status quo. It claimed for itself the intellectual heritage of international radical and critical criminology and a commitment to what it called practical intervention, while shunning or at least being highly sceptical of change based on legal evolution and improved management. In some ways the political circumstances of the time solved dilemmas of the relationship between theory and practice with which many criminologists of broadly critical persuasion were grappling in other countries. Under circumstances in which the freedom of the press was limited but where academic freedom generally allowed publication, there could be no criticism of studies of aspects of the criminal justice system (of detention without trial, for example) which did not necessarily attempt to advance any scientifically coherent explanation but sought simply to expose existing wrongs.[3] Such research was in itself a form of action.

This is not to suggest that the critical criminology of the time was politically neutral: far from it. There was no uncertainty about its opposition to the existing order and its commitment to study state crimes and condemn the practices of the South African state. Abstract questions about the relationship of criminology to the state in general were not particularly troubling, for the practitioners of this form of criminology were easily united in a commitment to the abolition of apartheid and its replacement by a loosely conceptualized ideal of a democratic society.

A feature of the critical criminology of the time was that it brought academic criminologists of this persuasion into close working relationships with disadvantaged black (African and coloured) communities who were facing the repressive force of the South African state. Practices of cooperation and working with communities in research projects were formed under political conditions where opposition to the regime was morally unproblematic to all concerned. The contributions to the 1989 conference also reveal the extent to which shared opposition to the status quo allowed an inclusive (critical) criminology to combine issues of human rights (arguments for the abolition of capital and corporal punishment, for example, but also the more general critiques of state lawlessness) with studies much more firmly anchored in the descriptions of the impact of the state agents of social control on specific communities. In particular, it brought criminologists and other social scientists into contact with practising lawyers who were also attempting to use the space that the law still provided for defending those involved in the struggle against apartheid.

From resistance to proactive intervention

Social and political changes in any society are gradual processes, and with the wisdom of hindsight it is apparent that even in 1989 there were signs that the balance of power in South African society was shifting. The speech of the then President F.W. de Klerk on 2 February 1990 (*Cape Times*, 3 February 1990) in which he announced the unbanning of the liberation movements, the intention to enter into political negotiations and, interestingly, although overlooked in mainstream comment at the time, the willingness to reconsider the death penalty, was a public signal that South Africa had now become a society in transition. The negotiation of this transition (attended, of course, by further crises) was to dominate South African public life for the next four years. These political changes had a profound impact on all three approaches to criminology in South Africa.

Afrikaner nationalist criminology, already in steep intellectual decline by the late 1980s, soon lost its dominant access to those in political power and thus much of its influence. Many of its senior practitioners retired, but their successors did not seek to develop new ideas that built upon the heritage of radical conservatism. Instead they stressed their political neutrality and scientific objectivity and began to put out cautious intellectual feelers towards their more critical colleagues, while attempting to establish for themselves a niche as teachers of apolitical (technocratic) programmes for the police, correctional officials and the burgeoning private security industry.

Legal reformist criminology underwent a revival and with it an important shift in emphasis. While the 1980s may have seen the rise of human rights lawyers as a group, the legal system as a whole had still been dominated by narrowly (legal) positivist concerns. The 1990s saw questions about the constitution and about the entrenched fundamental rights it should embody move quickly to the core of national political debate. The Interim Constitution, which was the product of the negotiating process, contained many indications of the future shape of the criminal justice system. Moreover, in the process of constitution making the established lawyers' associations were challenged to make good their claim that they supported equality before the law by two new groupings, the National Association of Democratic Lawyers (NADEL) and the Black Lawyers' Association (BLA), both of which had close links with the liberation movements. The result was that the organized profession began to play a far more active role in matters such as legal representation for poor persons. The courts too began to adopt a more liberal approach towards human rights. Thus, for example, in 1993 in the case *Minister of Justice v. Hofmeyr*, the Appellate Division of the Supreme Court recognized that the rights of a former emergency detainee had been violated and stated its conclusions in such wide terms that it established a legal basis for the generous recognition of the rights of all prisoners. This recognition predated the introduction of a constitution with an entrenched bill of rights.

In addition to the impetus given by the constitution-making process, many 'mainstream' lawyers were confronted in other ways during the transitional years of the early 1990s with issues of how a future criminal justice system should be structured. Crucial in this regard was the Commission of Inquiry Regarding the Prevention of Public Violence and Intimidation, which was established in 1991 under the chairmanship of Judge Richard Goldstone. Although in the form of a judicial commission of inquiry concerned with fact finding, it became involved in much wider policy issues that included self-initiated attempts to mediate in disputes that might lead to violence at both local and national levels, and to chart a course for the future. One such national initiative was its inquiry into the control of public demonstrations. Instead of merely investigating the facts and then making proposals for legislative reform, the Commission appointed a panel of criminologists and other experts from South Africa and abroad and set in motion a process in which this panel and the Commission worked closely with both the South African police and the major political movements then organizing mass demonstrations. The recommendations that were made by the panel (supported by reference to criminological theory) were for a system of control of public demonstrations in which decisions about the form that such demonstrations should adopt were taken jointly by the organizers, the local authorities and the police. The primary responsibility for policing the participants to ensure that the agreed conditions about matters such as routes and numbers were met rested with the organizers, who could appoint their own marshals with power to enforce the conditions. These proposals were eventually cast in legislation, which was

passed in late 1993 (but did not come into force until October 1996).
More significantly, the recommendations, which were accepted in principle by all parties, in practice became guidelines for the management of public demonstrations with immediate effect. The process of establishing these guidelines was a pointer towards how lawyers and criminologists could work together and at the same time elicit the cooperation of important actors in civil society (Brogden and Shearing, 1993).

The development of legal reformism as potentially a major factor in changing the criminal justice system could not but have an impact on those criminologists who from the 1970s onwards had been concerned to develop a criminology appropriate to a democratic South Africa. It did not follow, however, that they were simply absorbed into assisting legally driven reformism. One reason for this was institutional. From around the time that it became clear that a major political change was in the offing, these ranks of the critical criminologists were swelled by scholars affiliated to some of the historically black universities where critical thought had not previously been able to flourish and by researchers and activists not primarily linked to university departments teaching criminology but to new organizations, which, even if they are loosely affiliated to universities, were established primarily to do research with a strong 'community' focus. Particularly significant in this regard have been the Centre for the Study of Violence and Reconciliation, linked to the University of the Witwatersrand, and the Community Peace Foundation and the Community Law Centre, both loosely affiliated to the University of the Western Cape. At the same time public interest lawyers and even NICRO (National Institute for Crime Prevention and Reintegration), the major non-governmental organization dealing with offenders, began to appoint researchers who were sympathetic to critical criminology.

These institutional developments were less important than the reality that there was now a group of people whose primary and shared professional interest was the study of crime and the development of a criminal justice system which would meet the criteria implicit in the work of the critical criminologists of the previous decade. But, as we have seen, these criteria were themselves somewhat open-ended. What they did have in common was a commitment to community-based research and to solutions that favoured local autonomy.

Involvement in new modes of community ordering really came into its own during the protracted transitional period. For a long time urban black South African communities in particular had developed communal mechanisms of social ordering outside the official structures (Hund and

Kotu-Rammopo, 1983). These mechanisms existed in an uneasy relationship with the mainstream police and courts. In the late 1980s there were a number of prosecutions of people who administered what became known as people's courts in the townships, as the state saw them as a threat to its authority. Much of the research on these courts was inspired by the need for evidence which could be used by the defence in such prosecutions (for example *S v. Sipati and four others*, 1991).

The period of transition presented opportunities for the re-examination and reconceptualization of these forms of popular justice. Description and activism could be and were combined by critical criminologists working in this area. The objective was both to improve the ability of a particular community to maintain order and to allow the community to relate on its own terms to the formal state agents of social control. In practice, there were many variations both in the community structures and in the forms that intervention took. Two examples, both drawn from interventions in townships near Cape Town and relating to policing rather than to the community courts, can serve to illustrate the roles that were played by persons with criminological expertise during the period leading up to, and immediately after, the first democratic elections in 1994.

The first example is drawn from a report by Mncadi and Nina (1994) on an initiative of the Community Peace Foundation (of which they were both prominent members) in the long-established black township of Guguletu. The initiative took the form of a training programme not on policing, as was initially envisaged, but on 'community safety'. The organizers defined 'community safety' as 'a process of empowering and enabling community members to contribute to guaranteeing a safer environment' (Mncadi and Nina, 1994:19). The training deliberately did not involve the police directly, but focused instead on members of street committees, structures that the organizers had previously identified as having political credibility in the community and already exercising some forms of social control. The training concentrated on human rights issues, conflict resolution and the functioning of state agencies such as the police and the courts. At the end of the programme participants drafted their own guidelines on how public safety could best be maintained by street committees. After this initial stage the intention had been that the participants should go back to their street committees. As activists they should discuss the modification of the guidelines and eventually participate in the establishment of a community police forum that would coordinate links with the official police force. In reality the process was more complicated and took longer than the organizers had anticipated. It did not lead to the establishment of such a forum. Nevertheless, after an evaluation the authors concluded that the members of the street committees who had undergone the course were now able to act more effectively as promoters of public safety. The street committees on which they served and which had to make factual findings before intervening in disputes were now more likely to follow norms of due process. Moreover, they were now better able to negotiate with the police and the local authority.

An equally optimistic assessment of the value of intervention by persons with criminological expertise was reached by Ferndale, Malekane and Schärf (1994) in their evaluation of the role of expert mediators in a dispute about the construction of a police station in Khayelitsha, one of the newer, largest and most politically unstable black townships near Cape Town. (The details of this complex dispute are not important for current purposes.) Notwithstanding the fact that various political organizations in a particular part of Khayelitsha were opposed to the construction of the police station on grounds that the community had not been consulted, as well as for other symbolic reasons, and that the police did not see the necessity for such consultation, it was possible to achieve a compromise. The outcome of protracted negotiations was that a so-called community peace centre was to be built, including various community facilities and offices for other government departments, such as labour, as well as the police. Of interest is the extent to which this outcome was the product of the ideas of the mediators. The authors note that in this instance neither the community organizations nor the police had clear ideas of what they wanted to achieve. They conclude their report with a frank comment that reflects the optimistic interventionism of this form of criminology in late 1994:

> To compound matters the political parties to the negotiations around our new constitution didn't have a new vision other than not wanting the apartheid style of policing. Curiously, none of the estimated 40 000 people who left the country to acquire skills during the struggle returned having been trained in policing issues. Under these circumstances our form of intervention seemed worth a try.
>
> (Ferndale, Malekane and Schärf, 1994:38)

In addition to the strong commitment to direct involvement in new modes of community ordering, there were other, often overlapping, impulses influencing the specific issues to which progressive criminologists chose to pay attention in this period. One of these was a concern with the treatment of juveniles by the criminal justice system. From the mid-1980s onwards, the ill-treatment of juveniles at the hands of the authorities, both as detainees in the state of emergency and generally, had been a constant focus of critical criminology (McLachlan, 1984) and of those in the liberation struggle who recognized that exposing these abuses was an elective way of bringing the abuses of apartheid to international attention (Human Rights Commission, 1990). In the early 1990s such issues were widely publicized in South Africa itself and criminologists, together with human rights and welfare organizations, were involved in public actions with slogans such as 'Justice for Children: No Child Should be Caged' and even 'Free a Child for Christmas' (Juvenile Justice Drafting Consultancy, 1994). The criminological input was not limited to sloganeering. There was also a conscious attempt to build a coalition of progressive forces, which could unite around new ideas for dealing with juveniles. Central to the coalition was the notion that the juvenile offenders should as far as possible be kept out of the courts. What was required, though, was more than mere diversion. Recognition was to be given to the concerns of the community. Communities were to be involved in a process of reintegrative shaming of the offender, leading to a form of restorative justice. In adopting terms such as 'reintegrative shaming' and 'restorative justice', criminologists were making a conscious attempt to link their proposals for South Africa with what they perceived to be a similar communitarian and progressive approach to social ordering among groups such as the Maori people in New Zealand and the First Nations in Canada. In this respect juvenile justice was particularly important. In the transitional period it probably attracted more debate and development resources than any other criminal justice issue and therefore the ideas of how society should ideally be organized in the future were articulated most fully in this context. When the formal political change took place, draft legislation for a new juvenile justice system that would incorporate these ideas had already been prepared by a coalition of criminologists and human rights activists (Juvenile Justice Drafting Consultancy, 1994).

Another important development of the transitional period was the establishment of a specifically feminist element in progressive criminological discourse. As Desirée Hansson (1995), the leading South African feminist criminologist of the time, has explained, feminism was influential in moving progressive criminology generally towards a research practice which was participatory and action-oriented, in introducing new areas of research and in shaping the discourse in existing areas involving violence against women so as to reflect specifically feminist concerns with the empowerment of women. Feminist involvement in the process of negotiation leading to the new constitution complemented these developments and in turn stimulated consideration of what state mechanisms could best secure protection of women and the advancement of their rights (Stanton and Lochrenberg, 1995).

Criminological ideas and the new South African state

Just as the speech of 2 February 1990 heralded the period of transition, the coming into power of the first democratically elected government in May 1994 signalled if not its end, a new era in which criminological ideas would have to assert themselves within a very different framework. The fact that individuals who had been prominent either as supporters of, or active participants in, the development of progressive criminology were now in positions of power in the new government did not detract from the reality that the framework for change was now one in which both the party in power and, by extension, although to varying degrees, all organs of the state had a measure of legitimacy which they had previously lacked.

The new government soon indicated its intention to break with the past and to consult widely on how this should be done. All the criminal justice departments (Justice, Safety and Security (Police), Welfare and Correctional Services, which are all separate ministries) held (in some instances on their own and in others in combination with various human rights organizations, and in almost all instances sponsored by foreign governments) a series of consultative conferences at which serious efforts were made to involve what were called 'all stakeholders'. The result was a carousel of meetings at which critical criminologists and Supreme Court judges, policemen and community activists mingled and were able to express their views. On re-reading the proceedings of these many meetings, one is left with a sense of wonder at the passion with which all these different views were expressed, often repeatedly. The crucial question, though, is to what extent did they have an impact and, more particularly for purposes of this chapter, what role did the ideals and the work of criminologists play in bringing about change, if any? It is impossible to consider this question across the full range of criminal justice activities. A few examples must therefore suffice.

It is significant that perhaps the most dramatic changes to the criminal justice system in the immediate post-election era came about as a direct result of liberal legal reformism. In two of its earliest decisions the new established Constitutional Court interpreted the Constitution, which was ambiguous in this regard, as outlawing both the death penalty and corporal punishment (*S v. Makwanyane and another*, 1995; *S v. Williams*, 1995). The context of these decisions is interesting, for the abolition of both forms of punishment enjoyed the support of the leadership of the ANC (and indeed the moratorium on the death penalty declared in February 1990 by their predecessors in government had prepared some of the political way for change), but for the ANC to have acted to abolish them by legislation would have meant running the risk of alienating some of its support. Also noteworthy is that there was little input from criminologists in these particular cases. Although the new court would have accepted Brandeis briefs on the social impact of these forms of punishment, none were forthcoming. The success in legal reformism through the courts in these test cases has not meant that this course of action has continued to be influential. Instead, there appears to have been a conscious decision by the public interest lawyers not immediately to bring cases that would expose the administrative failures of the new government.

The success thus far, of a critical criminology committed above all to community involvement, has been less spectacular. In the area of policing it has perhaps been most successful in the sense that the requirement set by the Interim Constitution of community involvement in police matters has been spelt out in national legislation. The 1995 South African Police Services Act (sections 18 to 21 of Act 68) now provides that representative police forums be established at all police stations and further structures at area and provincial levels. However, both commentators who are critical of the idea of community control of policing (Van Vuuren, 1996) and those who are sympathetic to it agree that there have been considerable difficulties in establishing such structures and ensuring that they function smoothly. To a large extent they remain dependent on the input of non-governmental organizations (Schärf, 1996).

In the area of juvenile justice the formal results have been particularly disappointing. The saga of legislative attempts to keep juveniles awaiting trial out of prison is an illustration of an attempted reform that failed. Briefly, the position was that section 29 of the Correctional Services Act (Act 8 of 1959) in the form that it was inherited by the new government provided that juveniles should not be detained in a prison or in a police cell or lock-up unless such detention was necessary and no other place of secure custody was available. In the past these conditions had all too easily been regarded as having been met, and children were detained in numbers which were a legitimate cause for concern for the campaigns to which I referred earlier. However, narrower interpretation of the legal requirement of that detention as 'necessary' and the provision of more secure detention facilities for juveniles whose confinement while awaiting trial really was necessary could have eliminated them. Instead, the Act was amended. The existing requirements were retained but in addition a prohibition was placed on the detention of juveniles under the age of 14 in a prison and an absolute limit was imposed on their detention in a police cell for longer than 24 hours. The Act was also amended with the intention of making the detention of older juveniles in prison or police cells for longer than 48 hours virtually impossible.[4] The amendments were, however, not brought into effect at once. Instead provision was made for them to be brought into operation by proclamation in individual magisterial districts. The intention clearly was that the amendments would only be brought into effect when alternative places of detention were available for serious juvenile offenders. However, in May 1995 the amendments were suddenly made applicable to the whole country (Sloth-Nielsen, 1995a), and many juveniles regarded as highly dangerous offenders had to be released or, in those centres where places of safety were available, returned to such places, even though they were unable to provide truly secure detention. The result was an outcry in the media, which linked rising crime rates with the failure to detain the most dangerous juvenile offenders.[5] Subsequently, after some public squabbling in the government of national unity, Parliament adopted a private member's bill by a member of the African National Congress, which largely reinstated the status quo.[6] The new amendment was designed to be temporary, for a year only until further places of safety could be provided, but in May 1997 Parliament extended it without debate for a further year. Although a comprehensive juvenile justice legislation with imaginative provision for community participation may still be introduced (Community Law Centre, 1995; Inter-Ministerial Committee on Young People at Risk, 1996), the history thus far has made its acceptance less likely.

In the Department of Justice itself the results have been mixed. From the perspective of community involvement an important positive feature has been the development of the pre-existing but dormant system of lay assessors in the magistrates' courts (Moosa, 1995). (South Africa has no jury system and the use of mixed benches in which two lay assessors sit with a magistrate as triers of fact of equal status offers interesting possibilities of effectively combining professional expertise and local knowledge.) The introduction of lay assessors has not been without its difficulties, many of which have to do with how the assessors are selected and paid and whether they have any direct responsibility to the communities they represent.

The process of transformation in correctional services has been particularly complex too (Giffard and Dissel, 1996; Van Zyl Smit, 1997). In this instance the major difficulty has been that the transformation forum which was set up to oversee the process became embattled in the internal labour politics of the Department, to which was added an overlay of national party-political disputes. A further complication was that the representative of the prisoners' union on this forum was a person with whom the government representatives were not prepared to work after he declared his support for 'reformed' gang leaders in the Western Cape. The overall result was that the progressive criminologists involved in this sector were effectively sidelined and the transformation abandoned. Change would have to come from elsewhere.

Constraints on change

These somewhat superficial sketches of the to and fro of transformation in various criminal justice sectors are designed to demonstrate the complexity of the process rather than convey detailed information. In sketching some of the reform attempts in individual areas of criminal justice administration, I have not highlighted the sheer administrative difficulty of managing the separate government departments operating in the criminal justice sphere. Each of these national departments has had to deal with enormous practical problems of reincorporating their functional equivalents that had operated in the old 'independent' Bantustans. Equally complex has been the process of restructuring the departments internally so that they begin to reflect the full South African population while retaining the expertise of existing staff members. In many instances the change has been accompanied by loss of morale and claims of corruption. The fragmentation of departments that have responsibilities for different aspects of the criminal justice system has also proved to be a major headache. Notwithstanding the fact that an overall National Crime Prevention Strategy (1996) was announced, and that there were many new ministers and new civil servants, old divisions remained.

Another major constraint that all aspects of the transformation face is the increasing fear of crime and the related tide of what Bottoms (1995) has termed 'popular punitiveness'. It may be true that the extent of the increase in crime has been exaggerated, that media portrayal of crime concentrates excessively on crimes committed against whites and that whites sometimes use the fear of crime as a metaphor for general unease that they may feel about the new regime. The fact remains that even in terms of officially reported crimes, rates are very high, and that fear of violent crime in particular has reached a level where the government is faced with the reality that investment and the retention of highly skilled labour within the country are threatened (NEDCOR/ISS, 1997).

A highly publicized report reflecting the views of the business community has condemned lax administration in the criminal justice sphere and questioned the efficacy of government attempts to deal with crime (NEDCOR Project, 1996). While it accepted the National Crime Prevention Strategy in general and the principle of community policing in particular, it made the case for different priorities and 'acceptance of the international strategy of acting vigorously against any crime no matter how small' (NEDCOR Project, 1996:15).

In less measured terms, opponents of the government have been quick to adopt the politics of law and order, with the hitherto unsuccessful campaign for the reintroduction of the death penalty serving as a rallying point. In the Western Cape in particular, the Moslem-led PAGAD movement (People Against Gangsterism And Drugs) has used criminal policy as a rallying point for a campaign of civil disobedience (and in at least one instance, the lynching and murder of a gang leader – broadcast on national television while the police watched 'helplessly'). PAGAD's programme combines extreme law and order politics with a direct and radical challenge to the state to deliver on promises of fundamental social and economic change.

The immediate targets of PAGAD's campaigns, the organized gangs and drug dealers, have responded with considerable sophistication. The leaders have claimed that they themselves have been victim of the social inequities of apartheid. They have founded their own community-based organizations and even offered the state a 'deal' in terms of which they would provide considerable funds for 'community development' in return for immunity from prosecution (Schärf and Vale, 1996).

Thus far the response of the government to these various challenges has been somewhat hesitant. It has resisted the blandishments of the gang leaders and sought to distance itself from those who supported them. On the other hand, it has vacillated about whether to negotiate with PAGAD, and justified this hesitation by its recognition of PAGAD's strong community base. At the same time the government has announced various get-tough-on-crime campaigns ranging from an almost farcical police undertaking to arrest thousands of known criminals in a short period (raising the obvious question about why this had not been done before), through the introduction of mandatory minimum sentences, to the bizarre (and only half-heartedly denied) suggestion that disused mine shafts be used to house dangerous prisoners.

This somewhat erratic flirtation with policies of law and order stands in contrast to the establishment and operation of the Truth and Reconciliation Commission during the same period. In brief, the Commission was established by legislation that the new parliament passed to reflect the carefully negotiated compromise on how crimes committed with a political motive during the apartheid period should be handled after the first democratic elections (Werle, 1996). It consisted of three committees dealing respectively with finding the 'truth' in relation to human rights abuses, the determination of who qualified for amnesty for their political offences and the payment of (relatively limited) compensation to the victims of such offences. Several features of the Commission's work have impacted on the criminal justice system: not least the threat of criminal prosecution of those offenders who have not been granted amnesty either because they did not apply for amnesty or were refused it. The main focus, however, was on the relationship between truth and reconciliation. In its many public and televised hearings the Commission stressed in almost theological terms that findings of fact should be followed by forgiveness and expiation. Of particular interest is that the work of the Truth Commission itself has been justified by referring specifically to the ideals of reintegrative shaming and restorative justice and the need for establishing 'community' in South Africa (Villa-Vincenzio, 1996). This approach did not go unchallenged. Victims sought to compel prosecutions or at least to be allowed to bring civil actions against the state, if not against perpetrators who have been granted amnesty. Alleged perpetrators in turn sought to avoid testifying by seeking to rely on their right not to incriminate themselves. Although in some instances court orders compelled the Commission to adjust its procedures in its public human rights hearings in order to protect the rights of witnesses, these attempts have generally not been very successful. The Constitutional Court in particular adopted the position that under the special circumstances national reconciliation takes precedence over what would otherwise be constitutionally protected rights (*Azanian Peoples Organization (AZAPO) and others v. President of the Republic of South Africa and others*, 1996).

Prognoses

What do these developments and non-developments mean for the future of the different trends that I have identified in South African criminological thought?

For Afrikaner–nationalist criminology in its historical sense the general political developments are probably a death knell. The likelihood of the re-emergence of a criminology that articulates sympathetically the social causes of crime of (poor) white Afrikaners and attempts to develop it into a full-blown theory with empirical underpinnings is slim. More plausible, however, is the emergence from this quarter of a criminology which seeks to justify popular punitiveness and which is broadly sceptical of constitutionalism and human rights, that is, a criminology of the kind which we have seen gaining public support and academic respectability in the USA (see for example, Bennett, DiIullio and Walters, 1996). Among academic criminologists little of this kind has emerged thus far. There is the likelihood, as I have suggested, that the successors to the Afrikaner–nationalist criminological tradition (who may not be Afrikaners or nationalists themselves) will play a part in developing the technical skills required to operate the criminal justice system. The possibility cannot be excluded that such technical expertise will be promoted as if it presents value-free solutions, while in fact the proposed solutions deliberately undermine all aspects of the ideal of communal responsibility for crime control.

In the short term it is easy to predict that legal reformist criminology will continue to benefit from the, admittedly not undisputed, political support for constitutionalism in South Africa. The 'final' South African Constitution, like its predecessor, contains many provisions dealing with criminal justice matters.[7] In particular, the Bill of Rights section spells out the rights of arrested, detained and accused persons in such detail that its full implementation would have a major impact on the operation of the criminal justice system. Working out the logical implications of these primarily individual and defensive rights in the wider context of a constitution that also seeks to guarantee some social and economic rights, as well as the rights of democratic participation, is a major and fascinating intellectual task. The primary difficulty in applying these tools to change the criminal justice system is to decide how to deal strategically with predictable failures by the state to provide that which can now be demanded with the specific (or derived) sanction of the Constitution. It is inevitable that public interest lawyers will litigate on issues such as the right to legal counsel and the provision of services to prisoners, but the substantive results may be to expose the limits of the South African state, or the reluctance of the courts to order that the Constitution be enforced. Such actions will inevitably also face the criticism that they are undemocratic in the populist sense, and relatedly, that they seek to compel the deployment of scarce resources on unjustifiable priorities. Reformists may well end up undermining the political support for the Constitution upon which they rely so much for their increased legitimacy.

Radical criminology with a strong commitment to communitarianism is well entrenched in the sense that the centrality of community involvement in crime control has been established in virtually all policy debates about criminal justice in South Africa. Even where there has been little fundamental change, the rhetoric of community control is pervasive. It is prominent in the National Crime Prevention Strategy (1996) and even the reform proposals of business have found it necessary to pay lip service to the ideal.

What is unclear is whether the practices which this criminology now supports, that is, reintegrative shaming and restorative justice, will become the dominant features of South African criminal justice; or whether they will be employed only to deal with some problem juveniles and minor disputes that the central state does not regard as sufficiently important to justify expending resources. This question is one that has rightly concerned self-styled 'intellectual activists' (Nina, 1995:7) in this tradition. From colonial times at least until prior to the transitional period, alternative forms of communitarian justice, whether in terms of African customary law in rural areas or *makgotla* courts in townships, were sanctioned or at least tolerated by the state, but only in so far as they did not challenge it in any way. Even the draft proposals put forward for the community courts in 1996 by the Department of Justice, which in principle is sympathetic to community empowerment, would destroy the vitality of the community justice movement, both by limiting its jurisdiction and by making some but not all local leaders of this movement into petty officials (Schärf, 1996a).

The activists have recognized that the roles of what Daniel Nina (1995) has called 'state justice' and 'popular justice' have changed in post-apartheid South Africa. In this situation they support the idea first articulated by Brogden and Shearing (1993) that there should be a dual system of policing in which community activities and state actions complement each other. Brogden and Shearing resolve the dilemma of deciding where to draw the line between the two forms of intervention by redefining the question to ask how problems relating to the prevention of crime can best be solved. In this context the use of the state police becomes one option among many. The political challenge is then to construct a framework in which responsibility can be located within civil society without threatening constitutionally entrenched rights. The example they use is the ingenious solution that I described earlier, developed for the control of public demonstrations by the panel of experts that advised the Goldstone Commission.

The question still remains whether the approach of the Goldstone proposals for policing public demonstrations can be developed as a general paradigm for community involvement in criminal justice matters. Formidable obstacles remain (Van der Spuv, 1994, 1995). Central to these is the difficulty of dealing with the tensions between a plurality of individual and group interests which may cut across the ideal of the 'community' which is sufficiently coherent to develop organs of community justice that are acceptable to all its members. Shearing (1994:5) is aware of this difficulty and warns bluntly that 'we should stop thinking about communities as homogeneous neighbourhoods and start recognizing them as comprised of interest groups which are often in conflict'.

The same cannot be said of all supporters of community justice. The assumption is too easily made that individuals in a particular area share, or can be brought to see that they share, ideals which the community is deemed to have. Although attempts are made to ensure the recognition of due process and human rights in community structures, there is a reluctance to assert the priority of constitutional principle over community wishes in disputed cases. There is also the danger that the community structures may themselves be taken over by organized criminal groups. There is an underestimated potential for conflict between individuals who seek to rely on their newly entrenched constitutional rights to protect them against the jurisdiction of 'voluntary' street committees and people's courts and to ensure that they are not discriminated against either as a group (Jehovah's Witnesses in a township, for example) or as individuals because they reject such associations. Little attention is paid to the question of whether an individual should be able to rely on the Constitution to demand that the state enforces the criminal law, and on what would happen if this were to be done effectively.

The difficulties of a primarily communitarian approach are compounded when it comes to dealing with crime that cuts across communities or interest groups or, even more dramatically, the cross-border and international crime to which South Africa is now exposed. There is a considerable danger that outsiders, be they illegal immigrants in a township made up mostly of black South Africans, or black robbers captured in a white suburb, will be treated particularly harshly. What is clearly required in such cases is a strong centralized system of justice that can persuade all parties that it can act effectively. Only on condition of such efficiency are the further requirements that the system also act in accordance with minimum standards of due process and human rights likely to be acceptable. On this analysis a criminology that is truly committed to democracy beyond the local scale has to engage also with the question of internal reform of state criminal justice agencies (Brogden and Shearing, 1993).

Conclusion

All approaches to crime control in South Africa are confronted by the challenge created by the recent history of that country: the desire to have a system of criminal justice which meets high standards of human rights and due process by preventing victimization through crime and at the same time ensuring that the rights of those suspects, who may be innocent, are protected. Included in this is a very strong commitment to the ideal of equality for all before the law. This has long been expressed in relatively simple terms that condemn racial disparities in sentencing or in the treatment of sentenced offenders, for example. At the same time, the society remains divided and unequal.

The South African criminology that was firmly committed to a democratic society played an important part in defending the ideal of a universally equitable criminal justice system at the time when it was most threatened and also by providing the important sociological perspective that formal equality before the law was necessary, but insufficient, to achieve substantive justice. More than that: particularly since the transition it has thought imaginatively about, and contributed materially to, the development of alternatives that would enable those who were, and who may remain, relatively powerless in the society to share in the advantages that such a system could offer. These are substantial achievements and justify support for the further development of some forms of community participation and even control of aspects of the criminal justice system.

Nevertheless, I am not optimistic that South Africa is likely to be able to reform its system as a whole so that it is guided primarily by principles of reintegrative shaming and restorative justice dispensed in local communities with minimal outside interference. Local justice has found some support at a national level. However, with the winding up of the Truth and Reconciliation Commission (Borraine, 2001), my prediction is that public attention will focus primarily on crime committed by strangers and the interest in large-scale communitarian solutions will wane. (Solidarity as expressed through various forms of community policing and community justice will of course remain a primary concern for the internal ordering of relatively close-knit communities.) Too little has yet been done to achieve agreement on shared values across the spectrum of communities for one to be able to begin to dispense with a centralized criminal justice system developed and administered by an elected national government and supervised by a judiciary applying constitutional principles.

In any event, it is arguable that a community-based approach to all aspects of criminal justice may not be desirable. It may constrain those who wish to alter the balance of power within a particular community or who may see community solidarity as itself oppressive. Criminological research from the mid-1990s onwards has made us increasingly aware of the limits of the power of the modem central state and the constraints on its ability to control crime effectively (e.g. Garland, 1996), but an efficient, incorrupt and principled central criminal justice administration continues to be an important guarantor of individual freedom.

Stanley Cohen has pointed to the fact that in many parts of the world where the distinction between political dispute and criminal violence has been obliterated the 'remote prospect of democracy lies in a radical *separation* between crime and politics' (Cohen, 1996:19, emphasis in the original). In South Africa the distinction has not disappeared but it is certainly under challenge. The adoption of communitarian criminological rhetoric by members of organized crime groups and the extreme law-and-order politics of a community-based group like PAGAD both pose threats to the established constitutional order. In South Africa, as elsewhere, much more attention needs to be paid to the balance between the input that community solidarity can make to ensure a safer environment and the role that the state can and should continue to play. An a priori commitment to communitarian solutions may limit insights into how such a balance is best achieved.

Notes

* This chapter first appeared in the *British Journal of Criminology* (1999) 39, 2 and is reproduced with permission.
1. 'Progressive realism' was the term some of my Cape Town colleagues later attached to this last category (Hansson, 1995).
2. For a fuller consideration of the transplantation and distortion of 'international' criminological ideas, see Van Zyl Smit (1989).
3. See Foster, Davis and Sandler (1987) or more generally Davis and Slabbert (1985).
4. For details of these complex amendments, for example that the longer period of detention of 48 hours was only supposed to apply to a closed category of

serious offences and the confusion surrounding repeated periods of detention, see Sloth-Nielsen (1995).
5. A further factor is that in the absence of a reliable system of birth registration it is often difficult to determine the age of suspects, and when this is in doubt the courts have treated offenders as juveniles.
6. Sloth-Nielsen (1996). The 1996 amendment did contain some attempts to protect juveniles in prison and some additional procedural safeguards: for details see Skelton (1996). In practice, though, the position is much the same as before the first amendment.
7. Although, interestingly, it does not provide for community police forums.

References

Unpublished papers referred to may be obtained from the Social Research Project, Institute of Criminology, University of Cape Town, Private Bag, Rondebosch, 7701 South Africa.

Abel, R. (1995) *Politics by Other Means. Law in the Struggle Against Apartheid, 1980–1994*. New York and London: Routledge.

Bennett, W., J. DiIullio and J. Walters (1996) *Moral Poverty – and How to Win America's War Against Crime and Drugs*. New York: Simon and Schuster.

Borraine, A. (2001) *A Country Unmasked: Inside South Africa's Truth and Reconciliation Commission*. Cape Town: Oxford University Press.

Bottoms, A. (1995) 'The Philosophy and Politics of Punishment and Sentencing', in C. Clarkson and R. Morgan (eds) *The Politics of Sentencing Reform*. Oxford: Clarendon Press.

Brogden, M. and C. Shearing (1993) *Policing for a New South Africa*. New York and London: Routledge.

Channock, M. (1995) 'Criminological Science and the Criminal Law on the Colonial Periphery: Perception, Fantasy and Realities in South Africa, 1900–1930', *Law and Social Inquiry* 20, 911–39.

Cohen, S. (1996) 'Crime and Politics: Spot the Difference', *British Journal of Sociology* 47, 1–21.

Community Law Centre (1995) *Law, Practice and Policy: South African Juvenile Justice Today*. Belville: Community Law Centre.

Davis, D. and M. Slabbert (eds) (1985) *Crime and Power in South Africa: Critical Studies in Criminology*. Cape Town: David Philip.

Ferndale, C., L. Malekane and W. Schärf (1994) 'From Police Station to Community Peace Centre: A New Vision for South African Policing', *Imbizo* 2, 31–8.

Foster, D., D. Davis, and D. Sandler (1987) *Detention and Torture in South Africa: Psychological, Legal and Historical Studies*. Cape Town: David Philip.

Garland, D. (1996) 'The Limits of the Sovereign State – Strategies for Crime Control in Contemporary Society', *British Journal of Criminology* 36, 445–71.

Giffard, C. and A. Dissel (1996) 'Transforming Correctional Services', *Track Two* 5 (1), 7–9.

Hansson, D. (1995) 'Agenda-ing Gender, Feminism and the Engendering of Academic Criminology in South Africa', in N.H. Rafter and F. Heidensohn (eds) *International Feminist Perspectives in Criminology*. Buckingham: Open University Press.

Hansson, D. and D. van Zyl Smit (eds) (1990) *Towards Justice? Crime and State Control in South Africa*. Cape Town: Oxford University Press.

Human Rights Commission (1990) *Children and Repression 1987–1989*, Report SR-4. Johannesburg: Human Rights Commission.

Hund, J. and M. Kotu-Rammopo (1983) 'Justice in a South African Township: The Sociology of *Makgotla*', *Comparative and International Law Journal of South Africa* 16, 179–208.

Inter-Ministerial Committee on Young People at Risk (1996) *Discussion Document for the Transformation of the South African Child and Youth Care System*. Pretoria: Government Printer.

Juvenile Justice Drafting Consultancy (1994) *Juvenile Justice for South Africa: Proposal for Policy and Legislative Changes*. Cape Town: Institute of Criminology, University of Cape Town.

McLachlan, F. (1984) *Children in Prison*. Cape Town: Institute of Criminology, University of Cape Town.

Mncadi, M. and D. Nina (1994) 'A Year: A Training Programme in Guguletu on Community Policing', *Imbizo* 2, 18–24.

Moosa, E. (1995) 'Lay Assessors', *Imbizo* 314, 15–17.

National Crime Prevention Strategy (1996) *National Crime Prevention Strategy*, Document produced by Inter-departmental Strategy Team of the Departments of Correctional Services, Intelligence, Justice, Safety and Security and Welfare. Pretoria: Government Printer.

NEDCOR Project (1996) *The NEDCOR Project on Crime, Violence and Investment: Executive Summary of the Main Report*. Johannesburg: NEDCOR.

NEDCOR/ISS (1997) *Crime Index*. Midrand: Criminal Justice Information Centre.

Nina, D. (1995) 'Reflections on the Role of State Justice and Popular Justice in Post-Apartheid South Africa', *Imbizo* 314, 7–14.

Omar, D. (1990) 'An Overview of State Lawlessness in South Africa', in D. Hansson and D. Van Zyl Smit (eds) *Towards Justice? Crime and State Control in South Africa*. Cape Town: Oxford University Press.

Schärf, W. (1996) 'Community Policing, A Preliminary Critical Analysis', unpublished paper presented at the Workshop on Community Policing, Technikon SA, 7 May.

Schärf, W. (1996a) 'Comments and Recommendations about the Community Courts Discussion Document of the Department of Justice', unpublished, Institute of Criminology, University of Cape Town.

Schärf, W. and C. Vale (1996) 'The Firm – Organised Crime Comes of Age During the Transition to Democracy', *Social Dynamics*, 22 (2), 30–6.

Shearing, C. (1994) 'Participatory Policing: Modalities for Lay Participation', *Imbizo* 2, 5–10.

Skelton, A. (1996) 'Rethinking the Issue of Children in Prison', *Rights* 1, 20–4.

Sloth-Nielsen, J. (1995) 'No Child Should Be Caged – Closing Doors on the Detention of Children', *South African Journal of Criminal Justice* 8, 47–51.

Sloth-Nielsen, J. (1995a) 'Juvenile Justice Review', *South African Journal of Criminal Justice* 8, 331–43.

Sloth-Nielsen, J. (1996) 'Pre-trial Detention of Children Revisited: Amending Section 29 of the Correctional Services Act', *South African Journal of Criminal Justice* 9, 60–72.

Stanton, S. and M. Lochrenberg (1995) 'Victims of Justice', *Crime and Conflict* 2, 13–16.

Stevens, R. (1988) 'Misdaas in die Weermag', *Acta Criminologica* 1, 17–27.

Van Der Spuv, E. (1994) 'Community Policing in South Africa: A Comment', *Imbizo* 2, 39–42.

Van Der Spuv, E. (1995) 'The Secret to Successful Policing', *Crime and Conflict* 3, 23–6.

Van Zyl Smit, D. (1989) 'Adopting and Adapting Criminological Ideas: Criminology and Afrikaner Nationalism in South Africa', *Contemporary Crisis* 13, 227–51.

Van Zyl Smit, D. (1990) 'Contextualising Criminology in Contemporary South Africa', in D. Hansson and D. van Zyl Smit (eds) *Towards Justice? Crime and State Control in South Africa*. Cape Town: Oxford University Press.

Van Zyl Smit, D. (1997) 'Some Aspects of Correctional Reform in South Africa', *Acta Criminologia* 10, 46–55.

Van Vuuren, J.W.J. (1996) 'The Evolution and Status of Community Policing Forums in South Africa', *Acta Criminologica* 9, 100–7.

Villa-Vincenzio, C. (1996) 'A Different Kind of Justice: The South African Truth *Acta Criminologica*, 9, 100–7.

and Reconciliation Commission', unpublished paper.

Werle, G. (1996) 'Without Truth No Reconciliation: The South African Rechstaat and the Apartheid Past', *Verfassung und Recht in Ubersee* 29, 57–72.

Cases cited

Azanian Peoples Organization (AZAPO) and others v. President of the Republic of South Africa and others (1996) 4 SA 671 (CC).

Minister of Justice v. Hofmeyr (1993) 3 SA 131 (A).

S v. Makwanyane and another (1995) 3 SA 391 (CC).

S v. Sipati and four others (1991) Case No. G/SH 403/91 Regional Court, George, Cape Province.

S v. Williams (1995) 3 SA 632 (CC).

3
Criminological Discourses in Northern Ireland: Conflict and Conflict Resolution[1]

Kieran McEvoy and Graham Ellison

Introduction

Despite the centrality of the criminal justice system to political conflict, criminological literature in general has had surprisingly little to say with regard to such matters. Much of the discussion of political conflict has been left to lawyers, political scientists, military and terrorist theorists and those who write in the area of peace studies and conflict resolution. Within criminology, while a number of scholars have approached the topic both tangentially and directly (e.g. Lombroso, [1876] 1968; Schafer, 1974; Cohen, 1996; Hagan, 1997; Jamieson, 1998; Nikolic-Ristanovic, 1998), the conceptual links between political conflict and the concerns of criminology have never been of central concern of the discipline. As Ruth Jamieson (1998:480) has argued, criminology has been 'largely aloof and unmoved' by the connections between political conflict and criminological discourses.

In parallel with Dirk van Zyl Smit's concerns with regard to South Africa in this volume, we wish to assess the significance of criminological discourses both during the Northern Ireland conflict and in the subsequent era of the peace process. We will suggest that some of the central tenets of criminological thought provide a useful epistemological anchor to discussions of the Northern Ireland conflict and the conflict resolution process. In particular, the emphasis with criminology on the notion of the state as a key constitutive actor in the study of crime makes it a particularly useful paradigm in studying a conflict where the role and responsibilities of the state are a politically and ideologically charged issue.

Of course, by no means all forms of criminological discourse in, and on, Northern Ireland have retained such a focus. Indeed, we shall argue that a failure to provide an appropriate focus on the role of the state and its agencies during the conflict has been a defining characteristic of at least one strain of criminological discourse in the jurisdiction. That said, alternative frameworks, in particular critical criminology, have provided an alternative and arguably more useful template both to assess the role of the criminal justice system during the conflict and indeed as a guide to criminological praxis during the process of conflict resolution.

The structure of this chapter is as follows. The first section deals with criminology conducted during the Northern Ireland conflict, analysing such discourses under the very broad umbrellas of positivist and critical approaches. The second section considers the developments within criminology during the era of conflict resolution, looking in particular at the emergence of four themes which we argue are of general applicability outside the context of Northern Ireland. These are the notion of criminology as a political project; criminology as a moral project; criminology as an international and comparative project; and, finally, the relationship between criminology, human rights and conflict resolution. The chapter concludes with a discussion of the intersection of these various ideas in a society in transition and in particular the role of criminological discourses in the creation of post-conflict memory.

Positivism and the Northern Ireland conflict

Piers Beirne (1987) has suggested that there is a tendency in modern criminology to decide what it is that one is 'against' and to call it positivism. Mindful of that caveat, we believe that it is none the less possible to identify a set of criminological discourses during the Northern Ireland conflict which may be accurately described as positivistic. Such discourses have taken two basic forms: (a) those that engaged directly in the study of political violence as a largely security-driven endeavour designed better to understand and therefore either better manage or 'defeat' the terrorists; and (b) those that appeared to view criminology as primarily the study of ordinary crime and which left political violence to the study of other non-criminological disciplines such as political science, peace studies or studies of 'terrorism'.

Positivism and the study of terrorism in Northern Ireland

As Matza (1964) has argued, one central tenet of positivism within criminology has been to separate the study of crime from the workings of the state.[2] Once separated from the workings of the state, analysed as deterministic, different and pathological, positivist discourses generally hold out the promise of using 'science' to 'treat' the problems created by crime and criminality (Garland, 1997). As McEvoy has argued elsewhere (McEvoy and Gormally, 1997), many of the best-known studies of 'terrorism' in Northern Ireland share these central characteristics of criminological positivism.[3]

With varying shades of difference, a number of academics emerged over the period of the Northern Ireland conflict who wrote from this perspective (Clutterbuck, 1977, 1990; Tugwell, 1981; Wilkinson, 1981, 1986; Wright, 1991). While none would describe themselves as straightforward criminologists, their subject-matter was the standard fare of criminology, including issues such as violence, policing, victims of violence, the judiciary, prisons and so forth. Based almost exclusively outside Northern Ireland, much of the analysis was marred by a view of the conflict as the outplaying of tensions between the two main communities, overseen by an occasionally ill-judged but ultimately benign British state forced reluctantly into the role of a largely neutral umpire (O'Dowd, Rolston and Tomlinson, 1980; Miller, 1998). Such commentators were usually very clear 'whose side they were on'.[4] Human rights abuses such as the internment of 'paramilitary suspects' (directed largely against the Catholic population – see Spujt, 1986) were viewed as 'distasteful, imposed reluctantly and to be abolished as soon as the security situation allowed' (Tugwell, 1981:26). The torture of suspects was viewed as the result of poor logistical planning concerning the arrests[5] and the allegations of a shoot-to-kill policy and subsequent cover-up 'clumsy and inefficient' (Wright, 1991:200). The reason for poor police/community relations between the Royal Ulster Constabulary (RUC) and Catholic community, mirroring the explanation of the police themselves (Mulcahy, 2000), was attributed largely to IRA intimidation and repression.

The views of such commentators have apparently (at least until recently) been taken quite seriously within key policy-making circles concerning Northern Ireland.[6] Few of them appeared capable of countenancing the social or political origins of terrorist violence in any meaningful sense.[7] Violence was viewed as 'a dangerous disease' (Wilkinson, 1986:31) in need of more effective treatment. Psuedo-scientific descriptions of paramilitary organizations, evidently based on security briefings rather than any actual interviews or engagement with paramilitary activists, substituted for real scholarly analysis.[8] Lastly, and perhaps most importantly in the context of a peace process, the axiomatic legitimacy of the state assumed in such analysis to a large degree absolved it from any responsibility to engage politically with the other protagonists in the resolution of the conflict other than in attempts to marginalize terrorist organizations politically from their supportive constituencies.[9] In effect, what commentators of Wilkinson's kind did with regard to the Northern Ireland conflict was to divorce the study of violence from the workings of the state, pathologize those engaged in violence as 'desperate fanatics' (Wilkinson, 1981:63) and 'godfathers' (Clutterbuck, 1994:76), and view scientific advances in security and anti-terrorist strategy as the only way to manage or even defeat political violence. As 'terrorism' experts they arguably monopolized official discourses on criminological matters related to the conflict, challenged only by a handful of critical criminologists, human rights activists (Boyle, Hadden and Hillyard, 1980; Rolston, 1983; Rolston and Tomlinson, 1986, 1988; Hillyard, 1990; Jennings, 1990; Dickson, 1992), criminal justice lawyers (e.g. Greer, 1995; Jackson and Doran, 1995) and more progressive political scientists (Guelke, 1995; McGarry and O'Leary, 1995).

Positivism and the study of ordinary crime in Northern Ireland

The domination of official discourses with regard to conflict-related criminology in Northern Ireland did not mean that 'ordinary crime' was ignored. Rather, a number of competing theses about 'ordinary' crime and its relationship to the political violence emerged (for an overview see Morison and Geary, 1989; McEvoy, Gormally and Mika, 2001).

The first, drawn in particular from psychological studies of the impact of violence, began to emerge from the mid-1970s onwards. This genre argued that violence and civil disorder had a corrosive social and political impact generally, leading to an increase in ordinary crime, particularly among young people.[10] Such a view fitted within the broader range of scholarship on the relationship between crime and conflict which argues that the social and political upheaval related to conflict leads to a state of anomie, a breakdown in the bonds of social control and the opportunity for unchecked male aggression and destruction (Bonger, 1936; Durkheim, 1992; Ignatieff, 1994; Jamieson, 1998).

However, a central difficulty in the Northern Ireland context for the maintenance of such a position was the fact that official crime statistics generally showed lower rates of crime in Northern Ireland than in the rest of the UK and Irish Republic. These apparently low crime rates were explained by pointing to the hostility to the police, particularly within nationalist/republican communities and the activities of paramilitaries (e.g. in dissuading people from going to the police or in carrying out their own policing activities), which combined to produce lower reporting rates. Teleologically, paramilitaries were 'blamed' for the social and political upheaval which had occurred since the outbreak of the Troubles. Indeed, the low levels of 'ordinary' crime of the pre-Troubles Stormont era (Brewer, Lockhart and Rodgers, 1997) were used explicitly in official discourses to underpin and present a rose-tinted view of a more harmonious past (e.g. RUC, 1977). Paramilitaries were indisputably engaged in crimes themselves.[11] They could also therefore be held responsible for a broader decline in the bonds of social control, particularly among the younger generation.

A second thesis, which emerged during the late 1970s and early 1980s and has remained prominent since, suggested that Northern Ireland has a 'surprisingly low crime rate' *despite* the Troubles. This view suggested that Northern Ireland society had remained intact in spite of paramilitary violence, as evidenced by comparatively low levels of 'ordinary decent crime' (Heskin, 1981).[12] This analysis was supported by the statistical evidence then available from the Chief Constable's *Annual Reports* and the Northern Ireland Office's Commentaries on Northern Ireland Crime Statistics. As has been argued elsewhere (O'Mahony et al., 2000), crime indices were used again to underpin a political framework projecting a view of Northern Ireland as a decent, church-going, family-oriented low-crime society – a 'paradise on earth', as one former Tory minister described it – marred only by the actions of the 'men of violence'.

It is possible to argue that a third and arguably overlapping genre of criminological scholarship emerged in Northern Ireland which focused on ordinary crime in the jurisdiction. This style of criminology is something we have chosen to call 'don't mention the war' criminology. Focusing on issues such as car theft, crime prevention, juvenile delinquency and similar topics, an administrative criminology arguably emerged in Northern Ireland which was characterized by a largely technocratic and atheoretical treatment of crime in the jurisdiction which paid little substantive attention to the state's legitimacy deficits or the fact that the phenomenon was occurring in a conflict zone (e.g. PPRU, 1984; McCullough, Schmidt and Lockhart, 1990; McQuoid and Lockhart, 1994).[13] Often either funded or carried out by government, or consisting of written accounts of transposed models of work from the British 'mainland' with few alterations to take cognizance of local circumstances (Sanby-Thomas, 1992; Safer Towns, 1994; see also the critique by Crawford and Blair, 2000), such studies paid little substantive attention to the complexities of the relationship between paramilitary activity and ordinary crime, or indeed to the impact of the glaring legitimacy deficiencies of a police and criminal justice system predominantly focused on anti-terrorism.

In sum, therefore, and with the usual academic caveats regarding ideal types, we believe that it is possible to discern at least three genres of positivistic analysis of ordinary crime which emerged during the Northern Ireland conflict. Coupled with a similarly positivistic focus on political violence, such criminological discourses tended to blur rather than illuminate the complex relationship between the conflict, political violence and criminality. Of considerably more analytical use were the analyses which we have grouped below under the broad heading of critical criminology.

Critical criminology and the Northern Ireland conflict

We do not have space here for a proper analysis of the origins and complexity of critical criminological thought in Britain and elsewhere. For current purposes, however, it is sufficient to say that, following the work of the National Deviancy Symposium in the late 1960s (Cohen, 1988) and the seminal publication of *The New Criminology* (Taylor, Walton and Young, 1973), a loosely organized but broadly critical criminological tradition emerged in Britain. This genre of scholarship rejected positivist essentialism, and sought to locate the genesis of crime and interpretations of 'justice' within a wider nexus of class inequalities and power relations. As Colin Sumner notes, *The New Criminology* in particular 'put a brick through the windows of various establishments that had it coming to them' (1994:284). Critical criminologists insisted that crime control was an oppressive and mystifying process that could only be studied in relation to the wider political economy of capitalist society. Whereas positivist criminology focused on what it took to be the objective reality of crime, critical criminology located the study of crime within a study of class relations and structural inequalities. It focused upon the processes of criminalization, shifted attention to the operation of criminal justice agencies (particularly the police and the courts) in producing a criminal *other*, broadened the criminological scope to include the systemic analysis of white-collar crime, crimes of the powerful and crimes committed by the state (Chambliss, 1975; Box, 1987) and provided a base for a commitment to praxis and a normative commitment to social justice and social change.

Before we begin to assess the development of a critical criminology in relation to the Northern Ireland conflict, it is important to highlight a significant caveat. Northern Ireland has not produced a totalizing volume of critical criminological research (as per *The New Criminology*). Indeed, while in proportion to its size, Northern Ireland has been described as the most heavily researched area on earth (Whyte, 1990:viii), comparativelty little of this research has been directed at specific criminological or criminal justice concerns *per se*. Thus not only has there been a dearth of criminological research in Northern Ireland – even that which has an administrative or orthodox flavour – there has been an even greater absence of critical criminological research. A number of tendencies have contributed to this, and for the purposes of the current discussion three broad explanations can be delineated.

First, as we have noted above, the development of positivistic accounts of terrorism in particular arguably established a set of hegemonic discourses which dominated criminological discussions, resulting in a 'hierarchy of credibility' (Schlesigner, 1978) and a greater willingness on the part of researchers to 'believe' the official version of events (for a discussion see Miller, 1994, 1998). The poor quality of much of such analysis arguably contributed to the 'writing off' of criminology in other critical social science circles much in the same way as criminology had been dismissed more broadly in Britain until the NDC (National Deviancy Conference).[14]

Second, the wider dynamics of the conflict have undoubtedly impacted upon the ability of academics to conduct research on Northern Ireland. For locally based researchers, whose 'objectivity' was likely to be called into question particularly if the research had a critical flavour, such difficulties were compounded. Notwithstanding the sterling endeavours of a number of individuals – themselves often working in isolation – the climate for critical research veered from dismissiveness to active hostility, while the lack of funding was also a major problem (Ellison, 1997; Miller, 1998; Mulcahy, 1998). The Royal Ulster Constabulary was particularly reticent about being subjected to scrutiny, with the Chairman of the Northern Ireland Police Federation even going so far as to lambast 'parasitic and irrelevant academics who lionise paramilitaries' (*Irish News*, 7 June 1995). Indeed, it was not until 1991 that the first full-length micro-sociological study of the RUC was published by Brewer and Magee, albeit conducted under the relatively non-contentious ambit of 'routine policing'. That research too created considerable difficulties for its authors (Brewer and Magee, 1991). Even the most anodyne request to study routine aspects of policing or other aspects of criminal justice policy in Northern Ireland – issues that were examined with often banal regularity in Britain – were prohibited or discouraged in Northern Ireland.

Third, Northern Ireland has (until relatively recently) lacked a cohesive criminological and criminal justice research culture in which to furnish a composite picture about crime and criminal justice issues. While there were a number of academics with a primary interest in criminological and criminal-justice-related issues dotted throughout Northern Ireland's two universities, and a few more working with NGOs, it was only with the establishment of the Institute of Criminology and Criminal Justice at Queen's University, Belfast in 1995 that the discipline itself was given a unified and coherent focal point within Northern Ireland. The Institute was created precisely because of the shared view among academics and policy makers of the need for a central disciplinary resource.

None the less, with caveats in mind that the work referred to below does not represent a unified corpus, we have grouped together a range of critical criminological work conducted in and around the Northern Ireland conflict.

The first wave: the end of Stormont

Space does not permit a detailed analysis of the structural characteristics of Northern Ireland that impacted on the nature of nationalist mobilization in the late 1960s and that presaged the slide to violent confrontation (for detailed expositions see Farrell, 1976; Purdey, 1990; Ellison and Martin, 2000). Suffice it to note that before the onset of civil disturbances in the late 1960s Northern Ireland was a bleak and soulless place, at least from the accounts of English journalists who arrived there during the early years of 'the Troubles' (Limpkin, 1972; Fisk, 1975).[15] While the rest of Europe (and indeed the United Kingdom) may have been 'swinging' in the 1960s, Northern Ireland had all the hallmarks of a society time-warped in the 1950s. Its political system was unique in Western Europe: particularist and exclusivist, it remained essentially an oligarchy, with one-party government for over half a century; a political class whose elite membership was drawn from the ranks of the landed gentry, the nobility and propertied business classes, and who collectively had a firm commitment to *laissez-faire* and non-interventionism in virtually all aspects of government life (with the exception of internal security). This political stasis also meant that there was no social democratic 'political opportunity structure' (cf. Melucci, 1996) through which nationalist grievances could be directed, channelled and institutionalized.

In the absence of social democratic consensus about the basis of legitimacy, Northern Ireland had been governed from its inception by specially enacted 'emergency' legislation (the Special Powers Act). The jurisdiction was policed by the predominantly Protestant Royal Ulster Constabulary (RUC), and the exclusively Protestant Ulster Special Constabulary (USC), who were accorded wide executive powers, and whose officers shared an ideological affinity with, and normative loyalty to, the majority Unionist community (Ruane and Todd, 1996).

It would be an exaggeration to suggest that the ruling Unionist elite was haunted by the fear of communism and Bolshevism to the same extent as the National Party in South Africa. None the less, several leading Unionist MPs were members of the anti-communist British Empire Union, and during the early years of Northern Ireland's history, concerted efforts were made by the Ulster Unionist Labour Association to weed out 'Bolsheviks' from local labour associations, although as Bew, Gibbon and Patterson point out (1996:25), 'Bolsheviks' and 'republicans' were often regarded as synonymous.[16] Thus the onset of civil rights mobilization in the late 1960s was regarded by many in the Unionist Party to be a communist-inspired conspiracy to undermine the state (see Purdey, 1990). As such, the harsh response of the Unionist government, and in particular the activities of the RUC and the USC, refocused the demands of the civil rights campaigners away from political and social democratic reforms, to make the issue of policing and 'justice' 'the civil rights issue' (Ó Dochartaigh, 1997).

Consequently, early (critical) criminological concerns were located within a broader nexus of socio-political struggle which took cognizance of the deeply structured inequalities and anti-democratic tendencies of the Northern Ireland state, together with more immediate concerns with praxis – what was actually happening on the ground. For instance, in 1969, Gill Boehringer, the American criminologist then working in the Law Faculty at Queen's University conducted research into policing – mainly in working-class nationalist areas of Belfast which by this stage were effectively 'no-go' areas for the RUC – and developed a model of 'tiered' policing, which he argued would go some way to ameliorating the problems of legitimacy that typified state policing in such areas.[17] Other critical work from this period, while not expressly concerned with criminal justice and criminological issues *per se,* was heavily inspired by Ralph Miliband's *The State in Capitalist Society* (1969), which highlighted the totality and interconnectedness of relationships within the capitalist system. Thus any discussion of crime and the role of repressive state apparatus (the police, the law, the criminal justice system) could not be considered independently of the broader structural issues, and in Northern Ireland, the constitutional question. Michael Farrell's highly influential *Northern Ireland: The Orange State* (1976) is perhaps the best-known example of this genre, in which he outlined the dynamics of what he regarded as an 'imperialist and elaborate sectarian police state' built up without protest from the British and 'backed in the last resort by British forces' (1976:326).

Farrell's work locates the conflict in Northern Ireland within the broader context of an anti-imperialist struggle, while the civil rights protests in the late 1960s were interpreted as the first signs of a crisis in state legitimation. The RUC and the USC, together with repressive legislation in the form of the Special Powers Act, were thus geared to the maintenance and upholding of a blatantly sectarian and discriminatory political entity. Of course, the law and police as 'tools of the ruling class' thesis is now regarded as a somewhat crude and instrumentalist exposition of Marxian political economy (Taylor, Walton and Young, 1973) and indeed *The Orange State* was itself subjected to sustained critique by other Marxist commentators from within Northern Ireland for what they regarded as its over-deterministic and somewhat simplistic analysis of the conflict (see Bew, Gibbon and Patterson, 1979; O'Dowd, Rolston and Tomlinson, 1980). Nevertheless, in spite of these criticisms, what Farrell did in this work and in his subsequent volume *Arming the Protestants* (1983) (focused specifically on policing) was to draw attention to the fact that the criminal justice system itself could be a significant locus for conflict.

The Orange State was complemented in 1980 by a more reflexive Marxian account of 'the Troubles' by O'Dowd, Rolston and Tomlinson, under the title *Between Civil Rights and Civil War* (1980). Utilizing a Marxian framework, heavily influenced by Athussarian structuralism with a focus on the role of ideology, and a Gramscian conception of 'hegemony', the authors shifted the focus of debate away from the local circumstances of Northern Ireland to examine the role of the British state in the conflict. In particular they were highly critical of its attempts to position itself as a 'neutral umpire' arbitrating between two warring and atavistic factions. Indeed, as they suggest in their final chapter, the UK state is not 'above' the Northern Ireland problem; it is an integral part of that problem (1980:208).

The second wave: responding to criminalization

Following the change of government strategy with regard to conflict management in the latter part of 1970s to one of criminalization, critical research began to take a distinctly more criminological flavour as the strategy put the criminal justice system on the front line in the struggle to mobilize consensus against the terrorists (Tomlinson, 1980).[18] A number of strains of critical research emerged, all of which were more or less criminological in nature.

Legal reformist work, conducted largely by human rights activists and a few academics, was concerned primarily with human rights abuses committed by members of the security forces (Amnesty International, 1978, 1988; CAJ, 1983a,b, 1985; Walsh, 1983). While this work was crucial in exposing these abuses, it relied understandably heavily on 'blackletter' law and discourses of formal legal rationality, and did not really focus upon the permissive nature of the law itself and the fact that many state practices in Northern Ireland were often conducted – at least in terms of formal legal rationality – *within the law* (see Ellison, 1997; for a general critique of legal formalism see McBarnet, 1981; Lustgarten, 1987).

The overlapping genre of critical legal research developed an arguably more reflexive and theoretical understanding of the relationship between the law and the dynamics of conflict in Northern Ireland (e.g. Boyle, Hadden and Hillyard, 1975, 1980). Drawing explicitly upon the intellectual tradition of critical criminology itself, some of these researchers looked in particular at the processes by which political violence became criminalized (Rolston and Tomlinson, 1986, 1988) and the development of what amounted to a security–industrial complex in Northern Ireland. Hillyard (1987) also drew upon the conceptualization of 'authoritarian statism' expounded by Stuart Hall and his colleagues argued persuasively that Northern Ireland was becoming a testing laboratory for technologies of control and surveillance that were subsequently 'normalized' within a wider British context.

Finally, what we have chosen to term 'radical eclecticism', saw an academically amorphous group of scholars explore issues that fall within the broad ambit of criminology from a range of disciplines and generally critical paradigms beyond narrow legal or socio-legal concerns. For example, from within media and cultural studies a number of commentators highlighted the often selective and one-dimensional nature of media coverage of the conflict (Curtis, 1984; Rolston, 1991a; Miller, 1994), while from social psychology, Ed Cairns deconstructed the established psychological orthodoxy that suggested that violence could be medicalized or pathologized as something that existed within individuals, and suggested that instead it needed to be grounded within a complex interplay of social processes and the meanings that people use to make sense of their world (Cairns, 1994). In addition, from within anthropology, sociology and critical geography a number of ethnographic studies of urban, working-class community life in Belfast were conducted which, by locating elements of subcultural theory within a broader structuralist perspective, provided an important counter to the ideological components of the officially propagated discourse of criminalization (Burton, 1978; Jenkins, 1983; Dawson, 1984; Sluka, 1989). Such studies demonstrated the complexities of the relations between paramilitaries and local communities, wherein paramilitary activities were often not deemed to be 'criminal' as articulated in official state discourse or indeed holding their respective communities to ransom through a process of intimidation and terror. Rather, as was also demonstrated by a number of explicitly criminological studies, paramilitary activities such as informal justice and punishment of alleged anti-social offenders was often expected by local comunities who had little faith in the formal justice system (Morrissey and Pease, 1982; Munck, 1984, 1988; Hillyard, 1985; McCorry and Morrissey, 1989).

The third wave: the post-ceasefire period

Criminological discourses in Northern Ireland since the ceasefires are considered in some detail in the section below on criminology and conflict resolution. Suffice to say here that this period has seen a profound increase in the range and scope of criminological work in the jurisdiction. This has been due to a number of interrelated factors. The establishment of the Institute of Criminology and Criminal Justice at Queen's University, Belfast in 1995 gave the discipline a coherent focal point, brought together researchers, and facilitated the dissemination of ideas of individuals working in a range of criminological areas including policing, youth justice, crime surveys, prisons, restorative justice, and crimes of private space (e.g. Brogden and Nijhar, 2000; Ellison and Smyth, 2000; O'Mahony, 2000; O'Mahony et al., 2000; Wright and Bryett, 2000; McEvoy, 2001). Scholars in other departments in the two Northern Irish universities have also become increasingly active in criminological work (e.g. McWilliams and Spence, 1996; McElrath and McEvoy, 1999; Hillyard and Tomlinson, 2000; Knox and Monaghan, 2000; McElrath, 2000). Younger scholars who conducted their doctoral research in Northern Ireland but have since been employed elsewhere have begun to publish their analysis to good effect (e.g. Mulcahy, 1999, 2000; Pickering, 2000, 2001), and more established academics, albeit from other disciplines, have refocused their attention on matters criminological (McGarry and O'Leary, 1999) in light of the peace process. In addition, as is discussed in greater detail below, a rapprochement in relations between critical researchers and official funding bodies and a political climate which is much more facilitative of, and conducive to, the conduct of critical research has contributed in no small way to a profound shift in the academic and intellectual climate in Northern Ireland.

However, rather than offer an exposition of the breadth of that work, we have chosen to focus below on a number of themes which may be drawn from research, in particular that on the intersection between criminology and the conflict resolution process.

Criminology and conflict resolution: lessons from Northern Ireland

Before discussing the more generally applicable themes which have emerged in the era of conflict resolution, it is worth reiterating the centrality of criminological discourses to the process of peacemaking in Northern Ireland. For example, in the wake of the Good Friday Agreement, an independent commission on policing was established under the chairmanship of former Hong Kong governor Chris Patten and included a number of prominent criminological academics among its membership (Patten, 1999). An independent sentence review commission was established which oversaw the release of paramilitary prisoners belonging to organizations on ceasefire (Sentence Review Commission, 2000). A civil-service-led review team was established (with four independent members including three criminologists) to examine and make recommendations for reform of the Northern Ireland criminal justice system as a whole with the exception of policing and emergency laws (Criminal Justice Review, 2000). A victims' commission was established and reported on a range of victim-related issues (Bloomfield, 1998). There has been a proliferation of community-based restorative justice projects established in order to try to supplant paramilitary punishment violence (McEvoy and Mika, 2001). Finally, a human rights commission was established and has recently produced a draft Bill of Rights for Northern Ireland with recommendations on rights pertaining to a range of criminal justice matters, emergency laws, prisoners' rights, juvenile justice and related criminological topics (Human Rights Commission, 2001). In short, criminology has been at the very heart of the conflict resolution process.

Based on the Northern Ireland experience, we would argue that there is a range of at least four intersecting themes which, while felt acutely in the context of a political conflict, have a considerably broader applicability. These are the notion of criminology as a political project;

criminology as a moral project; criminology as an international and comparative project; and finally, the interrelationship between criminology, human rights and conflict resolution.

Criminology as a political project

First, as was suggested above, criminology follows established patterns of the other social sciences within conservative, liberal or critical paradigms – either supporting the established order, offering a reformist critique within the normative and legal structure of the state, or forming alliances with other progressive forces in the articulation of a radical alternative and transformative vision. Such a framework is true for any society. However, in a process of political conflict and conflict resolution, a brighter light shines on such paradigms, holding them up to closer scrutiny because the intellectual, political and social stakes are higher, and, arguably, the potential for transformation is greater.

In 1967, in his essay 'Social Structure, Social Control and Deviation', Lemert argued in his critique of Strain theory that Merton had an all too static view of cultural goals, social structure and social control. Instead he contended that it might be possible to view criminology in a more dynamic fashion as the study of deviance within a theory of social change (Lemert, 1967:26). If we see criminology as the study of the relationship between deviance, social control and social structure, then criminology in a conflict or a post-conflict situation is a more 'speeded-up' and arguably more lucid version of what is taking place in more 'stable' societies. The legitimacy deficiencies of the criminal justice system are more obvious and more obviously contested, often serving as the focal point around which the political fault lines of a conflict intersect (Bell, 2000). The ensuing political negotiations, assuming that none of the protagonists have achieved an outright military victory, often mean that the potential (at least) for progressive change to the institutions of the system is arguably greater, at least during the period of negotiation and transition (Teitel, 2000) than in more settled democracies.

In some respects it may be worthwhile drawing an imperfect analogy between criminology (or critical criminology at least) in a conflict zone such as Northern Ireland and the political and historical context of the NDC in Britain in the late 1960s (Rock, 1988). Cohen has described well his involvement in this group as a view of criminology offering 'a form of commitment, a way of staying in without on the other hand selling out, or playing the drab game of orthodox politics' (Cohen, 1988:80). In the politically charged environment of a conflict, with clear intellectual positions to 'be against' (such as a positivistic understanding of political violence or administrative criminology) and obvious instances of state and paramilitary repression and violence, criminology has arguably provided at least some criminologists in Northern Ireland with a tool for moral and political engagement. As was noted above, human rights activists in the jurisdiction have made similar interventions, by operating within the paradigm provided by international human rights standards (e.g. Mageean and O'Brien, 1999). By retaining a focus upon the parameters provided by the discipline, and using its conceptual and intellectual tools to make interventions on contentious issues such as police accountability, state killings, prisoner releases and so forth, criminology has offered a platform and some degree of protection from the charge that such interventions were politically motivated. After all, if criminologists cannot speak critically about prisons, policing, victims and the rest, then who can?

Criminology as a moral project

The increased awareness of the political character of criminology also allows a tentative relationship to be posited between criminology and morality.[19] Criminology has always been bound up with notions of morality. As Quinney has argued, 'the very stuff of the criminal law is moral ... A moral decision is taken when it is decided to protect others by the means of criminal law. Legal reform or legal revolution cannot be achieved by taking morality out of the law' (Quinney, 1972:24). The difficulty with the concept of morality, particular for broadly critical criminologists, is that it is normally associated with 'protagonists for law and order and severe penal sanctions' (Christie, 1981:10) or what Van Swaaningen has described as 'reactionary or crypto-religious connotations such as duty, shame or sin' (Van Swaaningen, 1997:250). However, as Van Swaaningen goes on to argue, it is possible to explore the links between criminology and morality through discourses such as social justice, human rights protection and participatory justice in order to develop a more critical and pluralist notion of morality (ibid.: 249–50).

Writing in 1979, Cohen suggested that there were two routes within critical criminology which offered pathways back to the moral dimension of criminal politics (Cohen, 1988:120).[20] Later, in 1985, having engaged with the dangers of community-based corrections, he answers the question 'so what is to be done?' with what he refers to as 'moral pragmatism'.[21] The role of the criminologist for Cohen is to serve 'three voracious gods': first, an overriding obligation to honest intellectual enquiry (however sceptical, provisional, irrelevant and unrealistic); second, a political commitment to social justice; and third (and potentially conflicting with both), the pressing and immediate demands for short-term humanitarian help (Cohen, 1998). His conclusion is that 'our task is the seemingly impossible, to combine detachment with commitment. There is only one universal guide for this: not to use intellectual scepticism as an alibi for political inaction' (ibid.:126).

For criminologists such as ourselves, who have lived through and worked on the Northern Ireland conflict, Cohen's outline of the moral dimension of the criminological project has a particular resonance. Criminology, or at least *good* critical criminology, in a conflict zone is a quintessentially *moral* project. In such a context, whether one is working on policing, prisons, victims of crime, or whatever, the criminological endeavour should be about not only better understanding the object of study but also showing the honest links between those topics and the contours of the conflict in order to try to make a difference. In such a situation, the obligation to try to use the analytical strengths of one's discipline to make a difference is perhaps more obviously morally compelling; it is only a question of degree rather than of principle.

Criminology as an international and comparative project

A third key feature of criminology in Northern Ireland, in particular during the conflict resolution era, has been a reliance upon the international and comparative dimensions of the discipline to reflect upon key themes in the jurisdiction. In the political context of increased globalization, integration within the European Union and elsewhere, cross-national policing on issues such as drugs, terrorism and so forth, international comparative criminology has developed into a major theme of the discipline in general (e.g. Neuman and Berger, 1988; Ruggiero and South, 1995; Nelken, 1997; Sheptycki, 2000), as has increasingly the comparative study of policy making (Downes, 1988; Rutherford, 1990, 1995).

A number of reasons have been put forward for doing comparative criminological work in general. For some commentators, the purpose of the work is to seek to transcend local cultural, political or national factors in order to arrive at genuine universal social scientific truths (Gottfredson and Hirschi, 1990). For others, it provides an opportunity to increase the explanatory potential of criminological theories by offering an essential antidote to ethnocentrism, and in particular to the hegemony of US-based criminological discourses (Beirne and Nelken, 1997:xiii). Comparative criminology, it is argued, allows one to see better what is actually going on in one's own country.[22] It may facilitate improvements in methodology and refine empirical enquiry (Beirne, 1983; Bennett and Lynch, 1990; Van Dijk and Mayhew, 1993). It may also sensitize western scholars to the less obvious imperial and colonial dimensions to their own intellectual traditions (Cohen, 1982).

To a greater or lesser extent all of these factors have played some part in encouraging the considerable increase in international and comparative criminological scholarship in Northern Ireland. While comparative research was a mainstay of related disciplines such as political science during the conflict (e.g. O'Leary and McGarry, 1993; Guelke, 1995), and while a number of criminological studies which were comparative in nature were published during the conflict (e.g. Rolston and Tomlinson, 1986; Brewer, 1988; Weitzer, 1990), the period since the ceasefires has seen a dramatic rise in such studies. Comparative criminological work has been carried out on issues such as policing and the protection of human rights (O'Rawe and Moore, 1997); the maintenance of order at public demonstrations (Jarman et al., 1998; Bryant and Jarman, 1999); the release of paramilitary prisoners (Gormally and McEvoy, 1995); the victims of paramilitary assaults in Northern Ireland (Knox and Monaghan, 2000) and the development of informal justice systems in Northern Ireland (McEvoy and Mika, 2002); and the role of the judiciary in criminal proceedings (Doran and Jackson, 2000). As well as such scholarship carried out by activists and academics, a number of the review bodies established under the terms of the Good Friday Agreement themselves stimulated rich strains of comparative research. The Independent Commission on Policing commissioned and drew heavily upon international and comparative research in reaching its conclusions (Patten, 1999). Similarly, the Review of the Criminal Justice System team commissioned and then published a wide number of research reports, almost all of which drew considerably on international and comparative data (e.g. Blair, 2000; Crawford and Matassa, 2000; Criminal Justice Review, 2000; Dignan, 2000; Walker and Tedford, 2000).

As well as the factors suggested above, a number of key dynamics have contributed to this increased output in international and comparative scholarship in the jurisdiction. First, and perhaps most empirically difficult to back up, has been a general sense that the peace process 'unfroze' international interest more generally in what was happening in Northern Ireland. After such a prolonged period of seemingly intractable conflict, the gradual emergence of the peace process enlivened international scholarly and media interest in the place (Miller, 1998; De Bréadún, 2001). It became easier to engender international interest in criminological work in the jurisdiction beyond those constituencies long interested in conflict generally or Irish affairs more specifically.

A second and related feature was that a range of funding sources became available which were not heretofore on the criminological horizon. Major charitable sources such as the Joseph Rowntree Foundation, the John Merck Fund and others provided funds for scholars to carry out comparative field work as well as to host major conferences as part of broader dissemination strategies (e.g. NIACRO, 1995a; CAJ, 1999). The ESRC Violence Programme funded one major conflict-related study (Knox and Monaghan, 2000), and of course, as noted above, both the Patten and Criminal Justice Reviews were given large research budgets and commissioned work of a comparative nature.

A third, and perhaps more interesting feature of this increase has been those scholars and activists who deliberately carried out international and comparative work in order to take forward particular peacemaking agendas. Nelken has argued that comparative criminology allows us to 'raise or sharpen awkward questions' (Nelken, 1994:223). International and comparative work on issues such as policing, prisoner release and marching have allowed scholars to go beyond local hegemonic understandings of the insolubility of particular problems. The 'ethnocentrism' referred to by Beirne and Nelken (1997) with regard to criminology in general could at times be equally applied to those of us who live and work in a complex zone of conflict such as Northern Ireland. Perhaps, at times we have appeared to revel in our complexity, celebrated our uniqueness and acquiesced in our intractability. The prolonged nature of our conflict, and its deep historical, political, cultural and social complexity have arguably transmogrified in some quarters among the elites of Northern Ireland into an intellectual resignation that little could be done to achieve change, a tired resignation to the view that 'nothing works'. However, comparative research which avoids simplistic or mechanistic transpositions from one jurisdiction to another but rather thematizes and frames complex questions into formats which are digestible to a lay audience can move debates beyond the localized context.[23] Such contexts have offered the potential for real criminological praxis in the process of peacemaking in Northern Ireland.

Criminology, conflict resolution and human rights discourses

As was noted above, the work of human rights activists and scholars during the Northern Ireland conflict has often dovetailed with that of criminologists on issues such as policing, emergency laws, the Diplock courts, extra-judicial killings and so forth (see, e.g., Amnesty International, 1988, 1992, 1994; Jennings, 1990; Dickson, 1992; CAJ, 1997; Ní Aoláin, 2000). There has occasionally been explicit collaboration between the two disciplines (e.g. Boyle, Hadden and Hillyard, 1980; O'Rawe and Moore, 1997). Lawyers and criminologists whose interests have straddled both disciplines have drawn considerably upon either analytical framework (e.g. Morison and Livingstone, 1995; Campbell, 1999; McEvoy, 2000). And of course, during the period of conflict resolution, the centrality of human rights to contemporary criminological discourses in the jurisdiction has been highlighted by the extreme prominence of international human rights standards in the recent major publications on policing, criminal justice and related matters.[24]

Other criminologists, also often spurred on by the exigencies of life in a political conflict, have also been spurred to engage with human rights discourses. As Van Zyl Smit argues in his chapter in this volume (Chapter 2), human rights were an important strand of both critical and what he refers to as 'legal reformist' criminology in South Africa. Similarly in Latin America, as Del Olmo has argued, the discourses of critical criminology on that continent have 'advanced the study of, and concern for, human rights as the first priority' (Del Olmo, 1999:37). Perhaps best known among criminologists who have worked explicitly within a human rights framework is (again) Stan Cohen (now at the London School of Economics), who became deeply involved in the human rights movement in Israel after moving to live and work there. From the early 1990s, Cohen began to write about human rights abuses, the ways in which they are framed or denied, and the intersection between these issues and his traditional work in criminology and the sociology of deviance (e.g. Cohen, 1993, 1996, 2001).

Cohen identified a number of major gaps in the criminological discourse with regard to human rights which are relevant for current discussion. First, he argued that criminologists had failed to recognize that human rights instruments have become a major source of 'moral enterprise and criminalisation' and that one could no longer simply point to the usual suspects of middle-class morality or the interests of corporate capitalism as primary criminalizing agents. Second, he argued that much of the radical criminological work on human rights had something of an ethnocentric American focus, preoccupied with the 'exposure' of the CIA's dirty wars, the surveillance of the FBI, and the global drugs war (e.g. Barak, 1991). Third, he pointed out that while criminologists ritually acknowledge the damage and harm caused by state crimes, there is little substantive or sustained engagement with the reality of gross human rights victimization. Rather, due to western ethnocentrism and success of a range of strategies of denial practised universally (including by criminologists), mainstream criminology has largely left work on human rights abuses for others (Cohen, 1993).

Cohen's pessimistic assessment of crimology's capacity to engage with human rights discourses may be (at least slightly) less true today than it was ten years ago. More recent contributions from American radical and peacemaking criminology have, while still focused on the repressive activities of US domestic law enforcement and foreign policy, become somewhat more international and less parochial than their predecessors (e.g. Friedrichs, 1997; Ross, 2000). That said, criminology's failure to engage substantively with the implications of international human rights, humanitarian law and variations of political conflict such as genocide or mass rape largely remain as valid a criticism (Jamieson, 1999; Day and Vandiver, 2000; Hoffman, 2000; Yacobian, 2000). Similarly, while a more explicitly rights-conscious criminology has emerged in the developing areas of animal rights (e.g. Benson, 1998), 'green' criminology (e.g. South, 1998) and related national and transnational issues concerning white-collar crime and workers' health and safety (e.g. Pearce and Tombs, 1998), and in what might be termed 'black-letter' criminal justice scholarship (Beatson, 1999), it is still something that is not quite mainstream.

Engagement in human rights discourses has a number of distinct advantages for criminologists. At a theoretical level, such discourses appeal because they offer some form of moral and intellectual anchor. With the demise of the old metanarratives of the cold war era of Marxism and liberalism, they have become a 'dominant narrative', the normative language of the future (Cohen, 1993:99) – 'the lingua franca of global moral thought, as English has become the lingua franca of the global economy' (Ignatieff, 2001:53). Human rights frameworks arrest the postmodern tendency towards 'plurality, contingency and difference', offering instead a meaningful and universalist set of standards which can give concrete meaning to general concepts of justice, discrimination and so forth (Sparks, 1994, cited in Van Swaaningen, 1997:234). They have become the key terrain for some of the most lively and stimulating debates in political science and critical legal studies on the role of the state, national justice systems, civil society and international legal order in the new global/transnational era – all issues which remain central criminological problematics (Alston, 1995; Van Ness and Aziz, 1999; Douzinas, 2000). Finally, at a very practical level in Britain at least, criminologists, like others who work on the justice system, must now come to terms with the implications of the Human Rights Act 1998 on their object of study.

The mainstreaming of human rights concerns within criminology generally, which arguably occurs in a more direct and immediate fashion in a zone of conflict, will mean that any criminologist writing about policing, prisons, courts, or any other aspects of the criminal justice system must inevitably take on board the human rights dimensions to their subject-matter. As in Northern Ireland, human rights considerations will become an epistemological given, a key feature of the criminological landscape.

Conclusion: criminology, transition and memory

In any violent political conflict, the criminal justice system is inevitably in the front line of the state's efforts to contain, manage or even criminalize political violence. The police, courts, prisons, and prosecution are all by necessity and design the central weapons in the state's efforts to respond to any such violence and civil disorder. The particular configurations of that response (e.g. police or army primacy, the use of emergency v. ordinary laws, military court v. jury trials, combatants treated as prisoners of war v. ordinary criminals – and the myriad of hybrids in between) are the key practical and ideological components of the way that a state chooses to fight the conflict. Thus the study of a criminal justice system provides a reference point for understanding the parameters of a conflict while it is ongoing. Similarly, as we have argued above in the case of Northern Ireland, the ways in which the criminal justice system responds during a period of conflict resolution (e.g. in areas such as prisoner release, police and criminal justice reform, the treatment of victims, the protection of human rights and so forth) are for many the litmus test to establish whether a society is truly emerging from the conflict.

In recent years much of the discussion concerning criminal justice in a post-conflict setting has focused on what is increasingly termed in legal and philosphical ciricles 'transitional justice'.[25] In Latin America, Eastern Europe, the former Soviet Union, and a number of countries in Africa, many societies have struggled with central questions concerning their criminal justice systems, often after considerable violence and injustice (e.g. Rosenberg, 1995; Mendez, 1997; Walicki, 1997). In such a transition, issues related to the past such as debates concerning the prosecution of those reponsible for committing atrocities and other conflict-related activities (Beigbeder, 1999; Osiel 2000) and truth commissions

and amnesties for past offences (Hayner, 1994; Boraine, 2001) come centre stage. Similar and interconnected issues related to the future, such as
the prospective role of those who have adminstered a criminal justice
system in times of conflict (normally when their duties have included
systemic abuses of the rights of its citizens) or new mechanisms
designed to ensure greater legitimacy and a clear break with the practices of the past (O'Donnell, Schmitter and Whitehead, 1986; Zalaquett,
1990; Linz and Stepan, 1996) – these too are core issues for a criminlogy
of conflict resolution to grapple with.

The practical and theoretical exigencies of criminological discourses
in a period of transition aruably provide us with a clearer view of some
fundamental criminological truisms.

The particular post-conflict mechanisms employed to reconcile the
past with the future, whether prosecutions of previous human rights
violators, amnesties, truth commissions or 'business as usual' (or variations containing some of these elements), are often dictated in large part
by prevailing political exigencies (e.g. Zalaquett, 1990). Criminal justice
in transition is perhaps more honestly framed by the prevailing political
circumstances than criminal justice in more settled times.

In turn, the contours of a post-conflict settlement in a national or
indeed international collective consciousness are inevitably largely
defined by the legal mechanisms ultimately chosen to achieve the transition. As Teitel has argued, 'the conception of justice that emerges in
times of political change is extraordinary and constructionist; it is alter-
natively constituted by, and constitutive of, the transition' (Teitel,
2000:6). Regimes in transition are forced to engage with the role that
criminal law plays in fermenting a society's sense of identity and collective memory.[26] Trials of war criminals or truth commission hearings are
social dramas wherein those involved self-consciously use the aspects of
spectacle traditionally associated with the criminal justice process to
embed particular messages about a society's past and future.

Finally, in transition, the criminal justice process is also required to
ask fundamental questions concerning its purpose and rationale. The
primacy of actuarial and managerial concerns, which it has been argued
have come to replace metanarratives regarding the role of criminal justice in many western countries (e.g. Feeley and Simon, 1992; Raine and
Wilson, 1997), are at least temporarily displaced as regimes must decide
if their movement from the past is to be driven primarily by retributive,
reparative or socially reconstructive concerns.

So how do these transitional themes relate to the Northern Ireland
context? Some critical republican commentators may dispute whether

a genuine 'transition' has actually occurred here, arguing, for example, that what has occurred is in effect a repackaging of the same British state, with the same criminal justice and policing infrastructure, largely staffed by the same individuals and operating within the same imperial framework (e.g. MacIntyre, 1995). Such a view, however, is to confuse revolution with transition. If we utilize the definition provided above by Teitel, we have no doubt that Northern Ireland is a jurisdiction in transition. While the extent of the transition is yet to be determined, that it is happening is beyond dispute.

With regard to the interplay between prevailing political exigencies and the criminal justice system, the relationship could hardly have been more obvious. Other than the intricate constitutional arrangements, as we have argued above, much of the Good Friday Agreement was taken up with the criminal justice system. The provisions which paved the way for prisoner release, police and criminal justice reform represented a largely explicit recognition that the legtimacy deficits of the system were key factors in the origins and perpetuation of the conflict and thus central to attempts at peacemaking.

As to the constructionist capacity of the legal mechanism employed to span the move from conflict and its relationship to the creation of memory of the conflict, the current picture is far less clear. Northern Ireland has seen comparatively little pressure from key civil society actors for a truth commission (Boraine, 1999). Similarly, while there have been attempts by various victims' groups and their anti-Agreement political allies to exclude Sinn Fein from government on the basis of previous IRA atrocities (Morgan, 2000), there has been little organized campaigning for 'war trials' of non-state combatants (or indeed state combatants) for acts carried out during the conflict. Instead Northern Ireland has seen a piecemeal approach to uncovering truth about certain key events.[27] These limited truth-finding investigations have only come about in the wake of intensive political lobbying by civil society and varying political forces. While a limited amnesty has been declared for a number of former paramilitaries 'on the run', a general amnesty for all former combatants would seem highly unlikely. The political will for such measures, or indeed for prosecutions for previous atrocities, does not exist. Thus, and perhaps inevitably, the capacity for legal or criminal justice mechanisms to build shared understandings of the past are circumscribed by the prevailing political winds which are not blowing in that direction.

There has, however, been some deep-rooted examination of the purpose and rationale of the criminal justice system during the period of transition in Northern Ireland. The centrality of human rights discourses to the reviews of policing and the criminal justice system, the real questioning of the use and effect of imprisonment,[28] the explosion of interest in the area of restorative justice – these are all examples of fundamental reassessments which are related to the transition. As Teitel has argued, 'values of mercy and reconcilation commonly considered to be external to criminal justice are an explicit part of transitional deliberation. The explicit politicization of criminal law in these periods challenges ideal understandings of justice and turns out to be a persistent feature of jurisprudence in the transitional context ...' (2000:217). Similar to Dirk van Zyl Smit in relation to South Africa, we too are somewhat sceptical whether such progressive deliberations will fundamentally alter the nature of the system once the process of transition has gone further down the road.

The institutional capacity of (elements at least) of the justice system to minimize, circumnavigate and otherwise thwart progressive criminological praxis has been well demonstrated (e.g. with regard to the implementation of the Patten Report) the further we have moved from the end of the conflict. Should the institutions of local governance survive, that resistance to change will be further complicated by the full devolution of criminal justice powers and the oversight of policing to local politicians. The outplaying of that process in the Northern Ireland context is just too uncertain to predict at this juncture. That said, Northern Ireland will not be a dull place in which to be a criminologist or indeed to do criminology.

Notes

1. A number of the ideas in the second section of this chapter were first presented in a paper delivered by Kieran McEvoy at the British Criminology Conference in Leicester, 2000. We are grateful for the comments of a number of those who attended that conference.
2. Other commonly identified features of positivism include determinism, wherein psychological or social factors compel individuals towards criminality; differentiation, wherein criminals can be differentiated from non-criminals because of biological, psychological or sociological traits; and pathology, wherein criminality could be explained because something had 'gone wrong' at a biological, psychological or social level (see, e.g., Taylor, Walton and Young, 1973; Wilson and Herrnstein, 1985; Beirne, 1987; Gottfredson and Hirschi, 1990).
3. In common with other jurisdictions undergoing political conflict from the 1970s onwards, the *science* of 'terrorism studies' emerged in order to assist western states in tackling the phenomenon, studying the links between

terrorist groupings, their relations with sponsoring states such as Libya or Iraq and a range of other security-related issues (McClintock, 1985; Chomsky, 1988; Cockburn, 1990; Rolston, 1991b). The well-funded production of such scholarship provided an academic basis for a series of technocratic discourses on terrorist violence, assumed that the democratic credentials of Western states were axiomatic and justified a predominantly security-focused approach to tackling such violence which largely underplayed its political origins (Herman and O'Sullivan, 1990, 1991; Gearty, 1996). This discipline is enjoing something of a renaissance following the attacks of 11 September 2001 by Islamic militants on American civilian targets.

4. For example, in the preface to his 1977 book Richard Clutterbuck outlines his rationale for the study of terrorism: 'a society needs an awareness of what the terrorists are trying to achieve, and a high degree of public co-operation with its police and soldiers. We need to understand how this kind of war is fought on both sides if we are to know how best to help those who are fighting, win it' (Clutterbuck, 1977:ii).

5. 'Interrogation is a slow business and requires much patience, especially if, as in this case, some of those arrested resist violently. ... Arresting 342 in one night vastly exceeded the capacity for interrogation in Northern Ireland' (Clutterbuck, 1977:69).

6. Among the most influential of these commentators was Professor Paul Wilkinson, based at the University of St Andrews. Wilkinson, who was himself targeted by the IRA, has been described as Britain's 'primary expert on terrorism' (Gearty, 1996). In 1996, over a year after the first IRA ceasefire, the government commissioned a review of the anti-terrorism legislation in the United Kingdom to be carried out by a senior judge Lord Lloyd. In the main body of the Report, Lord Lloyd states, 'It seemed desirable at the outset to seek an academic view as to the nature of the terrorist threat ... There was nobody better qualified to undertake such a task than Professor Wilkinson' (Lloyd, 1996, Vol. 1:viii). Lord Lloyd was so impressed by the resulting submission that he took the highly unusual step of publishing it as an adjunct, Volume 2, of his Report. Wilkinson's part of the Report views the UK as the bulwark of democratic freedoms facing an actual or potential 'threat' from different variants of terrorism (Lloyd, 1996, Vol. 2:79). Its conclusion concurs largely with that of Lord Lloyd himself, that a permanent panoply of anti-terrorist legislation is required, built very much on the offences and police powers contained in the 'emergency' legislation passed to deal with the Northern Ireland conflict (Lloyd, 1996, Vol. 2:81).

7. 'If we attach any meaning and value to our Western Judaeo-Christian, liberal and humanist values and the ethical and legal systems that have been shaped by this tradition, we must logically recognise the *criminal* [our emphasis] nature of terrorism ... It is a moral crime, a crime against humanity, an attack not only on our security, our rule of law and the safety of the state, but on civilised society itself' (Wilkinson, 1986:66).

8. 'Thus the present strucure [of the IRA] comprises four levels; the godfathers, the hard core, the volunteers and the auxiliaries' (Clutterbuck, 1994:158).

9. See McEvoy and Gormally (1997) for a more sustained critique of this genre of scholarship and its implications.

10. The Chief Constable's *Annual Report* for 1979, looking back at the previous ten years, argued that 'the general lawlessness brought about by a decade of terrorism has lowered community restraint and personal discipline' (RUC, 1979:2). Juvenile-justice-related research refers to papers prepared and circulated within government departments in the mid-1970s which express the view that 'at some stage the prolonged period of civil disorders could produce an increasing volume of juvenile delinquency' (NIO circular, 1976, cited in Powell, 1982; Caul, 1983).

11. Between the various Republican and Loyalist factions, paramilitaries have been responsible for almost 90 per cent or over 3200 of conflict-related deaths including civilian and security force casualties, with the security forces responsible for 360 killings between 1969 and 1999 (McKittrick et al., 1999; Ní Aoláin, 2000). Thousands more have been injured in bombings, shootings and other acts of political violence (Fay, Morrissey and Smyth, 1999). In order to fund their respective campaigns, paramilitaries have been responsible for a range of other offences, including robberies, kidnapping, extortion, smuggling and, in the case of Loyalist paramilitaries and Republican splinter groups, the dealing and distribution of illicit drugs both for organizational funds and personal gain (Bowyer Bell, 1993; McEvoy, McElrath and Higgins, 1998; Silke, 1999).

12. A more sophisticated variant of this thesis is advanced by Brewer, Lockhart and Rodgers, who argue that increased ghettoization as a result of the conflict had the effect of creating more tight-knit communities with a greater prominence given to the role of extended families. They argue convincingly that 'political violence has, ironically, protected Northern Ireland from some of the worst vagaries of community breakdown and dislocation witnessed in Britain's inner cities. The knock on effects of this for ordinary crime levels in Northern Ireland are positive, irrespective of the other effects of terrorism, especially on the families of its victims' (Brewer, Lockhart and Rodgers, 1997:216).

13. In a subtle and not unsympathetic account of similar criminological research in Britain, Loader has described this genre as 'jobbing criminology' by which he means 'the practice of going from criminological job to criminological job either unburdened by intellectual agendas, or else committed only to narrowly construed and pre-established policy goals' (Loader, 1998:197). As Loader argues, we may all become 'jobbers' from time to time. He goes on to suggest that such an intellectual tradition is marked by a number of 'closures' concerning the study of crime and social regulation. These are: (a) the pursuance of a chronically limited range of explanatory avenues, structuring enquiries around the question of what works, leaving unexamined the connection between crime control and questions of social structure; (b) the 'bracketing off' of the political dimensions of its subject-matter (e.g. the relationship between 'Neighbourhood Watch' and the official promotion of active citizenship); and (c) the lack of any articulated ethical standpoint, the 'forgetting' that the process of crime control is not just about effectiveness but also to do with social justice and that success in such a policy can consequently be assessed in normative as well as instrumental terms (ibid.: 197–8).

14. Even within critical social science circles, criminological concerns have been somewhat marginalized. For example, in an otherwise reflexive and critical

anthology published under the title *Rethinking Northern Ireland* (Miller, 1998), wherein scholarly attention is drawn to a plethora of topics such as colonialism, feminism and nationalism, politics and culture, demography and spatial segregation, only one chapter comes anywhere near to addressing criminological or criminal justice issues, and even then only tangentially under the rubric of 'British policy' in Northern Ireland (see Tomlinson, 1998).

15. Swings in public parks were routinely chained on Sundays in many local council areas and laws prohibiting the Sunday opening of pubs were only relaxed in the late 1980s.

16. In a similar vein, an early collection of essays under the title *Ulster Under Home Rule*, edited by the then Professor of Jurisprudence at Queen's University, F.H. Newark, and published in 1955, is peppered with frequent and disparaging remarks about 'Socialism'. Indeed, Newark himself branded a mildly critical report into the operation of the Special Powers Act, and published in 1936, as having been written by a 'body well leavened with individuals whom we now recognise as Communists and fellow travellers' (1955:49). The body in question was the National Council of Civil Liberties!

17. Boheringer's research is notable in many respects, not least because he recognized that *policing* is not necessarily the business of the state police, and that as a process grounded in the very essence of ordering and governance, it should be an organic, 'bottom-up' affair, emanating from within the community (see Shearing and Stenning, 1987; Shearing, 2001).

18. Criminalization was introduced in the wake of the Gardiner Committee report in 1976. It was in essence a strategy designed to delegitimize and depoliticize those involved in paramilitary violence by removal of the practical and symbolic state recognition of the political nature of terrorist violence. Internment without trial was ended, as was 'Special Category Status' (in effect *de facto* prisoner-of-war status) for convicted paramilitary prisoners and the police were given primary responsibility for security policy (Cunningham, 1991; Ellison, 2000; McEvoy, 2001).

19. As Peter Young has argued, criminology may be described as the process of 'practical reasoning to take forward particular political or moral agendas' (Young, 2000).

20. One relates to the focus on the definitional question of criminology, extending the definition of crime and criminology's subject-matter to include imperialism, racism, sexism, colonialism, capitalism and exploitation. This, Cohen argues, is more that an exercise in expansive subject demarcation but rather it 'announces a moral stance; not just that we should "study" all these evils but that we should condemn them, condemn them as if they were like or worse than the crimes that fill our current textbooks and our criminal justice system' (Cohen, 1988:120). The second route he suggests is the recognition that the working class also suffers from crime and shares an interest in aspects of bourgeois ideology (e.g. the demand for justice) and the recognition that there is no monolithic criminal consciousness, that crimes may be committed for a range of reasons including brutalization by the sytem, voluntarism or primitive political rebellion (ibid.: 121).

21. The moral element refers to the affirmation of doing good and doing justice. The pragmatic end stands against 'all forms of premature theoretical and political closure, all quests for cognitive certainty which rule out certain

solutions as being conceptually impure or politically inadmissible' (Cohen, 1985:252–3).

22. 'The reason for doing comparative research may have as much to do with understanding one's own country better as it has to understanding anyone else's. Comparative enquiry has as one of its chief concerns the effort to identify the way a country's types of crime and of crime control resonate with other aspects of its culture. Many claims about crime causation or about crime control which purport to be universal in fact take their sense and limits of applicability from such cultural connections' (Nelken, 1994:221).

23. As Dave Wall, former chief executive of NIACRO (Northern Ireland Association for the Care and Resettlement of Offenders), the agency which was responsible for the international comparative research on prisoner release, has argued: 'The international and comparative dimension to this research has considerably informed the emerging debate in Northern Ireland on the prisoner issue. It has allowed us all to think the unthinkable, to recognise that whatever the local exigencies, prison release is a necessary part of conflict resolution and to look pragmatically and sensitively as to how this might be achieved' (NIACRO, 1995b:1).

24. For example, the Independent Commission on Policing described the role of human rights in their deliberations thus. 'It is a central proposition of this report that the fundamental purpose of policing should be, in the words of the Agreement, the protection and vindication of the human rights of all ... There should be no conflict between human rights and policing. Policing means protecting human rights' (Patten, 1999:18). Similarly the civil-service-led Criminal Justice Review stated that 'We also believed that we would consider the issues within our terms of reference from a human rights perspective, a perspective that underpins and runs through the Belfast Agreement itself. As a result we have paid a great deal of attention to international and domestic human rights obligations, and considered all of the issues before us from a human rights perspective' (Criminal Justice Review 2000:4). Each chapter of that report begins with a review of the relevant international human rights standards and their implications for the element of criminal justice under consideration. In addition, a separate research report was commissioned on human rights and criminal justice (Livingstone and Doak, 2000).

25. Teitel's discussion on the meaning of transition is useful here. She uses the phrase transitional justice to refer to what happens in a 'post revolutionary period of political change within a bounded period spanning two regimes ... Within one school of thought transition is demarcated by objective political criteria, chiefly procedural in nature. Thus, for some time, the criteria for transition to democracy have focused on elections and related procedures ... For others, the transition ends when all the politically significant groups accept the rule of law.' She suggests a move away from the former (defining transition purely in terms of democratic procedures such as electoral processes) towards a broader enquiry which looks in particular at normative understandings associated with the rule of law in political flux (Teitel, 2000:5).

26. As Mark Osiel has argued, 'in the last half century, criminal law has increasingly been used in several societies with a view to teaching a particular interpretation

of the country's history, one expected to have a salubrious impact on its solidarity' (Osiel, 1997:6). In such a context, the criminal justice process looks both forward and backwards. 'As an aim for criminal law, the cultivation of collective memory resembles deterrence in that it is directed towards the future, where enhanced solidarity is sought. But, like retribution, it looks to the past, to provide the narrative content of what is to be shared in memory' (ibid.:18).

27. These have included, among others, the establishment of the Bloody Sunday Inquiry, chaired by Lord Saville, investigating the deaths of the fourteen civilians killed by the paratroopers in 1972, a judicial investigation into allegations of security force collusion in the murder of two human rights lawyers as well as garda involvement in the deaths of two RUC officers and an inquiry in the Irish Republic into allegations of British security force involvement in a series of bombings in Dublin and Monaghan in the early 1970s.

28. The current Draft Bill of Rights for Northern Ireland stipulates that 'A person convicted of a crime shall be given a custodial sentence only as a measure of last resort. The State shall develop and encourage the use of alternatives to prosecution and custodial sentences.' It also provides that 'The State shall take effective measures to ensure that favourable conditions are created for the reintegration of prisoners into society' (Human Rights Commission, 2001:10).

References

Alston, P. (ed.) (1995) *The United Nations and Human Rights: A Critical Appraisal.* Oxford: Oxford University Press.

Amnesty International (1978) *Report of a Mission to Northern Ireland.* London: Amnesty International.

Amnesty International (1988) *Northern Ireland: Killings by the Security Forces and Supergrass Trials.* London: Amnesty International

Amnesty International (1992) *Fair Trial Concerns in Northern Ireland: The Right of Silence.* London: Amnesty International.

Amnesty International (1994) *Political Killings in Northern Ireland.* London: Amnesty International.

Barak, G. (ed.) (1991) *Crimes by the Capitalist State: An Introduction to State Criminality.* Albany: State University of New York Press.

Beatson, J. (1999) *The Human Rights Act and the Criminal Justice and Regulatory Process.* Oxford: Hart Publishing.

Beigbeder, Y. (1999) *Judging War Criminals: The Politics of International Justice.* New York: St Martin's Press – now Palgrave Macmillan.

Beirne, P. (1983) 'Generalization and its Discontents: Some Remarks on the Comparative Study of Crime', in I. Barak-Glantz and E. Johnson (eds) *Comparative Criminology.* Beverly Hills, CA: Sage.

Beirne, P. (1987) 'Adolphe Quetelet and the Origins of Positivist Criminology', *American Journal of Sociology* 92 (5), 1140–69.

Beirne, P. and D. Nelken (1997) *Issues in Comparative Criminology.* Aldershot: Ashgate.

Bell, C. (2000) *Peace Agreements and Human Rights.* Oxford: Oxford University Press.

Bennett, R. and J. Lynch (1990) 'Does a Difference Make a Difference? Comparing Cross-National Crime Indicators', *Criminology* 28, 153–82.

Benson, T. (1998) 'Rights and Justice on a Shared Planet: More Rights or New Relations?', *Theoretical Criminology* 2 (2), 149–75.

Bew, P., P. Gibbon and H. Patterson (1979) *The State in Northern Ireland 1921–72: Political Forces and Social Classes*. Manchester: Manchester University Press (2nd edn 1996, London: Serif).

Blair, C. (2000) *Crime Reduction, Reducing Criminality*. Belfast: HMSO.

Bloomfield, K. (1998) *We Will Remember Them*. Belfast: HMSO.

Bonger, W. (1936) *An Introduction to Criminology*. London: Methuen and Sons.

Boraine, A. (1999) *'All Truth is Bitter': A Report of the Visit of Dr Alex Boraine, Deputy Chairman of the South African Truth and Reconciliation Commission, to Northern Ireland*. Belfast: NIACRO.

Boraine, A. (2001) *A Country Unmasked: Inside South Africa's Truth and Reconciliation Commission*. New York: Oxford University Press.

Bowyer Bell, J. (1993) *The Irish Troubles: A Generation of Violence*. Dublin: Gill & Macmillan.

Boyle, K., T. Hadden and P. Hillyard (1975) *Law and State: The Case of Northern Ireland*. London: Robertson.

Boyle, K., T. Hadden and P. Hillyard (1980) *Ten Years on in Northern Ireland: The Legal Control of Political Violence*. Belfast: Cobden Trust.

Box, S. (1987) *Power, Crime & Mystification*. London: Tavistock.

Brewer, J. (ed.) (1988) *The Police, Public Order and the State: Policing in Great Britain, Northern Ireland, the Irish Republic, the USA, Israel, South Africa, and China*. Basingstoke: Macmillan – now Palgrave Macmillan.

Brewer, J. and K. Magee (1991) *Routine Policing in a Divided Society*. Oxford: Clarendon Press.

Brewer, J., B. Lockhart and P. Rodgers (1997) *Crime in Ireland, 1945–95: 'Here be Dragons'*. Oxford: Oxford University Press.

Brogden, M. and P. Nijhar (2000) *Crime, Abuse and the Elderly*. Devon: Willan Publishing.

Bryant, D. and N. Jarman (1999) *Monitoring the Police, Parades and and Public Order*. Belfast: Democratic Dialogue.

Burton, F. (1978) *The Politics of Legitimacy: Struggles in a Belfast Community*. London: Routledge and Kegan Paul.

Cairns, E. (1994) *A Welling up of Deep Unconscious Forces: Psychology and the Northern Ireland Conflict*. University of Ulster, Coleraine: Centre for the Study of Conflict.

CAJ (Committee on the Administration of Justice) (1983a) *Emergency Laws: Suggestions for Reform in Northern Ireland*. Belfast: CAJ.

CAJ (Committee on the Administration of Justice) (1983b) *Procedures for Handling Complaints Against the Police*. Belfast: CAJ.

CAJ (Committee on the Administration of Justice) (1985) *Plastic Bullets and the Law*. Belfast: CAJ.

CAJ (Committee on the Administration of Justice) (1997) *The Misrule of Law: A Report on the Policing of Events during the Summer of 1996*. Belfast: CAJ.

CAJ (Committee on the Administration of Justice) (1999) *The Agreement and a New Beginning to Policing in Northern Ireland. Conference Report*. Belfast: CAJ.

Campbell, C. (1999) 'Two Steps Backwards: The Criminal Justice (Terrorism and Conspiracy) Act 1998', *Criminal Law Review*, Dec. 941–59.

Caul, B. (1983) 'Juvenile Offending in Northern Ireland – A Statistical Overview', in B. Caul, J. Pinkerton and F. Powell (eds) *The Juvenile Justice System in Northern Ireland*. Jordanstown: Ulster Polytechnic.

Chomsky, N. (1988) *Culture of Terrorism*. London: South End.

Christie, N. (1981) *Limits to Pain*. Oxford: Martin Robertson.

Clutterbuck, R. (1977) *Guerrillas and Terrorists*. Chicago: Ohio University Press.

Clutterbuck, R. (1990) *Terrorism, Drugs and Crime in Europe After 1992*. London: Routledge.

Clutterbuck, R. (1994) *Terrorism in an Unstable World*. London: Routledge.

Cockburn, A. (1990) 'The Smoking Gun Speaks: A Former Assassin has Revealed US Involvement in El Salvadorian Political Murders', *New Statesman & Society* 13 (111), 114–15.

Cohen, S. (1982) 'Western Crime Control Models in the Third World: Benign or Malignant?', *Research in Law, Deviance and Social Control* 4, 85–119.

Cohen, S. (1985) *Visions of Social Control*. Cambridge: Polity Press.

Cohen, S. (1988) 'Footprints in the Sand: A Further Report on Criminology and the Sociology of Deviance in Britain', republished in S. Cohen, *Against Criminology*. Oxford: Transaction Books.

Cohen, S. (1993) 'Human Rights and Crimes of the State: The Culture of Denial', *Australian and New Zealand Journal of Criminology* 26 (2), 97–115.

Cohen, S. (1996) 'Crime and Politics: Spot the Difference', *British Journal of Sociology* 47 (1), 1–21.

Cohen, S. (1998) 'Intellectual Scepticism and Political Commitment: The Case of Radical Criminology', in P. Walton and J. Young (eds) *The New Criminology Revisited*. Basingstoke: Macmillan.

Cohen, S. (2001) *States of Denial: Knowing about Atrocities & Suffering*. Cambridge: Polity Press.

Chambliss, W. (1975) *Criminal Law in Action*. London: Addison-Wesley Longman.

Crawford, A. and C. Blair (2000) *Community Safety Centre Review and a Strategy for Northern Ireland*. Belfast: HMSO.

Crawford, A. and M. Matassa (2000) *Community Safety Structures: An International Literature Review*. Belfast: HMSO.

Criminal Justice Review (2000) *Review of the Criminal Justice System in Northern Ireland*. Belfast: HMSO.

Curtis, L. (1984) *Ireland: The Propaganda War*. London: Pluto Press.

Dawson, G. (1984) *Planning in the Shadow of Urban Civil Conflict: A Case Study from Belfast*. Liverpool: Department of Civic Design, University of Liverpool.

Day, E. and M. Vandiver (2000) 'Criminology and Genocide Studies: Notes on What Might Have Been and What Still Could Be', *Crime, Law and Social Change* 34, 43–59.

De Bréadún, D. (2001) *The Far Side of Revenge: Making Peace in Northern Ireland*. Dingle: Brandon.

Del Olmo, R. (1999) 'The Development of Criminology in Latin America', *Social Justice* 26 (2), 19–45.

Dickson, B. (1992) 'Northern Ireland's Emergency Legislation: The Wrong Medicine?', *Public Law* 10, 592–624.

Dignan, J. (2000) *Restorative Justice Options from Northern Ireland*. Belfast: HMSO.

Doran, S. and J. Jackson (eds) (2000) *The Judicial Role In Criminal Proceedings*. Oxford: Hart Publishing.

Douzinas, C. (2000) *The End of Human Rights: Critical Legal Thought at the Turn of the Century*. Oxford: Hart Publishing.

Downes, D. (1988) *Contrasts in Tolerance: Post-war Penal Policy in The Netherlands and England and Wales*. Oxford: Oxford University Press.

Durkheim, E. (1992) *Professional Ethics and Civil Morals*. London: Routledge.

Ellison, G. (1997) 'Professionalism in the Royal Ulster Constabulary: An Examination of the Institutional Discourse', unpublished D.Phil. thesis, University of Ulster.

Ellison, G. and G. Martin (2000) 'Policing, Collective Action & Social Movement Theory: The Case of the Northern Ireland Civil Rights Campaign', *British Journal of Sociology* 51 (4), 681–99.

Ellison, G. and J. Smyth (2000) *The Crowned Harp: Policing Northern Ireland*. London: Pluto Press.

Farrell, M. (1976) *Northern Ireland: The Orange State*. London: Pluto Press.

Farrell, M. (1983) *Arming the Protestants: The Formation of the Ulster Special Constabulary*. Dingle: Brandon.

Fay, M.T., M. Morrissey and M. Smyth (1999) *Northern Ireland's Troubles: The Human Costs*. London: Pluto Press.

Feeley, M. and J. Simon (1992) 'The New Penology: Notes on the Emerging Strategy of Corrections and its Implications', *Criminology* 30 (4), 449–74.

Fisk, R. (1975) *The Point of No Return: The Strike Which Broke the British in Ulster*. London: Times Books.

Friedrichs, D. (ed.) (1997) *State Crime: Volume I, Defining, Delineating and Explaining State Crime; Volume II, Exposing, Sanctioning and Preventing State Crime*. Aldershot: Ashgate.

Garland, D. (1997) 'Of Crime and Criminality: The Development of Criminology in Britain', in M. Maguire, R. Morgan and R. Reiner (eds) *The Oxford Handbook of Criminology* (2nd edn). Oxford: Oxford University Press.

Gearty, C. (1996) 'Introduction', in C. Gearty (ed.) *Terrorism*. Aldershot: Ashgate.

Gormally, B. and K. McEvoy (1995) *Release and Reintegration of Politically Motivated Prisoners in Northern Ireland: A Comparative Study of South Africa, Israel/Palestine, Italy, Spain, The Republic of Ireland and Northern Ireland*. Belfast: NIACRO.

Gottfredson, M. and T. Hirschi (1990) *A General Theory of Crime*. Stanford, CA: Stanford University Press.

Greer, S. (1995) *Supergrasses: A Study in Anti-terrorist Law Enforcement in Northern Ireland*. Oxford: Clarendon Press.

Guelke, A. (1995) *The Age of Terrorism and the International Political System*. London: Tauris.

Hagan, F. (1997) *Political Crime: Ideology and Criminality*. Needham Heights, MA: Allyn & Bacon.

Hayner, P. (1994) 'Fifteen Truth Commissions – 1974 to 1994: A Comparative Study', *Human Rights Quarterly* 16 (4), 598–655.

Herman, E. and G. O'Sullivan (1990) *The Terrorism Industry: The Experts and Institutions that Shape our View of Terror*. London: Pantheon Books.

Herman, E. and G. O'Sullivan (1991) 'Terrorism as Ideology and Cultural Industry', in A. George (ed.) *Western State Terrorism*. Cambridge: Polity Press.

Heskin, K. (1981) 'Societal Disintegration in Northern Ireland: Fact or Fiction?', *The Economic and Social Review* 12, 97–113.

Hillyard, P. (1985) 'Popular Justice in Northern Ireland: Continuities and Change', *Research and Law, Deviance and Social Control* 7, 247–67.

Hillyard, P. (1987) 'The Normalisation of Special Powers: From Northern Ireland to Britain', in P. Scraton (ed.) *Law, Order and the Authoritarian State: Readings in Critical Criminology*. Milton Keynes: Open University Press.

Hillyard, P. (1990) 'Political and Social Dimensions of Emergency Law in Northern Ireland', in A. Jennings (ed.) *Justice Under Fire: The Abuse of Civil Liberties in Northern Ireland*. London: Pluto Press.

Hillyard, P. and M. Tomlinson (2000) 'Patterns of Policing and Policing Patten', *Journal of Law and Society* 27 (3), 394–415.

Hoffman, M. (2000) 'Emerging Combatants, War Crimes and the Future of International Humanitarian Law', *Crime, Law and Social Change* 34, 99–110.

Human Rights Commission (2001) *Making a Bill of Rights For Northern Ireland: A Consultation by the Northern Ireland Human Rights Commission*. http://www.nihrc.org/update/new_page_1.htm.

Ignatieff, M. (1994) *Blood and Belonging: Journey into the New Nationalism*. London: Vintage Books.

Ignatieff, M. (2001) *Human Rights as Politics and Idolatry*. Princeton, NJ: Princeton University Press.

Jackson, J. and S. Doran (1995) *Judge Without Jury: Diplock Trials in the Adversary System*. Oxford: Clarendon Press.

Jamieson, R. (1998) 'Towards a Criminology of War in Europe', in V. Ruggiero, N. South and I. Taylor (eds) *The New European Criminology: Crime and Social Order in Europe*. London: Routledge.

Jamieson, R. (1999) 'Genocide and the Social Production of Immortality', *Theoretical Criminology* 3 (2), 131–46.

Jarman, N., D. Bryan, N. Caleyron and C. De Roas (1998) *Politics In Public: Freedom of Assembly and the Right to Protest: A Comparative Analysis*. Belfast: Democratic Dialogue.

Jenkins, R. (1983) *Lads, Citizens and Ordinary Kids: Working Class Youth Lifestyles in Belfast*. London: Routledge and Kegan Paul.

Jennings, A. (ed.) (1990) *Justice Under Fire: The Abuse of Civil Liberties in Northern Ireland*. London: Pluto Press.

Knox, C. and R. Monaghan (2000) *Informal Criminal Justice Systems in Northern Ireland*. http://www.busmgt.ulst.ac.uk/research/ESRC.

Lemert, E. (1967) *Human Deviance, Social Problems and Social Control*. Englewood Cliffs, NJ: Prentice Hall.

Limpkin, C. (1972) *The Battle of the Bogside*. Harmondsworth: Penguin.

Linz, J. and A. Stepan (1996) *Problems of Democratic Transition and Consolidation*. Baltimore, MD: Johns Hopkins University.

Livingstone, S. and J. Doak (2000) *Human Rights Standards and Criminal Justice*. Belfast: HMSO.

Lloyd, Lord (1996) *Inquiry into Legislation Against Terrorism*. Cmnd Paper 3420.

Loader, I. (1998) 'Criminology in the Public Sphere: Arguments for Utopian Realism', in P. Walton and J. Young (eds) *The New Criminology Revisited*. London: Macmillan Press – now Palgrave Macmillan.

Lombroso, C. (1876) *L'Uomo Delinquente*, translated as *Crime, its Causes and Remedies* 1968 by Henry Horton. New Jersey: Patterson Smith.

Lustgarten, L. (1987) 'The Police and the Substantive Criminal Law', *British Journal of Criminology* 27, 1.

MacIntyre, A. (1995) 'Modern Irish Republicanism: The Product of British State Strategies', *Irish Political Studies* 10, 97–122.

Mageean, P. and M. O'Brien (1999) 'From the Margins to the Mainstream: Human Rights and the Good Friday Peace Agreement', *Fordham International Law Journal* 22 (4), 1499–539.

Matza, D. (1964) *Delinquency and Drift.* New York: Wiley.

McBarnet, D. (1981) *Conviction: Law, the State and the Construction of Justice.* London: Macmillan – now Palgrave Macmillan.

McClintock, M. (1985) *The American Connection (vol. 1), State Terror and Popular Resistance in El Salvador.* New York: Zed Books.

McCorry, J. and M. Morrissey (1989) 'Community, Crime and Punishment in West Belfast', *Howard Journal* 28 (4), 289–92.

McCullough, D., T. Schmidt and B. Lockhart (1990) *Car Theft in Northern Ireland.* CIRAC Paper No. 2. Belfast: Extern Organisation.

McElrath, K. (2000) *Unsafe Haven: The United States, the IRA and Political Prisoners.* London: Pluto Press.

McElrath, K. and K. McEvoy (1999) *Ecstasy Use in Northern Ireland.* Belfast: HMSO.

McEvoy, K. (2000) 'Law, Struggle and Political Transformation in Northern Ireland', *Journal of Law and Society* 27 (4), 542–71.

McEvoy, K. (2001) 'Human Rights, Humanitarian Law and Paramilitarism in Northern Ireland', in C. Harvey (ed.) *Human Rights, Equality and Democratic Renewal in Northern Ireland.* Oxford: Hart Publishing.

McEvoy, K. and B. Gormally (1997) 'Seeing is Believing: Positivist Terrorology, Peacemaking Criminology, and the Northern Ireland Peace Process', *Critical Criminology: An International Journal* 8 (1), 9–31.

McEvoy, K. and H. Mika (2001) 'Punishment, Politics & Praxis: Restorative Justice and Non-Violent Alternatives To Paramilitary Punishments In Northern Ireland', *Policing and Society* 11 (3–4), 359–82.

McEvoy, K. and H. Mika (2002) 'Restorative Justice and the Critique of Informalism in Northern Ireland, *British Journal of Criminology* 42 (3) 534–562.

McEvoy, K., B. Gormally and H. Mika (2001) 'Conflict, Crime Control and the "re" Construction of State/Community Relations in Northern Ireland', in G. Hughes et al. (eds) *Crime Prevention and Community: New Directions.* Milton Keynes: Open University Press.

McEvoy, K., K. McElrath and K. Higgins (1998) 'Does Ulster Still Say No?: Drugs, Politics and Propaganda in Northern Ireland', *Journal of Drug Issues* 28 (1), 127–54.

McGarry, J. and B. O'Leary (1995) *Explaining Northern Ireland: Broken Images.* Oxford: Blackwell.

McGarry, J. and B. O'Leary (1999) *Policing Northern Ireland: Proposals for a New Start.* Belfast: Blackstaff Press.

McKittrick, D., S. Kelters, B. Feeney and C. Thorton (1999) *Lost Lives: The Stories of the Men, Women and Children who Died as a Result of the Northern Ireland Troubles.* London: Mainstream Publishing.

McQuoid, J. and B. Lockhart (1994) *Self Reported Delinquency and Other Behaviours Amongst Young People in Northern Ireland.* Belfast: Extern Organisation.

McWilliams, M. and L. Spence (1996) *Taking Domestic Violence Seriously: Issues for the Civil and Criminal Justice Systems*. Belfast: HMSO.

Melucci, A. (1996) *Challenging Codes: Collective Action in the Information Age*. Cambridge: Cambridge University Press.

Mendez, E. (1997) 'In Defence of Transitional Justice', in A. McAdams (ed.) *Transitional Justice and the Rule of Law in New Democracies*. Notre Dame, IN: University of Notre Dame Press.

Miliband, R. (1969) *The State in Capitalist Society*, London: Weidenfeld and Nicolson.

Miller, D. (1994) *Don't Mention the War: Northern Ireland, Propaganda and the Media*. London: Pluto Press.

Miller, D. (ed.) (1998) *Rethinking Northern Ireland: Culture, Ideology and Colonialism*. London: Longman.

Morgan, A. (2000) *The Belfast Agreement: A Practical Legal Analysis*. London: The Belfast Press Limited.

Morison, J. and R. Geary (1989) 'Crime, Conflict and Counting', *Howard Journal* 28 (1), 9–26.

Morison, J. and S. Livingstone (1995) *Reshaping Public Power: Northern Ireland and the British Constitutional Crisis*. London: Sweet & Maxwell.

Morrissey, M. and K. Pease (1982) 'The Black Criminal Justice System in West Belfast', *Howard Journal* 21, Spring, 59–166.

Mulcahy, A. (1998) 'The Dynamics of the Police Legitimation Process in Northern Ireland', unpublished Ph.D. thesis, Arizona State University.

Mulcahy, A. (1999) 'Visions of Normality: Peace and the Reconstruction of Policing in Northern Ireland', *Social and Legal Studies* 8(2), 277–95.

Mulcahy, A. (2000) 'Policing History: The Official Discourse and Organizational Memory of the Royal Ulster Constabulary', *British Journal of Criminology* 40 (1), 68–87.

Munck, R. (1984) 'Repression, Insurgency and Popular Justice: The Irish Case', *Crime and Social Justice* 21 (2), 81–94.

Munck, R. (1988) 'The Lads and the Hoods: Alternative Justice in an Irish Context', in M. Tomlinson, T. Varley and C. McCullagh (eds) *Whose Law and Order? Aspects of Crime and Social Control in Irish Society*. Belfast: Sociological Association of Ireland.

Nelken, D. (1994) 'Whom Can You Trust?: The Future of Comparative Criminology', in D. Nelken (ed.) *The Futures of Criminology*. London: Sage.

Nelken, D. (1997) 'Understanding Criminal Justice Comparatively', in M. Maguire, R. Morgan and R. Reiner (eds) *Oxford Handbook of Criminology* (2nd edn). Oxford: Oxford University Press.

Neuman, W. and R. Berger (1988) 'Competing Perspectives on Cross-National Crime: An Evaluation of Theory and Practice', *Sociological Quarterly* 29, 81–213.

Newark, F. (1955) 'The Law and the Constitution', in T. Wilson (ed.) *Ulster Under Home Rule*. Oxford: Oxford University Press.

NIACRO (1995a) *Conference Report of the International Conference on the Early Release and Reintegration of Politically Motivated Prisoners*. Belfast: NIACRO.

NIACRO (1995b) Press release prepared for *International Conference on the Early Release and Reintegration of Politically Motivated Prisoners*. Belfast: NIACRO.

Ní Aoláin, F. (2000) *The Politics of Force: Conflict Management and State Violence in Northern Ireland*. Belfast: Blackstaff Press.

Nikolic-Ristanovic, V. (1998) 'War and Crime in the Former Yugoslavia', In V. Ruggiero, N. South and I. Taylor (eds) *The New European Criminology: Crime and Social Order in Europe*. London: Routledge.

Ó Dochartaigh, N. (1997) *From Civil Rights to Armalites: Derry and the Birth of the Irish Troubles*. Cork: Cork University Press.

O'Donnell, G., P. Schmitter and L. Whitehead (eds) (1986) *Transitions from Authoritarian Rule: Comparative Perspectives*. Baltimore, MD: Johns Hopkins University.

O'Dowd, L., B. Rolston and M. Tomlinson (1980) *Northern Ireland: Between Civil Rights and Civil War*. London: CSE Books.

O'Leary, B. and J. McGarry (eds) (1993) *The Politics of Ethnic Conflict Regulation*. London: Routledge.

O'Mahony, D. (2000) 'Young People, Crime and Criminal Justice: Patterns and Prospects for the Future', *Youth and Society* 32 (1), 60–80.

O'Mahony, D., R. Geary, K. McEvoy and J. Morison (2000) *Crime, Community & Locale: The Northern Ireland Communities Crime Survey*. Aldershot: Ashgate.

O'Rawe, M. and L. Moore (1997) *Human Rights on Duty: Principles for Better Policing, International Lessons for Northern Ireland*. Belfast: CAJ.

Osiel, M. (1997) *Mass Atrocity, Collective Memory and the Law*. New Brunswick, NJ: Transaction Publishers.

Osiel, M. (2000) 'Why Prosecute? Critics of Punishment for Mass Atrocity', *Human Rights Quarterly* 22 (1), 118–48.

Patten, C. (1999) *Report of an Independent Commission on Policing in Northern Ireland*. Belfast: HMSO.

Pearce, F. and S. Tombs (1998) *Toxic Capitalism: Corporate Crime and the Chemical Industry*. Aldershot: Dartmouth.

Pickering, S. (2001) 'Undermining the Sanitized Account: Violence and Emotionality in the Field in Northern Ireland', *Britain Journal of Criminology* 41 (3), 485–501.

Powell, F. (1982) 'Justice and the Young Offender in Northern Ireland', *British Journal Of Social Work* 12, 565–86.

PPRU (Policy Planning and Research Unit) (1984) *Commentary on Northern Ireland Crime Statistics 1969–1982*. Occasional Paper 5, Belfast: Department of Finance and Personnel.

Purdey, B. (1990) *Politics in the Streets: The Origins of the Civil Rights Movement in Northern Ireland*. Belfast: Blackstaff Press.

Quinney, R. (1972) 'The Ideology of Law: Notes for a Radical Alternative to Legal Repression', *Issues in Criminology* 7, 1–27.

Raine, J. and M. Wilson (1997) 'Beyond Managerialism in Criminal Justice', *Howard Journal* 36 (1), 80–95.

Rock, P. (ed.) (1988) *A History of British Criminology*. Oxford: Oxford University Press.

Rolston, B. (1983) 'Reformism and Sectarianism: The State of the Union after Civil Rights', in J. Darby (ed.) *Northern Ireland: The Background to the Conflict*. Belfast: Appletree Press.

Rolston, B. (ed.) (1991a) *The Media and Northern Ireland: Covering the Troubles*. Basingstoke: Macmillan – now Palgrave Macmillan.

Rolston, B. (1991b) 'Review of Bew and Patterson (1985) and Boyle and Hadden 1985 (1985)', *Journal of Law and Society* 13 (2), 257–62.

Rolston, B. and M. Tomlinson (eds) (1986*) The Expansion of European Prison Systems; Working Papers in European Criminology.* Stockholm: European Group for the Study of Deviance and Social Control.

Rolston, B. and M. Tomlinson (1988) 'The Challenge Within: Prisons & Propaganda in Northern Ireland', in M. Tomlinson, T. Varley and C. McCullagh (eds) *Whose Law and Order?* Belfast: Queen's University Bookshop.

Rosenberg, T. (1995) *The Haunted Land: Facing Europe's Ghosts After Communism.* New York: Random House.

Ross, J.I. (2000) *Controlling State Crime* (2nd edn). New Brunswick, NJ: Transaction Publishers.

Ruane, J. and J. Todd (1996) *The Dynamics of Conflict in Northern Ireland.* Cambridge: Cambridge University Press.

RUC (1977) *Annual Report of the Chief Constable.* Belfast: Royal Ulster Constabulary.

RUC (1979) *Annual Report of the Chief Constable.* Belfast: HMSO.

Ruggiero, V. and N. South (1995) *Eurodrugs: Drug Use, Markets and Trafficking in Europe.* London: UCL Press.

Rutherford, A. (1995) *Transforming Criminal Policy: Spheres of Influence in the United States, The Netherlands and England and Wales During the 1980s.* Winchester: Waterside Press.

Safer Towns (1994) *Addressing Drug Misuse: Issues and Approaches.* Belfast: Extern Organisation.

Sanby-Thomas, M. (1992) *Preventative Strategies to Reduce Car Theft in Northern Ireland.* Extern Report No. 2. Belfast: Extern Organisation.

Schafer, S. (1974) *The Political Criminal: The Problem of Morality and Crime.* New York: The Free Press.

Schlesinger, P. (1978) *Putting Reality Together.* London: Constable.

Sentence Review Commission (2000) *Annual Report of the Northern Ireland Sentence Review Commission.* Belfast: Northern Ireland Office.

Shearing, C. (2001) 'A Nodal Conception of Governance: Thoughts on a Policing Commission', *Policing and Society* 11 (3–4), 259–72.

Shearing, C. and P. Stenning (eds) (1987) *Private Policing.* Newbury Park, CA: Sage.

Sheptycki, J. (ed.) (2000) *Issues in Transnational Policing.* London: Routledge.

Silke, A. (1999) 'Ragged Justice: Loyalist Vigilantism in Northern Ireland', *Terrorism and Political Violence* 11 (3), 1–31.

Sluka, J. (1989) *Hearts and Minds, Water and Fish: Support for the IRA and INLA in a Northern Ireland Ghetto.* Greenwich, CT: JAI Press.

South, N. (1998) 'A Green Field for Criminology? Proposals for a Perspective', *Theoretical Criminology* 2 (2), 211–33.

Sparks, R. (1994) 'Postmodernism and Misgivings About Human Rights', paper presented to the American Society of Criminology, Miami, 17 November.

Spujt, R. (1986) 'Internment and Detention Without Trial in Northern Ireland 1971–1975', *Modern Law Review* 49, 712–39.

Sumner, C. (1994) *The Sociology of Deviance: An Obituary.* Buckingham: Open University Press.

Taylor, I., P. Walton and J. Young (1973) *The New Criminology: For a Social Theory of Deviance.* London: Routledge and Kegan Paul.

Teitel, R. (2000) *Transitional Justice.* New York: Oxford University Press.

Tomlinson, M. (1980) 'Reforming Repression', in L. O'Dowd, B. Rolston and M. Tomlinson (eds) *Between Civil Rights and Civil War.* London: CSE Books.

Tomlinson, M. (1998) 'Walking Backwards into the Sunset: British Policy and the Insecurity of Northern Ireland', in D. Miller (ed.) *Rethinking Northern Ireland: Culture, Ideology and Colonialism*. London: Longman.

Tugwell, M. (1981) 'Low Intensity Conflict in Northern Ireland', in D. Charters, D. Graham and M. Tugwell (eds) *Low Intensity Conflict*. Ottawa: Department of National Defence.

Van Dijk, J. and P. Mayhew (1993) 'Criminal Victimization in the Industrialized World: Key Findings of the 1989 and 1992 International Crime Surveys'. The Hague: Netherlands Ministry of Justice.

Van Ness, P. and N. Aziz (eds) (1999) *Debating Human Rights: Critical Essays from the United States and Asia*. London: Routledge.

Van Swaaningen, R. (1997) *Critical Criminology: Visions From Europe*. London: Sage.

Walicki, A. (1997) 'Transitional Justice and Political Struggles of Post Communist Poland', in J. McAdam (ed.) *Transitional Justice and the Rule of Law in New Democracies*. Notre Dame, IL: Notre Dame University Press.

Walker, N. and M. Tedford (2000) *Designing Criminal Justice: The Northern Ireland System in Comparative Perspective*. Belfast: HMSO.

Walsh, D. (1983) *The Use and Abuse of Emergency Legislation in Northern Ireland*. London: Cobden Trust.

Weitzer, R. (1990) *Transforming Settler States: Communal Conflict and Internal Security in Northern Ireland and Zimbabwe*. Berkeley, CA: University of California Press.

Whyte, J. (1990) *Interpreting Northern Ireland*. Oxford: Clarendon Press.

Wilkinson, P. (1981) *British Perspectives on Terrorism*. London: Allen & Unwin.

Wilkinson, P. (1986) *Terrorism and the Liberal State*. London: Macmillan – now Palgrave Macmillan.

Wilson J. and R.J. Herrnstein (1985) *Crime and Human Nature*. New York: Simon and Schuster.

Wright, J. (1991) *Terrorist Propaganda: The Red Army Faction and the Provisional IRA 1968–86*. New York: St. Martin's Press – now Palgrave Macmillan.

Wright, J. and K. Bryett (2000) *Policing and Conflict in Northern Ireland*. New York: St Martin's Press – now Palgrave Macmillan.

Yacobian, G. (2000) 'The (In)significance of Genocidal Behaviour in the Discipline of Criminology', *Crime, Law and Social Change* 34, 7–19.

Young, P. (2000) 'Cross Border Criminological Cooperation in Ireland', paper delivered at Queen's University Belfast, June.

Zalaquett, J. (1990) 'Confronting Human Rights Violations Committed by Former Governments: Principles Applicable and Political Constraints', *Hamline Law Review* 13 (3), 623–60.

4
Conflict Prevention and the Human Rights Framework in Africa

*Rachel Murray**

Introduction

A brief glance at Africa would suggest that the methods adopted to deal with conflict prevention have achieved little success (Deng and Zartman, 1991; Ramcharan, 1991). It is equally clear, however, that there are complex causes of conflict (van Walraven, 1998) and that one cannot view conflict in a narrow sense, but must take account of political, economic and social factors to truly understand its causes and process (Tesha, 1999). The focus of this chapter is not on the management of conflicts but on their prevention, as it is clear that it is more effective to contain conflicts than to deal with them once they have occurred.[1] I will argue that that a human rights approach to conflict offers us an epistemological and practical basis for better understanding and preventing conflicts in the first place.[2]

Human rights violations (broadly defined)[3] often predate conflicts. Arbitrary arrests and detentions, oppression of political opposition groups and individuals, difficulties in socio-economic conditions and border controls, for example, often increase before more serious conflict situations develop. Monitoring the situation of human rights over a period of time can therefore provide indicators of impending disputes (OAU/IPA, 1998:17–18).[4] Conversely, once conflicts begin, human rights violations often increase in frequency and seriousness, creating what Tesha has referred to as a 'vicious circle' (Tesha, 1999:22). However, despite this symbiotic relationship, human rights and conflicts are often dealt with separately, and this is apparent not only in the practice of international bodies such as the UN and the African political institution, the Organization of African Unity (OAU),[5] but also in the theoretical division between the disciplines of international humanitarian law (the 'laws of war') and human rights law (MacBride, 1970; Forsythe, 1982; Kuitenbrouwer, 1999). There is a presumption that:

> human rights law is designed to operate primarily in normal peacetime conditions and within the framework of the legal relationship between a state and its citizens. International humanitarian law, by contrast, is chiefly concerned with the abnormal conditions of armed conflict and the relationship between a state and the citizens of its adversary.
>
> (Fleck, 1995:9)

The two areas of law are treated separately, despite the recognition that they share a common concern and similar values, and that the two can even apply to the same situations (Forsythe, 1982; Meron, 1987). Indeed, instruments such as the European Convention on Human Rights and those adopted under the United Nations (human rights law) were drawn up in response to the atrocities which occurred during the conflict of World War II. Despite this commonality, the traditional lack of coherence of this dichotomy and the loopholes that such a division creates (see Eide, 1979; Meron, 1987; Murray, 2000: esp. 127–31) are slowly being challenged with the recognition by some institutions, among these the African mechanisms, of the weaknesses of such an approach. Events such as the genocide in Rwanda in 1994 made it clear that even though conflicts on such a scale may traditionally have been the domain of humanitarian law, human rights institutions cannot sit idly by. Conversely, international institutions' involvement in peace-keeping has sometimes extended beyond conflict situations to monitor and deal with states post-conflict.

As the Foundation for Inter-Ethnic Relations has argued:

> The separation of humanitarian law and human rights law and of human rights from conflicts fails to recognise that the relationship between societal tensions and human rights violations in this context is significant. The root of tension may be the systematic violation of the rights of certain groups and individuals. On the other hand, human rights violations can arise from a perceived incompatibility of aspirations between authorities and sections of the population. In this sense, conflict prevention and the human dimension are strongly interlinked.
>
> (Foundation for Inter-Ethnic Relations, 1997:19)[6]

To be fair, some of the major institutional players have increasingly come to recognize the interconnectedness of such issues and to eschew the notion of human rights as belonging institutionally to the designated human rights organs. For example, the Organization for Security and Co-operation in Europe (OSCE), which is the largest regional security organization in the world with 55 participating states, defines security as linked with, among other matters, peace, *human rights* (my emphasis) and economics (OSCE, 1992). Similarly, the issue as to whether the UN Security Council was mandated to consider human rights matters was upheld specifically by the International Criminal Tribunal for Rwanda's decision in *Prosecutor v. Joseph Kanyabashi* (Case No. ICTR-96-15-t), where the Tribunal held that 'the protection of international human rights is the responsibility of all UN organs, the Security Council included, without any limitation, in conformity with the UN Charter'.

Africa is of particular interest in this regard. Internal conflicts occur often on the continent and many states fluctuate between situations of conflict and peace. Indeed, it can be argued that the traditional understanding of the concept of the state, which is at the core of the relationship between human rights and conflict prevention, is itself a hindrance as an (arguably) western concept superimposed on traditional African structures. Such a tension often results in an odd combination of attempts at reconciling individualistic presumptions regarding the importance of national identity propounded by the West with ethnic divisions and a more pronounced sense of community.

This chapter will therefore focus upon the extent to which the Organization of African Unity, the entity created during the process of decolonization, deals with these tensions. In particular I want to focus on the extent to which the OAU and its conflict mechanism consider human rights to be part of their mandate. Second, I want to examine in particular the human rights arm of the OAU, the African Charter on Human and Peoples' Rights and its Commission, to determine the extent to which it can and will consider issues of conflicts within its human rights mandate. Finally I wish to critically analyse the recent moves to establish an early warning system and the relationship between such a system, the protection of human rights and the prevention of conflict.

Human rights within the context of conflicts: the approach of the OAU

The Organization of African Unity (OAU) was set up in order to

> promote the unity and solidarity of the African States; defend the sovereignty of members; eradicate all forms of colonialism; promote

international cooperation having due regard for the Charter of the United Nations and the Universal Declaration of Human Rights; coordinate and harmonize Member States economic, diplomatic, educational, health, welfare, scientific and defense policies.

(OAU, 2001)

The Charter was drawn up in 1963, and there are currently 53 nations party to it. The Charter stipulated that dispute resolution through peaceful settlement was of central importance to the OAU,[7] and although human rights are only mentioned in the preamble, they are linked with issues of conflict.[8]

In recent years there has been an increased recognition of the relationship between human rights and conflict in the OAU as a whole. In 1990 a *Declaration on Fundamental Changes Taking Place in the World* (OAU, 1990) noted that an 'increasingly interdependent world calls for greater international solidarity and peace and prosperity should be shared for the common good of humanity'. In addition, the Assembly of Heads of State and Government, the highest political body of the OAU, has expressly reaffirmed adherence to Article 13 of the African Charter on Human and Peoples' Rights[9] and the *Universal Declaration on Democracy* (Inter-Parliamentary Council, 1997) by holding that the principles of 'good governance, transparency and human rights are essential elements for building representative and stable government and contribute to conflict prevention'.[10]

A conflict mechanism

Recognizing the need for a more permanent and consistent approach to dispute settlement,[11] in 1993, after much deliberation, the OAU adopted the 'Cairo Declaration', establishing a mechanism for conflict prevention, management and resolution (OAU, 1993). The Cairo Declaration itself indicated a need to look more widely and consider the root causes of conflict, noting that 'freedom, equality, justice and dignity' cannot be achieved unless 'conditions for peace and security [were] established and maintained' (OAU, 1993: paras 1 and 2).

The mechanism had three aims: prevention, management and resolution. The focus was clearly upon the first, but where conflicts have occurred its function was to 'undertake peace-making and peace-building functions in order to facilitate the resolution of these conflicts ... civilian and military missions of observation and monitoring of limited scope and duration may be mounted and deployed' (OAU, 1993: para. 15).

The decisions of the conflict mechanism are taken by a central organ which functions at heads of state, ministerial and ambassadorial levels. The Secretariat of the OAU provides the administrative support for the conflict mechanism at the OAU headquarters in Addis Ababa, under the Conflict Management Centre with a small number of staff. There is also a military arm of the conflict mechanism, the Field Operations Section (FOS)[12] and a peace fund was set up specifically to support financially the activities of the mechanism.[13]

Recent developments

Consideration of the early warning system will be examined further below, but a number of recent activities may assist in the integration of human rights and prompt a more comprehensive awareness of conflict situations. The establishment of the Women's Committee on Peace and Development,[14] which acts as an advisory body on gender, peace and development to the OAU and UN's Economic Commission for Africa, is expressly required to take into account international human rights instruments in its functioning. The International Panel on Eminent Personalities to Investigate the Genocide in Rwanda and Surrounding Events (IPEP), a temporary body mandated to examine and report on the genocide, although having no express mention of human rights, had to be guided by 'relevant international and OAU Conventions' (OAU, 1998b) and it is clear that considering the genocide inevitably involved examination of wider notions of human rights. In addition, the Secretary-General himself plays a role in dealing with conflicts, and the present Secretary-General, Dr Salim Ahmed Salim, has indicated the importance of human rights in his speeches and presentations on many occasions (Salim, 1996), and has condemned violations of human rights by some states (OAU, 1999b,c). His approach, however, has not always been consistent, and this may be due to a reluctance to submit comments on 'more influential' countries (Amnesty International, 1998b:17). This reflects the attitude of the OAU as a whole, which suggests that inclusion of human rights within the work of the OAU, in general, leaves much room for improvement (Amnesty International, 1998b:2).

Apart from the OAU's lack of willingness to become involved in difficult conflict situations in general, the lack of integration of human rights in its work is perhaps explained by the relationship with its African Commission on Human and Peoples' Rights. This eleven-member, independent body was set up in 1987 under the African Charter on Human and Peoples' Rights, an instrument to which all African states are now party. The Commission is mandated to promote and protect human rights, and operates by examining reports submitted by states and adopting decisions on communications from individuals and NGOs on alleged violations of the rights in the Charter. Despite being under the auspices of the Ethiopian-based OAU, the Commission's Secretariat is situated in The Gambia. A consequence of this is that there seems to be a perception that human rights matters are distinct from other OAU work, and that any such issue is delegated to the Commission to deal with. Exacerbated by the geographical isolation of the Commission, there has thus been little knowledge of the Commission's operations, or sometimes even of its existence, among the various OAU organs and departments and little relationship between it and the rest of the OAU. This, therefore, has had an impact on the extent to which conflicts and human rights can be integrated. What is worth considering, also, is the extent to which the African Commission itself sees conflicts as part of its human rights mandate.

The African Commission on Human and Peoples' Rights: conflict in the context of human rights?

The substantive provisions of the Charter appear to place conflict within the context of human rights. Article 23(1) states that 'all peoples shall have the right to national and international peace and security. The principles of solidarity and friendly relations implicitly affirmed by the Charter of the United Nations and reaffirmed by that of the Organization of African Unity shall govern relations between States'. Article 23(2), affirmed by the Commission's interpretation, interestingly suggests that it is expected that most conflicts will come from inside the state rather than being external threats. The inclusion of peoples' rights within the Charter also offers the potential for preventing conflicts,[15] of which the work of the OSCE Commissioner on Minorities could be seen as a precedent. Indeed, it has been recognized that 'questions involving minorities ... are often intimately connected to problems which go to the very heart of the existence of states, impacting upon the relationship between regions and the centre, and border questions as well as the essence of the territorial integrity of states' (Foundation for Inter-Ethnic Relations, 1997:17).[16] This, along with other Articles of the Charter which will be considered below, indicates that conflicts are perceived to be part of the mandate of the Commission.

In light of this, various methods are available to the Commission to enable it to highlight potential conflicts.[17] The individual communication procedure under Article 58 of the Charter speaks expressly of 'a series of serious or massive violations' of the Charter rights.[18] The importance of this procedure, not only for highlighting abuses, but also for potentially dealing with possible conflicts, is clear:

> the prevalence of internal conflicts in Africa, most of which are accompanied by massive violations of human rights, suggests the need for strengthening human rights mechanisms in Africa ... However, the issue of providing a mechanism for non-state groups to voice their grievances regarding systematic discrimination and violations of human rights remains critical. Recourse to a legitimate international mechanism where such grievances can be aired and pressures brought to bear upon the offending government to change its behaviour will be an important development in the protection of human rights in Africa.
>
> (OAU/IPA, 1998:22–3)

Other methods include: on-site missions, the assignment of Commissioners to particular states for promotional purposes (African Commission, 1998a), the inter-state communication procedure, the reporting mechanism, the ability to adopt interim measures, the holding of extraordinary sessions and the work of the Commission's Special Rapporteurs.[19]

An early warning mechanism for Africa?

Despite being seen as the central focus of the OAU conflict mechanism, there is at present no early warning mechanism in the system. The limited number of staff at the Conflict Management Centre in the OAU Secretariat has meant that few persons can analyse and process data collected from news agencies and other organizations, for example, and alert the central organ to potential conflicts.

Separate from these developments, the African Commission has also been considering the establishment of its own early warning mechanism. A nine-point plan was drawn up by one of the Commissioners as a result of discussions, and a subsequent meeting on Article 58 organized by Interights in 1996 (African Commission, 1998c). This action plan requires the Commission to 'act promptly in cases of massive violations of human rights or emergency situations'. In this respect it could undertake a number of actions, including 'on-site visits, make diplomatic approaches and contact national and international organisations concerned with human rights', authorize a group or member to compile a report, or organize meetings 'near the state or at its [the Commission's] headquarters' if the state is not cooperative. The Commission could also make a public report itself on an emergency situation. That this is a preventive initiative is clear from the proposal to organize focal points, in collaboration with member states and NGOs linked to the Commission, collect information, give warning of emergency situations and be ready to discuss emergency situations on its agenda on a regular basis.

It has been suggested that the Commission could use NGOs as 'indicators from particular countries and indicators of the potential massive violations, for example, simmering ethnic tension with a repressive regime' (Murray, 2001) and that situations of concern could be reported to the heads of state of the OAU (African Commission, 1998c).

An indication of how responsive the Commission could be was given when during one session the representative of Amnesty International made a statement to the Commission that several persons were due to be executed in Rwanda the following day and urged the Commission to contact the authorities, urging them to suspend the executions until it had the opportunity to consider the matter. The Commission agreed to send a fax to the African and international media. Although the action was in vain, it did indicate the willingness of the Commission to operate and work with NGOs to respond to urgent issues. However, the Commission appeared unwilling to adopt this method as a general approach, refusing to respond in the same way to a similar request from an NGO in Sierra Leone. Its reticence could perhaps be explained by its fear of embroiling itself in a contentious situation, or perhaps it was eager not to appear to be at the beck and call of any NGO that called on it to act immediately. This is a pity, as it reduces the intervention of the Commission and could arguably give the impression that it failed to respond to human rights violations or the potential for them to occur.

Despite these parallel moves by the African Commission and the OAU, there has been little collaboration between them. There has been some indication by the OAU of the need to take a human rights perspective into the work of the conflict mechanism with the Ambassadorial Human Rights Seminar in 1997 (OAU, 1997), recommending, among other matters, that human rights be made a permanent issue on the agenda of the central organ. At a second seminar held in 1998 it was recognized that 'conflicts constituted both a cause and effect of human rights violations' and a link between poverty and conflicts and the

Conflict Division was encouraged to include human rights in its work (OAU, 1998c: para. 6).

The African Commission, similarly, has envisaged, in its nine-point plan, that it will report such situations to the OAU Assembly or the Chairman, as well as ministerial conferences of the OAU, and publicize such situations. Despite recent calls for this greater coordination between the Commission, the OAU conflict mechanism and the Secretary-General (of the OAU) (Murray, 2001),[20] the nine-point early warning proposal has not yet been formally adopted.[21] Thus any real collaboration or an attempt to combine efforts has been lacking. Given the recognition that a wide variety of information should be obtained, including that on violations of rights,[22] the importance of a close cooperation with the African Commission is inevitable. The OAU itself has recognized that it cannot operate an early warning system without being able to 'depend on a number of other actors within and outside Africa', with the need to set up information networks and sub-regional and regional centres (OAU, 1998a:8). The OAU should be building on its existing mechanisms.

The African Commission is in the ideal position. A continual monitoring of the human rights situation in a state will provide indicators to potential conflicts. The African Commission, however, is unique in its mandate to monitor the civil and political, as well as economic, social and cultural and peoples' rights in the Charter.[23] This enables it to consider the wider social and political situation in any given African state and to gain an in-depth understanding of potential developments and conflicts. There are already links with electoral monitoring, which is a way of predicting potential disputes between the OAU and the African Commission, with Commissioners acting as observers in election monitoring in some states.[24] It is this 'holistic approach to conflict prevention' which is essential (Foundation for Inter-Ethnic Relations, 1997:27).

There are precedents for a human rights approach to conflict prevention with the position of the OSCE High Commissioner for National Minorities and its early warning system (see further Cissé, 1996). The High Commissioner is mandated to be 'an instrument of conflict prevention at the earliest possible stage'. He provides 'early warning' and, as appropriate, 'early action' with regard to tensions involving minority issues which have not yet developed beyond an early warning stage, but, in the judgement of the High Commissioner, have the potential to develop into a conflict within the OSCE area, affecting peace, stability or relations between participating states (OSCE, 1992).

The African Commission can provide the OAU bodies with information obtained not only through the receipt of communications in relation to specific states, but also, probably most importantly, from its close relationship with NGOs across Africa and their general willingness to assist the Commission and provide it with information. However, unless a structure is adopted, as with the OSCE High Commissioner, the collection of this information may be rather *ad hoc*.[25] The – at least perceived – independence of the African Commission will be an important factor, as it has been in the work of the High Commissioner on National Minorities (Foundation for Inter-Ethnic Relations, 1997:20).

There are obvious difficulties, however, with the need to transmit such information quickly to the OAU and with the need for the Conflict Division of the OAU to process and act upon it accordingly. Such problems have also been identified with regard to the UN engaging in early warning, with criticism including a 'fragmented' approach among the political bodies, a lack of expertise in early warning among those sitting on the human rights treaty bodies, and lack of time to respond to the situations (Stavropoulou, 1996:431). What is important, however, is that the African Commission is an essential catalyst and provider of information from a wider perspective. It should be central and integral to the work of the conflict mechanism's early warning system, not merely secondary.

Conclusion

From a wider perspective, and as indicated elsewhere in this volume, human rights is central to an understanding of the relationship between criminology, state criminality and conflict resolution at the national and international levels. The manner in which a state treats its citizens is reflected in the criminal law, with more oppression indicated by increasingly draconian laws relating to arrest, detention and freedom of expression, to name a few. Preventing such initial actions from developing into conflict situations on a wider scale requires a recognition of these as first steps along that road. Genocide and the scale of human rights violations that it entails cannot occur without being sanctioned and organized by the authorities, one conclusion to a process begun by changes in criminal legislation.

The OAU's interest in conflicts has been *ad hoc*, and a sense of commitment to dealing with them only recent, through the provision of the conflict mechanism. However, the most important aspect of the mechanism, the preventive aspect, has yet to be implemented fully. In the course of its considerations, the OAU would do well to continue the approach, albeit limited, followed by its other bodies, to integrate human rights. Some moves in recent years do give cause for hope; for example, a ministerial conference in Mauritius in April 1999 affirmed concretely that 'observance of human rights is a key tool for promoting collective security, durable peace and sustainable development' and that 'respect for human rights is indispensable for the maintenance of regional and international peace and security and the elimination of conflicts' (OAU, 1999g).[26] In addition, the Constitutive Act of the African Union also makes reference to human rights, although it is limited in relation to the African Commission itself. The procedures available to the African Commission to deal with disputes indicate some attempt to place conflicts within a human rights framework. However, the extent to which they have been used to their full extent by the Commission falls sadly short.

If viewing conflict from the perspective of human rights law offers a better way of predicting conflicts, it is clear that the OAU needs to go further in practical terms, ensuring that collaboration occurs between its various departments and the Conflict Division as well as improving collaboration between the OAU and the African Commission. This would improve the likelihood of a stronger, coordinated response to a situation. In considering their establishment of an early warning system, the OAU and the African Commission must envisage concrete measures of working together on a single system which will not continue to underline the unrealistic separation of concepts of human rights and conflicts. Understanding the causes of conflicts is complex, but monitoring the wider human rights situation might be more productive in predicting problems.

Notes

* The author would like to thank Peter Billings, Richard Clements, Kieran McEvoy and Steven Wheatley for their invaluable comments on this draft. This chapter is a version of a paper presented to the International Law Association's series of talks in Cardiff, November 1999. Most of the documents and information on the Organization of African Unity were obtained through visiting its Secretariat, made possible with the kind financial assistance of the Society of Public Teachers of Law. This chapter is an amended version of the article produced in *Journal of African Law* (2001) and I am grateful to the journal for their permission to reproduce some of those arguments here.
1. 'Our prime task should be to engage in the earliest possible preventative diplomacy, so that ideally we need never cry out an early warning of imminent

conflict, let alone have to engage in conflict management' (Van Der Stoel, 1994:9).

2. As the previous UN High Commissioner for Human Rights has stated, 'It will be important in the future to have as early notice as possible of situations in which various elements of the United Nations human rights programme could play a role in preventing the outbreak of serious violations of human rights' (UN High Commissioner for Human Rights: para. 66, as cited in Adelman, 1998:47). This has also been recognized by others (e.g. Schmid, Jongman and Gupta, 1994; UN, 1998: paras 49 and 72). For a discussion of the role and importance of human rights in peacekeeping see de Rover and Gallagher (1995), Clapham and Henry (1995). For a contrary view, essentially suggesting that the linkage of human rights to peacekeeping may jeopardize the impartiality and integrity of the former, see Marx (1996) and van Baarda (1994).

3. Where human rights encompasses civil and political rights as well as economic, social and cultural rights and peoples' rights.

4. As has been noted, 'upholding of human rights and fundamental freedoms, the promotion of the rule of law, protection of the rights of minorities, concern for migrants and the establishment, development and safeguarding of democratic institutions ... are critical components of conflict prevention measures. Violations of commitments in these areas can lead to distrust, tension, and societal conflicts. Disrespect for these values at the national level can have international consequences such as mass migration' (Foundation for Inter-Ethnic Relations, 1997:11).

5. As Adelman notes, although the UN Departments of Humanitarian Affairs and Humanitarian Early Warning System and its Integrated Regional Information Network System meet regularly, the UN Commission for Human Rights is not included (Adelman, 1998:47).

6. See also Amnesty International (1998a).

7. Article 3(4) cites the 'peaceful settlement of disputes by negotiation, mediation, conciliation or arbitration' as one of the principles of the Organization. In this respect, the Charter provided specifically for a Commission of Mediation, Conciliation and Arbitration, viewed as one of the 'principal institutions' of the Organization, along with the Assembly of Heads of State and Government, the Council of Ministers and the General Secretariat. It never, however, functioned. The reasons for failure to use this organ, and for taking the more *ad hoc* approach which was adopted by the OAU until the 1990s, were many, including: dislike of 'judicial structures' and preference for more amicable methods; its ability to deal only with the resolution of conflicts and not take a preventive role; and the limitations of the mandate to only inter-state disputes (Salim, 1996:11).

8. 'Convinced that it is the inalienable right of all people to control their own destiny; Conscious of the fact that freedom, equality, justice and dignity are essential objectives for the achievement of the legitimate aspirations of the African peoples; ... Persuaded that the Charter of the United Nations and the Universal Declaration of Human Rights, to the Principles of which we reaffirm our adherence, provide a solid foundation for peaceful and positive co-operation among states' (OAU Charter Preamble, 1963).

9. Article 13 stipulates: '1. Every citizen shall have the right to participate freely in the government of his country, either directly or through freely chosen

representatives in accordance with the provisions of the law. 2. Every citizen shall have the right of equal access to the public service of his country. 3. Every individual shall have the right of access to public property and services in strict equality of all persons before the law.'

10. In addition, in the OAU Assembly's *Decision on the Illicit Proliferation, Circulation and Trafficking of Small Arms and Light Weapons* (OAU, 1999d) it stressed the impact of 'illicit proliferation, circulation and trafficking of light weapons on the increased involvement of children as soldiers and the psycho-social trauma thereof and the need to comply with the African Charter on the Rights and Welfare of Children and the Convention on the Rights of the Child'. Furthermore, the OAU Council of Ministers urged states to ratify the African Charter on the Rights and Welfare of the Child (OAU, 1999e). More recently, at the 4th Extraordinary Summit of the Assembly in September 1999 the Assembly adopted a *Draft Sirte Declaration* (OAU, 1999f) which noted 'important measures' that have been undertaken to facilitate the work of the Secretariat and a move to a phase characterized by: 'conflict resolution, democratisation, observance of human rights, economic integration and social emancipation'. Progress should be guided by the African Charter on Human and Peoples' Rights, among other instruments and declarations and it noted that the new OAU Convention against terrorism 'constitutes a major and positive achievement towards promoting human rights values, stability and socio-economic development in Africa'.

11. In its *Declaration on Fundamental Changes* (OAU, 1990) the Assembly of Heads of State and Government reaffirmed cooperation in peace and quick resolution of conflicts and that the primary responsibility fell on African governments to solve African conflicts. It recognized the impact that the end of the cold war had had on Africa.

12. The central organ 'may also seek, from within the Continent, such military, legal and other forms of expertise as it may require in the performance of its functions' (OAU, 1993: para. 19). Since its inception the FOS has organized three mixed civilian/military missions to: Rwanda, Burundi and the Comoros, although there have been difficulties in carrying out their functions, particularly in the last two cases: the Neutral Military Observer Group in Rwanda, in October 1993, remained there to supervise the ceasefire and prompt negotiations to sign the Arusha Peace Accords, until the UN entered. The Observer Mission in Burundi in July 1996 was there to prevent the conflict escalating. The Observer Mission to the Comoros in August 1998 was aimed at monitoring the situation and deterring an escalating crisis. It was not permitted to be on Anjouan, one of the islands, by the current authorities.

13. 'For the purpose of providing financial resources to support exclusively the OAU operational activities relating to conflict management and resolution' (OAU, 1993: para. 23). It consists of financial appropriations from the regular budget of the OAU, voluntary contributions from states and other sources in Africa. The OAU has also accepted voluntary contributions from outside Africa, which provide the much of the financial support. As is often the case, there is an acknowledgement that the mechanism is severely lacking in the funds required (OAU, 1999a:3).

14. This is set up in collaboration with the United Nations Economic Commission for Africa (ECA). Its task is to advise both the OAU and the ECA

on 'peace, stability, gender and development' and will have a close relationship with the conflict mechanism. See C/M.Dec.337(LCVI), endorsed by the 33rd Ordinary Session of the Assembly of Heads of State and Government in May 1997. Rule 1 of its Terms of Reference states that its aim is to 'ensure and enhance the participation of women in development and conflict prevention, management and resolution'.

15. See discussion by the Commission on this matter (African Commission, 1999).

16. As Pityana states, 'indigenous people therefore are not necessarily minorities and such an expression is considered inappropriate' (African Commission, 1999:2–3). Furthermore, he argues that inclusion of the term 'peoples' within the African Charter was 'designed to balance the individualism that had come to be associated with the western elaboration of human rights with the collective ideas of African anthropology'. The drafters of the Charter would hardly have intended for a 'people' to equate with a state, but peoples were 'tribal communities who are essential elements of African society ... [a people] must be construed as referring to identifiable ethnic communities which owe allegiance to a sovereign state'.

17. For fuller consideration of methods available to deal with 'serious or massive' violations which relate to conflict situations, see Murray (1999).

18. This reads: '1. When it appears after deliberations of the Commission that one or more communications apparently relate to special cases which reveal the existence of a series of serious or massive violations of human and peoples' rights, the Commission shall draw the attention of the Assembly of Heads of State and Government to these special cases. 2. The Assembly of Heads of State and Government may then request the Commission to undertake an in-depth study of these cases and make a factual report, accompanied by its findings and recommendations. 3. A case of emergency duly noticed by the Commission shall be submitted by the latter to the Chairman of the Assembly of Heads of State and Government who may request an in-depth study'. How one defines 'serious or massive violations' is not clear (see Murray, 2000).

19. Special Rapporteur on Summary, Arbitrary and Extra-Judicial Executions, Special Rapporteur on Prison and Other Conditions of Detention, Special Rapporteur on Women's Rights. All of them are Commissioners. The Special Rapporteur's Terms of Reference are wide enough to encompass matters dealing with conflict. In addition, Article 11 of the *Draft Protocol on the Rights of Women in Africa* notes, in relation to the 'right to peace', that 'women shall have the right to participate in the promotion and maintenance of peace and to live in a peaceful environment. States parties shall take all appropriate measures to involve women: (a) in programmes of education for peace and a culture of peace; (b) in the structures for conflict prevention, management and resolution at local, national, regional, continental and international levels; (c) in the local, national, sub-regional, regional, continental and international decision-making structures to ensure physical, psychological, social and legal protection of refugee, returnee and displaced women; (d) in all levels of structures established for the management of camps and asylum areas. 2. States Parties additionally shall reduce military expenditure significantly in favour of spending on social development, while guaranteeing the

effective participation of women in the distribution of these resources' (African Commission, 2000).

20. Distinctions have been drawn between 'early warning' and 'early action', whereby some participants felt that the Commission should be concentrating on the latter given that 'warnings' had been sent in response to the crises in Rwanda in 1994 and Nigeria in 1995 but had failed to prompt the necessary action from the government.

21. At the 26th session, it was decided that Commissioner Dankwa consider the matter further but that in the meantime emergencies be noted to the Chairman of the Commission, who might take action.

22. 'The objective of early-warning information is to prevent perceived or actual threat to the values of the Organization ... The values range from the protection of human and peoples' rights, promotion of democracy and security for all' (OAU, 1998a:7).

23. Stavropoulou argues with regard to economic, social and cultural rights that it is very difficult to identify indicators; as to implementing and monitoring them, this is 'even more complicated than for civil and political rights' (Stavropoulou, 1996:429).

24. There are problems of being involved at the early stages of the election, however (OAU, 1998a:12).

25. 'There is no systematic or institutionalised structure for gaining increased awareness of any given situation or the actions which should be taken in reaction to particular developments. The High Commissioner's action is rather dependent on ad hoc reaction to developments which come to his attention via a wide-ranging analysis based on a variety of reports and contacts' (Foundation for Inter-Ethnic Relations, 1997:25).

26. The fact that these were mentioned only in the preamble to the Declaration and nowhere in the substantive text suggests that there is little cause for celebration at this stage.

References

Adelman, H. (1998) 'Humanitarian and Conflict-Orientated Early Warning: A Historical Background Sketch', in K van Walraven (ed.) *Early Warning and Conflict Prevention. Limitations and Possibilities*. The Hague: Kluwer Law International.

African Commission on Human and Peoples' Rights (1998a) *Geographical Distribution of Countries for Promotional Activities*, DOC/OS/36e (XXIII).

African Commission on Human and Peoples' Rights (1998b) *Activity Reports of Commissioners: N. Barney Pityana*, DOC/OSA/53(a) (XXIV).

African Commission on Human and Peoples' Rights (1998c) *Mechanisms for Urgent Response to Human Rights Emergencies under Article 58 of the African Charter on Human and Peoples' Rights*, DOC/OS/52 (XXIV).

African Commission on Human and Peoples' Rights (1999) *Situation of Indigenous Peoples in Africa*, DOC/OS (XXVI)/130.

African Commission on Human and Peoples' Rights (2000) *Draft Protocol to the African Charter on Human and Peoples' Rights on the Rights of Women in Africa (Final Version)*, 13 September 2000, CAB/LEG/66.6.

Amnesty International (1998a) *Human Rights Integral to Regional Security*, 23 July, AI Index: IOR 64/01/98.

Amnesty International (1998b) *Organization of African Unity. Making Human Rights a Reality for Africans*, AI Index: IOR 63/01/98, August.

Cissé, C. (1996) 'Conflict Prevention by the OAU. The Relevance of the OSCE High Commissioner on National Minorities', *African Yearbook of International Law* 4.

Clapham, A. and M. Henry (1995) 'Peacekeeping and Human Rights in Africa and Europe', in A. Henkin (ed.) *Honoring Human Rights and Keeping the Peace – Lessons from El Salvador, Cambodia and Haiti*. Aspen, CO: Aspen Institute.

Deng, F. and I. Zartman (1991) (eds) *Conflict Resolution in Africa*. Washington DC: The Brookings Institution.

Eide, A. (1979) 'The New Humanitarian Law in Non-International Armed Conflict', in A. Cassese, *The New Humanitarian Law of Armed Conflict*. Naples: Editoriale Scientifica, sr1, 277–309.

Fleck, D. (1995) *Handbook of Humanitarian Law of Armed Conflicts*. Oxford: Oxford University Press.

Forsythe, D. (1982) 'Human Rights and Internal Conflicts: Trends and Recent Developments', *California West Journal of International Law* 12, 287–308.

Foundation for Inter-Ethnic Relations (1997) *The Role of the High Commissioner on National Minorities in OSCE Conflict Prevention: An Introduction*. The Hague: Foundation for Inter-Ethnic Relations.

Inter-Parliamentary Council (1997) *Universal Declaration on Democracy*. 161st Session, Cairo, 16 September.

Kuitenbrouwer, K. (1999) 'Ethnic Conflicts and Human Rights: Multidisciplinary Perspectives', in P. Baehr, F. Baudet and H. Werdmöler (eds) *Human Rights and Ethnic Conflicts*. Utrecht: Netherlands Institute of Human Rights.

MacBride, J. (1970) 'Human Rights in Armed Conflict', *Revue Droit Pénal Militaire et Droit de la Guerre* 9, 373–91.

Marx, R. (1996) 'A Non-Governmental Human Rights Strategy for Peace-keeping', *NQHR* 14, 127–45.

Meron, T. (1987) *Human Rights in Internal Strife: Their International Protection*. Cambridge: Grotius.

Murray, R. (1999) 'Serious or Massive Violations under the African Charter: A Comparison with the Inter-American and European Mechanisms', *NQHR* 17 (2), 109–33.

Murray, R. (2000) *The African Commission on Human and Peoples' Rights and International Law*. Oxford: Hart Publishing.

Murray, R. (2001) 'Report of the 1999 Sessions of the African Commission on Human and Peoples' Rights', *HRLJ*, 172–194.

OAU (1963) *Charters of the Organization of African Unity*. Addis Ababa: OAU.

OAU (1990) *Declaration on Fundamental Changes Taking Place in the World*. Addis Ababa, 11 July, AHG/Dec.141(XXXV).

OAU (1993) *Declaration of the Assembly of Heads of State and Government on the Establishment, within the OAU, of a Mechanism for Conflict Prevention, Management and Resolution*, AHG/Decl.3(XXIX), Cairo, Egypt, June.

OAU (1997) *Report of the First Seminar for African Ambassadors on Strengthening the African Human Rights System organised by the OAU in Collaboration with the ICJ and the African Commission on Human and Peoples' Rights, 6–7 May, Ethiopia*.

OAU (1998a) *OAU Mechanism for Conflict Prevention, Management and Resolution,* Addis Ababa.

OAU (1998b) *Press Statement on the Establishment of an International Panel of Eminent Personalities to Investigate the Genocide in Rwanda and Surrounding Events,* Ouagadougou, 3 June.

OAU (1998c) *Report of the Second Seminar for African Ambassadors on Strengthening the African Human Rights System organised by the OAU and the ICJ,* 8–9 September Ethiopia.

OAU (1999a) *Report of the Secretary-General on the OAU Peace Fund,* CM/2106(LXX).

OAU (1999b) *Report of the Secretary-General on the Conflict in Sierra-Leone,* CM/2099(LXX)-f.

OAU (1999c) *Report of the Secretary-General on the Situation in the Islamic Federal Republic of the Comoros,* CM/2099(LXX)-c.

OAU (1999d) *Decision on the Illicit Proliferation, Circulation and Trafficking of Small Arms and Light Weapons,* AHG/Dec.137(LXX).

OAU (1999e) *Decision on the Report on the 'African Conference on the Use of Children as Soldiers',* CM/Dec.482(LXX).

OAU (1999f) *Draft Sirte Declaration,* EAHG/Draft/Decl.(IV) Rev.1.

OAU (1999g) *Grand Baie Declaration,* CONF/HRA/DECL(I).

OAU (2001) Website of the Organization of African Unity. http://www.oau-oua.org.

OAU/IPA (1998) *Report of the Joint OAU/IPA Task Force on Peacemaking and Peacekeeping in Africa,* New York, March.

OSCE (1992) *Helsinki Document II.*

Ramcharan, B. (1991) *The International Law and Practice of Early-Warning and Preventative Diplomacy: The Emerging Global Watch.* Dordrecht: Martinus Nijhoff.

Rover, C. de and A. Gallagher (1995) 'Human Rights Training for UN Peace-Keepers: Lessons from Mozambique', *NQHR* 13, 217–35.

Salim, S.A. (1996) 'Lessons from a Decade of Conflicts: Prospects of Peace and Security by the Year 2000', presentation by HE Salim Ahmed Salim, Secretary-General, Conference of African Ministers of Planning and UNDP Resident Representatives, 31 January–2 February.

Schmid, A., A. Jongman and D. Gupta (1994) 'Early Detection of Emerging Political and Humanitarian Crises: An Early Warning Model for Assessing Country Proneness to Conflict Escalation'. Leiden: PIOOM (unpublished).

Stavropoulou, M. (1996) 'Human Rights and Early Warning in the United Nations', *NQHR* 14, 419–33.

Tesha, T. (1999) 'Addressing the Challenges of Peace and Security in Africa', Addis Ababa, Ethiopia: Conflict Management Centre, Occasional Paper Series No.1/1999.

United Nations (1998) *The Causes of Conflict and the Promotion of Durable Peace and Sustainable Development in Africa. Report of the Secretary-General,* General Assembly, Security Council, 52nd Session, 53rd year, Report of the UN Secretary-General on the Work of the Organization of African Unity, S/1998/318, 13 April.

Van Baarda, T. (1994) 'The Involvement of the Security Council in Maintaining International Humanitarian Law', *NQHR* 12, 137–52.

Van Der Stoel, M. (1994) Keynote Speech of the High Commissioner on National Minorities, to the Seminar on Early Warning and Preventative Diplomacy, Warsaw, 19–21 January, in *CSCE, Office for Democratic Institutions and Human Rights Bulletin*, 2 (2), 7–13.
Van Walraven, K. (1998) (ed.) *Early Warning and Conflict Prevention. Limitations and Possibilities*. The Hague: Kluwer Law International.

Cases cited

Prosecutor v. Joseph Kanyabashi (Case No. ICTR-96-15-t).

5

Critiquing the Critics of Peacemaking Criminology: Some Rather Ambivalent Reflections on the Theory of 'Being Nice'

Jim Thomas, Julie Capps, James Carr, Tammie Evans, Wendy Lewin-Gladney, Deborah Jacobson, Chris Maier, Scott Moran and Sean Thompson *

Introduction

Nobody is very likely to consider a doctrine true merely because it makes people happy or virtuous – except perhaps the lovely 'idealists' who become effusive about the good, the true and the beautiful and allow all kinds of motley, clumsy and benevolent desiderata to swim around in utter confusion in their pond (Nietzsche, 1966:49). In the past decade, a growing number of scholars have attempted to integrate 'being nice' with theoretical precepts. Peacemaking criminology reflects one such attempt. Perhaps because it blends scholarship and praxis with an ideology of social harmony and unity, peacemaking criminology (PMC) risks being seen as something less than a rigorous intellectual position, and more as a philosophical belief system. As a consequence, one goal for advocates lies in expanding the tenets of PMC beyond the pale of co-ideologues in order to avoid the criticism that PMC is just another effusively 'feel good' doctrine promulgated by confused idealists.

The essays in this volume attest both to the recent growth of the peacemaking perspective in criminology, especially the restorative justice variant, and to the diversity of ways that practitioners have attempted to implement its tenets in research and in practice. Yet the increased interest in peacemaking criminology in the past decade has also led to corresponding questions about its practical utility and intellectual consistency. Is the perspective useful as a means to reduce crime? Or is it simply a catchall phrase used by politically and intellectually diverse advocates, with little substantive value beyond mobilizing for group hugs and a mass chorus of 'We Shall Overcome?' This chapter examines whether it is simply a muddle-minded means for idealists to become 'effusive about the good, the true, and the beautiful'.

Our entry into this project began when the volume's co-editor, Kieran McEvoy, accepted the suggestion that our graduate seminar on the US criminal justice system write a collective article. For some of us, criminal justice is a practitioners' field in which peacemaking seems quite alien. For others of us, peacemaking is something we do in our daily lives, something that seemed unrelated to our academic pursuits. A few of us are actively involved in attempts to humanize prisons. All of us were sceptical of the perspective of peacemaking criminology, not so much for what it represents, but for the apparent confusion surrounding the central tenets, the lack of clear strategies for implementation, and the inability or refusal of many adherents to address the hard questions of how we, individually or collectively, ought to respond to specific instances of violence of all types.

Although some of our commentary may seem critical, we are unequivocally sympathetic to the perspective, and it influences much of our own work. Yet we have collective reservations about adopting the term as a mantle around which to wrap either our research or our praxis without first assessing what we wear when we don it. Many of our concerns seem either unaddressed by advocates, or, worse, ignored as irrelevant to peacemaking goals. This risks reducing PMC to a feel-good ethos while limiting adherents to preaching to the choir. In re-examining our own views about PMC, we begin by summarizing its primary characteristics. Next, we examine several criticisms of the perspective, and finally we identify its potential utility for mainstream scholars, policy makers and practitioners.

We offer two preliminary caveats to guide readers. First, our collective intellectual ambivalence occasionally translates into discursive mood swings as we attempt to balance the extreme PMC positions with those we consider more credible. However, it is likely that these swings reflect the diversity of PMC advocates at least as much as our own attempts to sort through them. Second, the occasional critical tone of our own effort reflects in part our agreement with critics on some points and our frustration with some of the leading PMC advocates to address the critics. None the less, if we successfully balance our swings, our commentary suggests ways to address some of the most severe criticisms by illustrating the perspective's potential for intellectual development and social action.

What is peacemaking criminology?

Perhaps we take peacemaking criminology too seriously. Then again, perhaps we should ask why we ought to take it seriously at all. It probably depends on how we define it, where we see it located in the pantheon of social theory (if at all), and on what practical, ideological or substantive relevance it has. There is no doubt that the perspective has become more visible in recent years. One irony, however, is that the more visible it becomes, the less substance it seems to have. Who, after all, can dispute that it's better to be nice than not nice, and that pain and suffering should be avoided?

The first difficulty in assessing peacemaking criminology begins with identifying a clear, reasonably encompassing definition, or even isolating a group of precepts that binds adherents. The perspective is not a theory, because it lacks an identifiable core of readily testable postulates or claims, contains more vision than explanation, and does not seem amenable to modification when confronted with contentious factual or other challenges. In fact, many advocates of the perspective seem to avoid addressing criticisms. It is not a systematic philosophy, because it contains no well-articulated premises or rigorous method for critiquing, testing or advancing knowledge. Although identified with the discipline of criminology, peacemaking criminology is not a discipline, because it possesses no integrating set of systematic theories or method or immediately obvious policy-oriented guidelines. Therefore, we begin our exploration of PMC by viewing it as a perspective, or a stance from which to view and comment upon objects within our gaze.

A peacemaking perspective in the social sciences is hardly new. Three decades ago, Curle (1971) articulated a detailed theory of strategies for replacing conflict with peace, and journals such as *Humanity and Society* have long nurtured a social science humanistic perspective. But, as the bibliographic entries in this volume indicate, the emergence of a distinctly criminological form of 'peacemaking', although it emerged over 20 years ago, has mushroomed primarily in the past decade. The growth occurred largely as a response to the perceived futility of the war-making metaphor that dominates crime control research and scholarship (Pepinsky, 1998a; Arrigo, 1999; Kraska, 1999) and in part as a response to the need to integrate criminal justice theory and practice within a broader framework of basic human needs.

Although the origins of PMC are often attributed to Richard Quinney (Akers, 1997; McEvoy and Gormally, 1997), the seeds of a kinder, gentler mainstream criminology that responded to human needs rather than reacted to human misdeeds were sown especially by the works of Tifft (1979), Tifft and Sullivan (1980) and Pepinsky (1979). In arguing for minimalist state control structures and spiritual rejuvenation as the preconditions for a just society, Tifft (1979) offered one of the earliest systematic attempts to establish a base for a criminology of peacemaking. Tifft's responsive anarchism was a call for a society based on love, one that attends to essential human needs. Stressing empathy for the plight of others, he argued that existing social structures and forms of interaction perpetuate human misery, and that crime and misery are irrevocably intertwined. Spiritual rejuvenation requires empathy with those who, because of their social position, are more likely to be relegated to life conditions characterized by structural inequality, existential despair and physical or mental suffering.

Developing a similar theme of a humanist social science, Pepinsky (1979:250) observed that, 'rather than trying to find out what is, the humanist uses data to calculate what can be'. In doing so, he contributed to criminology a transformative set of ideals to guide the emerging perspective as a research direction. In later refinements, Pepinsky (1988) argued that there is a direct relationship between violence and social unresponsiveness that occurs through processes of depersonalization. Like Tifft, Pepinsky challenged us to rethink our conceptualization of crime and suggested that an act of crime is conventionally defined by nuances of context and motive, a distinction he rejects (Pepinsky, 1988:551–3).

The articulation of an explicit peacemaking perspective in criminology arguably began with the works of Richard Quinney (1988a,b,c), and was further developed by others, such as Anderson (1989) and Pepinsky (1988, 1995, 1998a). Pepinsky and Quinney (1988a) reshaped the perspective with 20 articles by peacemaking proponents in a single collection that addressed the PMC tradition, integrated PMC with other genres such as feminism, and then connected the perspective to radical/critical criminology. Their collection not only increased the visibility of the perspective, but it also cast a wider intellectual and ideological net than had previous works by uniting scholars who had been writing on the periphery of explicit peacemaking issues.

Quinney, the prime mover in shifting PMC from the fringes of criminological awareness towards the centre, was the most articulate in arguing that conventional criminological theory was impoverished. For Quinney, 'No amount of thinking and no amount of public policy have brought us any closer to understanding and solving the problems of crime' (Quinney, 1988a:67). What is needed, he argued, is a fundamentally new paradigm, one that recognizes that crime is but one form of violence among many, including war, debilitating social formations, destructive forms of interaction, and structural factors that suppress human potential. This requires a proactive approach to crime and justice characterized by a focus on universal social justice as the prerequisite of elimination of predatory behaviour.

However, the diversity of practitioners' views clouds a clear image of the contours, implications and content of peacemaking criminology. Despite, or more likely because of, the growing diverse interest the perspective, like six Pirandellian characters, it remains in search of a unifying set of authors to provide it with a unique identity. Many proponents view peacemaking criminology as simply a term used to bridge the macro-micro theoretical and policy chasms between social structure, the criminal justice system and the individual.

What, then, is peacemaking criminology? Few, if any, leading adherents see it as a theory. Most would accept Sullivan's view that:

> peacemaking criminology is a perspective, a way of looking at the world which on the most intimate of levels means human relationships – how we form them, how we maintain them, and how we restore them when things go wrong.
>
> (Sullivan, email communication, 2 December 1999)

Although not all agree with Mika's coalition-building vision of PMC, he none the less confronts the definitional problem in an attempt to recast it as a way of pulling and holding diverse ideological groups around a core of shared humanism:

> I prefer to think of peacemaking criminology even more informally, where it is a comfortable conversation between individuals who subscribe to a very broad range of critical, dialectical, and reflexive orientations to justice.
>
> (Mika, 1999)

Although helpful, these definitions are vague on content and ambiguous on practices, leading both critics and sympathetic observers to judge the perspective abstruse and lacking practical substance. For example, Akers (1997:183) sees PMC as little more than a vague utopian vision that, while laudable, is of little use as an explanatory model for crime or for processing offenders. The tendency of leading proponents of the perspective to ignore or dismiss such criticisms creates such credibility problems and feeds the view that PMC advocates are merely lovely idealists swimming around in confusion.

Addressing the critics

Is PMC internally consistent such that it even makes sense to talk about it as a coherent body of thought, other than 'it's nice to be nice'? Or does it offer something substantively new with which to supplement, even replace, conventional criminological theory? In pulling together the most salient criticisms of PMC, we drew from five sources.

First, published commentaries directed attention to problems that conventional scholars identify with PMC. However, unlike the acrimonious debates surrounding the emergence of critical criminology in the 1970s (Taylor, Walton and Young, 1974; Inciardi, 1980), PMC has not yet generated such passionate opposition. We attribute this partly to the relative newness of the perspective, partly to the degree to which critical perspectives have become mainstream, and partly to the possibility that PMC is not taken seriously by mainstream scholars either as a threatening alternative perspective or, more damning, as a viable intellectual position.

Electronic discussions groups, or 'listservs', provided a second source of criticisms. The discussion group of the Critical Criminology Division of the American Society of Criminology (http://www.soci.niu.edu/ ~critcrim) was particularly useful, and we also drew from other groups specializing in peacemaking issues such as restorative justice and opposition to capital punishment. A private discussion group created to discuss peacemaking provided additional critiques.

Third, we solicited email commentary both from PMC critics and advocates.

Fourth, Web publications provided additional commentary. However, because of the inconsistency and often poor quality of Web material, we used it primarily as heuristic guidelines.

Finally, we drew most heavily from conference sessions and formal and informal discussions with critics and advocates attending the 1999 annual meetings of the American Criminological Association in Toronto.

Because many of the criticisms of PMC came from sympathetic observers, and because many of the observers expressed friendship with or collegial affiliation with leading PMC advocates, their comments were used with permission on the condition of anonymity.

One might ask, as did one advocate, 'Why bother responding to critics at all? It's better to just do peacemaking rather argue'. There are several compelling reasons for responding to criticisms of PMC. First, many criticisms, such as as PMC's similarity to functionalism, are based on misconceptions that, if unaddressed, take on an iterative, self-perpetuating character. Second, responding to critics moves PMC away from the perception that it is only a 'feel good' philosophy that elevates ideology above critique and discourse. Third, by raising critical issues, we can generate discussion of demonstrable shortcomings in the perspective as a way of overcoming them. Fourth, addressing criticisms against PMC also helps identify differences within the perspective by illustrating the various intellectual traditions that influence practitioners. Finally, addressing the intellectual and other problems increases PMC's credibility, and it is hoped, raises recognition of its viability.

From published literature, electronic sources and conference interactions we selected the most common or (to us) most interesting criticisms and sorted them into five broad thematic categories. We call these categories 'syndromes' to capture the image of symptomatic imbalance between PMC and scholars expressing discomfort with it.

The five syndromes focus on the criticisms that PMC is incompatible with Marxian/radical theories; is theoretically akin to functionalism; is inherently conservative; reflects overwhelming intellectual chaos; and lacks intellectual or empirical credibility.

Some of the criticisms are relatively simple and can be expressed briefly. Others, more complex, require further elaboration. We respond directly to three of the critical syndromes, but two others – those of 'chaos' and 'conservatism' we expand in separate sections.

The Marxian/radical syndrome

Although there is little in PMC that is explicitly Marxist, it is often associated with Marxian, radical/critical or conflict theories because some of the most visible proponents are associated with those theories. For example, Quinney's early works (1970, 1974, 1977) reflect influences of phenomenology, Marx and conflict theory, prompting one commentator to describe him as 'conventional, conflict oriented, critical, neo-Marxist, and more recently prophetic' (Friedrichs, 1980:48–9). Others, such as Tifft and Pepinsky, have also been classified as critical criminologists (Friedrichs, 1980; Thomas and O'Maolchatha, 1989) or within the radical conflict perspective (Williams and McShane, 1994; Beirne and Messerschmidt, 1995:533–4).

However, the peacemaking perspective seems to some critics the antithesis of traditional 'radical' positions such as conflict theory, critical theory or Marxian-oriented perspectives. Akers (1997:184), for example, has argued that it is contradictory to claim Marx as a significant theoretical basis, because of Marx's own emphasis on class conflict and non-rejection of violence as the means for social change. In this view, the Marxian war-making metaphor of social struggle and the necessity of class conflict lie in opposition to a vision of peacemaking. Bohm (1997:132) notes that PMC can be criticized for extreme idealism and excessive focus on transforming individuals rather than transforming society. Some radical theorists suggest that PMC advocates have sacrificed the radical/Marxian emphasis on social action to utopian contemplation:

> we challenge progressive academics to also think about Marx's simple, but profound thesis that while the *philosophers have only interpreted the world in different ways, the point is to change it.* We believe that it is time for criminologists to stop *thinking* about peace and to start *making* it.
>
> (Currie and MacLean, 1995:108; all emphasis in original)

Others within the Marxian tradition are sceptical of the ultimate value of PMC to significantly change repressive structural conditions, arguing that

> reforming subparts of the totality to make them more user friendly (informal) is actually 'another turn of the ideological screw' (Rick Abel) whereby folks are co-opted into believing that something important has changed when it has not and that instead of dealing with the wider structural issues, these are further masked. Then, if the outcomes are more humane but problems persist, the mainstream can blame the alternatives for failing, being too lenient etc., and thereby excuse themselves while holding on to power.
>
> (Henry, 2000)

Whether PMC diverges from or contradicts Marxian or any other theory may be a matter of profound indifference to PMC advocates, but because the criticism is used to discredit PMC, it is worth addressing.

The functionalist syndrome

A second concern with peacemaking criminology raised by critics at the American Society of Criminology conference centres on a perceived congruence with functionalism. While this criticism was neither the most common nor the most serious, it is one of the most interesting, both because of the nature of the claim and because it has been used against Marxian-oriented perspectives in the past.

The view that PMC resembles functionalism is based on the perception that both share the concept of 'harmony' as central to the position, that both are excessively utopian, and that because Marx was an (alleged) functionalist, PMC's Marxian/critical roots also carry functionalist baggage. Unlike the core of conflict theory, which holds that conflict is a fundamental part of the social process and that all societies rest upon constraint of some members by others (e.g. Chambliss and Seidman, 1971), the leading PMC advocates reject the necessity of conflict, or 'negative peace', which is any coercive apparatus – such as the criminal justice system – used against people who challenge a preferred social order (Quinney, 1998:358). Because the basis of peacemaking lies on establishing harmony and reducing the structural conditions, status hierarchies and interactional styles that facilitate conflict, some sceptics have suggested that, if we substitute 'consensus' with 'peacemaking', we have a variant of functionalism. In this view, the telos of peace or harmony is seen as driving social behaviour and institutions. Because of functionalism's tenets that all social systems are based on consensus (Parsons, 1937) or that crime is 'normal' (Durkheim, 1951), it is seen by some as inherently conservative (Bohm, 1997:84) or at best as fulfilling the liberal ideal of the world (Smith, 1966). Dahrendorf (1958) argued that functionalism is another form of utopian theory, and as such, neither fruitful nor realistic. Others (e.g. Fallding, 1972; Szymanski, 1972) have argued that Marx was, in fact, a functionalist. Hence, for some critics it then follows that because the peacemaking perspective also is based on consensus and harmony, is utopian, and underlies Marxian perspectives, it is likewise a *de facto* conservative teleological view.

The conservative syndrome

A third criticism also suggests that PMC is conservative, not because of ideological or theoretical assumptive premises, such as those found in functionalism, but because of an irony inherent in the core values of advocates. In this view, voiced especially by political militants and community activists, the emphasis on peace and the overriding tenet to reject conflict, especially violence, ultimately supports, even strengthens, an oppressive status quo by espousing a passive, impotent and generally ineffective belief system that leads to martyrdom rather than social change. For example, some critics point to Quinney's (1993) existential reflections espousing personal and intellectual mysticism and holistic spiritualism as evidence of the 'beastly beatitudes' of PMC. Others cite Quinney's (1988a:348) observation that peacemaking criminologists need not directly engage in conflict, but can instead bear witness to the suffering brought about by exploitation, poverty, greed, hate and inequality as evidence of excessive pacifism at best, 'acquiescence to evil' at worst. In the critic's view, victims do not need witnesses, they need warriors:

> Kitty Genovese [a woman stabbed to death in New York City while 38 people witnessed the attack and failed to report it] had witnesses who watched over nearly two hours as her assailant stabbed her to death. She didn't need witnesses. She needed someone to intervene. And that's my problem with peacemaking criminologists. They are silent on the question of how we should intervene in unpleasantness.
> (Anonymous conference critic, 1999,
> American Society of Criminology Meetings)

Some critics judge that the spiritual unity advocated by peacemaking criminologists presupposes a hive mentality that would replace democratic pluralism with homogeneous passivity (anonymous conference critic, 1999, American Society of Criminology). In the view of these critics, direct conflict, whether in the form of hostile arguments, direct confrontation or even the necessity of physical intervention, may be necessary to fight injustice or reduce harm. Failure to do otherwise, in this view, is simply self-indulgent intellectualist idealism that a privileged few can enjoy at the expense of others less fortunate.

The chaotic syndrome

A fourth criticism centres on the seemingly chaotic diffusion of intellectual threads, a tendency to hyperbole, seemingly naive or contradictory views, and the lack of a clear definition of 'peacemaking'. These critics point to the ideological, polemical, discursive and intellectual diversity of those advocating a peacemaking approach to justify the claim that PMC is little more than a hodgepodge of disconnected ideas. In this view, PMC is a dogmatic ideological ideal, one not requiring serious thinking and therefore not deserving of being taken seriously. Unfortunately, these critics are aided by the occasional hyperbole or shoddy thinking of adherents, especially by those who push the limits of pacifism by remaining silent on the question of how to deal with violence and those who commit it.

For example, the argument that we should expunge not only deeds, but words or even thoughts that are 'warlike', that generate 'negative peace', or that make others feel bad, seems not only unrealistic, but dangerously utopian. Gilligan (1997) is among those extending the peace metaphor beyond advocating social justice by calling for social arrangements that eliminate destructive emotional states, such as feelings of shame. For Gilligan, the emotion of shame is the primary cause of all violence. This would seem not only to lack empirical credibility, but also subverts the work of other scholars associated with PMC. For example, Braithwaite (1989), often cited by peacemaking scholars as a significant exemplar, argues the opposite: a society's capacity to instil in an offender the recognition of an offence and to generate a corresponding internalization of empathic responsibility – shame – constitutes a powerful social control mechanism. Unlike Gilligan, who sees shame as a necessary, albeit insufficient, cause of violence, Braithwaite sees it both as a means of social control and as a peaceful way to redress a wrong after a violation has occurred. Such an irreconcilably bipolar spectrum on such fundamental concepts makes it difficult for some to find a credible intellectual core.

Other critics point to the view that holding persons, including offenders, responsible for their actions reinforces the war-making rather than peacemaking model. Perhaps because he is considered a leading PMC scholar, Harold Pepinsky often becomes targeted as one of the more extreme examples of polemical aerobics. In advocating what he describes as the Navajo style of response to social breaching, Pepinsky argues that healing and reconciliation through dialogue are preferable to the concept of responsibility:

> Everyone leaves a truly balanced conversation free to choose what s/he does next. To the Navajo as to me, it is a contradiction in terms to make someone responsible; rather, a peacemaking process liberates one's heart to be in tune with others and to continue taking turns in interaction. Participating in a balanced conversation stimulates one's assumption of responsibility.
>
> (Pepinsky, 1998b)

The principle of balance and reconciliation underlies the practice of restorative justice, a form of conciliatory social response to offences, seen as a way to implement PMC programmes. Critics note that the underlying assumptions of this approach include the belief that there is a consensus on a 'spiritually correct' and universal normative order; that participants possess the ability to assess an offence and resolve it; that all parties participate willingly and are not subject to norms subtly coercing obedience; and that status and other power asymmetries will not intrude in the process.

However, one criminal justice practitioner responsible for integrating restorative justice programmes both within and outside of the conventional criminal justice process became somewhat more critical of the ideal following his own experiences:

> I have been thinking about the concept [of restorative justice] in terms of my own tribe's history and culture ... I'm sceptical about the concept working effectively. Restorative justice is derived from communities that could restore balance because of several constraints. Religion has traditionally played a major role. In the sage tradition, in order to pay respect to Wa-kon-da [God], one would live a very structured and purposeful life. Daily ceremonies, adherence to many tribal customs, and the structure of the society itself, depended upon these beliefs. Furthermore, each of the twenty-four tribal clans had their own specific sets of ceremonies and brought their own unique contributions to the tribe as a whole. If a tribal member was not in harmony, loosely defined here, the clan or tribal priests would take notice.
>
> (Personal communication, anonymous Illinois criminal justice agency practitioner, February 2000)

In this view, the appeals for implementing the perceived peaceful practices of other cultures make nice rhetoric, but they are at best misguided and at worst dangerously misconceived for several reasons (Levrant et al., 1999). First, peacemaking practices may hide deeper control elements that are far less peaceful, of which the 'balanced conversation' is the most visible outcome. Second, the practices may be just one social response among many, and reserved only for less serious transgressions. Third, restorative practices in other cultures may be more than an attempt to reconcile victim and offender; they may also be a means of mediating between other competing caste, class or kinship groups. Finally, restorative practices emerge from and are located within a cultural context of duties, obligations and expectations. Therefore, seeing them as something that can be readily translated into a viable practice in our own system may be unrealistic.

'Balanced healing conversations' between victims and offenders may seem a nice ideal, sceptics argue, but they tend to be reactive rather than proactive, and there is little evidence that they contribute – even in cultures that practice them – less frequent predations than in cultures that do not. Further, the definition of 'balanced conversation' might not be shared by all participants, and the call for what some see as 'forced reconciliation' can be seen as perpetuating, even intensifying, the feelings of powerlessness and predation by victims. Critics suggest that this type of excessive hyperbole and linguistic gerrymandering contributes to the confusion of PMC's core ideas. Although Pepinsky is not alone in the use of hyperbole, some critics find his style typical of a 'cavalier use of words and twists of phrase that leaves readers shaking their head'.

> (Anonymous conference critic, 1999,
> American Society of Criminology)

Among the examples provided in the 1999 American Society of Criminology conference discussions was the rejection of prisons (Mathiesen, 1998) or the call to govern them democratically (Pepinsky, 1998a:2), the suggestion that a surgeon who accidentally causes a patient's death during a heart operation should be deemed a criminal (Pepinsky, 1988:546), and that 'obedience' is part of the warlike culture and should be opposed (Pepinsky, 1998b). One ASC conference critic, citing Pepinsky (1998b), argued that some PMC advocates tend to exaggerate the war-making metaphor of conventional criminology with questionable lexicological twists:

> We follow the war making approach when we join others in trying to separate or disconnect our destiny from that of our enemies – those who in our eyes embody violence. 'Offenders' is a word we use for enemies. We follow the peacemaking approach when we accommodate victims instead, weaving ourselves together in trust that we have friends to be safe with whenever violence threatens or hurts.
>
> (Pepinsky, 1998b:242)

Some critics argue that the heart of peacemaking necessarily requires that individuals, as moral agents, accept and act upon their responsibility to others. Further, the goal of peacemaking is, at a minimum, to promote acquiescence to a harmonious and egalitarian social order and the acceptance of one's duty, which is a form of obedience, to the normative authority of the principles of peace. Therefore, it arguably follows that rejection of concepts such as responsibility, shame or obedience subverts one essential goal of peacemaking, which is to socialize social members to follow a pre-ordained set of pre- and proscriptive harmony-inducing norms. In addition, say critics, rhetorical ploys that rely on selective lexicological twists or evoke simplistic metaphors and images subvert clear thinking and conceal the problems of PMC as an intellectual position and as a viable instrument of praxis.

The (in)credibility syndrome

A fifth criticism is that, allegedly like many critical/radical theories, peacemaking criminology lacks empirical credibility (e.g. Inciardi, 1980). The perspective contains no explanatory postulates, and its claims are inherently unamenable to hypothesis construction and testing. Akers (1997:183–5), for example, argues that PMC fails to offer a theory of either crime or the criminal justice system that can be evaluated empirically. He argues that although its social goals may be compatible with some religious tenants, and although it might be possible to construct testable claims, it remains a philosophy and a utopian vision rather than a testable body of ideas.

Critics variously identify several difficulties with testing peacemaking postulates. First, the concept of peace, or at least variables reflecting the concept, cannot easily be operationally defined. Second, the concept of peace, or at a minimum indicators of it, must be conceptualized as an independent variable, a task associated with positivism, which many PMC advocates reject as either intellectually or ideologically viable. The common response that 'peace is the absence of conflict' is unsatisfactory, because one can have peace, even 'positive peace' (Quinney, 1998:358), in a context of social oppression. Third, the factors that 'cause' or are associated with peace are not easily identified. There is, suggest critics, no compelling reason to think that 'fairness', 'responsiveness' or even the vague concept of 'justice' are necessary a priori conditions of peace.

Is it possible to satisfy the structural requisites for peace (even if we could identify them) and yet have the peace process subverted by conflict-laden interactional processes resulting from power asymmetries in gender, race or class? For example, interactional processes that facilitate a positive group identity or personal status for all those involved in an interaction could be classified as a peaceful interaction. Enough of these collectively might create overall peace. However, if these conformed to an accepted social order in which power relations were concealed as the result of ideological blinders, such as can occur in subtle forms of interaction influenced by racial or sexual cues, by what criteria do we evaluate 'lack of peace', especially if unnecessary forms of social domination are invisible? Fourth is the problem of finding reliable data, qualitative or quantitative, with interaction as the unit of analysis. Fifth, critics suggest that even if data were obtainable, the development of a conceptual representation of the chain by which peace results would be insurmountable. Finally, even if the 'causes' of peace were established, it would be difficult to demonstrate that the absence of these attributes leads to non-peace.

If unanswered, these criticisms would seem to leave PMC with neither practical nor intellectual utility or credibility. The task before us now is to sort out those criticisms possessing merit and those that do not and then to assess what remains in the balance.

Responding to critics

One problem in working through the various criticisms – and this may be the primary problem in trying to define it – lies a little-discussed intellectual tension between adherents. Arguably, those working within PMC are primarily influenced by either Enlightenment or Romantic intellectual traditions. Although both traditions share several modernist characteristics, such as a humanist ontological and epistemological centring and a primacy of human agency as a force in progressive social change, they are separated by a fundamentally different worldview of humanity and knowledge:

> Whereas for the Enlightenment–scientific mind, nature was an object for observation and experiment, theoretical explanation and technological manipulation, for the Romantic, by contrast, nature was a live vessel of spirit, a translucent source of mystery and revelation. The scientist too wished to penetrate nature and reveal its mystery; but the method and goal of that penetration, and the character of that revelation, were different from the Romantic's. Rather than the distanced object of sober analysis, nature for the Romantic was that which the human soul strove to enter and unite with in an overcoming of the existential dichotomy, and the revelation he sought was not of mechanical law but of spiritual essence. While the scientist sought

truth that was testable and concretely effective, the Romantic sought truth that was inwardly transfiguring and sublime.

(Tarnas, 1991:367)

For some, perhaps a minority, PMC possesses a way to integrate Enlightenment principles of progress and humanism into theory and practice (Mika, 1987, 1992; Mika and Zehr, 1998; McEvoy, 2003). Others, influenced more by Romanticism's de-emphasis of reason and celebration of the 'inner soul', view peacemaking criminology as a spiritual enterprise. Quinney's nine observations on which his own foundation for peacemaking lies embody a rejection of many Enlightenment principles and embrace a Romantic style that typifies much PMC:

> (1) Thought of the Western rational mode is conditional, limiting knowledge to what is already known. (2) The truth of reality is emptiness; all that is real is beyond human conception. (3) Each life is a spiritual journey into the unknown and the unknowable, beyond the egocentric self. (4) Human existence is characterized by suffering; crime is suffering; and the sources of suffering are within each of us. (5) Through love and compassion, beyond the egocentric self, we can end suffering and live in peace, personally and collectively. (6) The ending of suffering can be attained in a quieting of the mind and an opening of the heart, in being aware. (7) Crime can be ended only with the end of suffering, only when there is peace – through love and compassion found in awareness. (8) Understanding, service, justice: All these flow naturally from love and compassion, from mindful attention to the reality of all that is here and now. (9) *A criminology of peacemaking* [italics in original], the non-violent criminology of compassion and service, seeks to end suffering and thereby eliminate crime.

(Quinney, 1991:3–4)

PMC's critics tend toward an Enlightenment-based critique of PMC's 'Romantic wing'. This one-sided focus exaggerates the empirical weaknesses while ignoring the Enlightenment-influenced aspects.

Although the implications of PMC as a merging of two traditions are beyond the scope of this chapter, our discussion emphasizes the shared features of Romantic and Enlightenment advocates. Our own thinking lies firmly within the Enlightenment tradition, but as in most attempts to create dichotomies, the two traditions sometimes overlap in our thinking and discourse.

Distinguishing between the Enlightenment and Romanticist characteristics of PMC is useful for at least four reasons. First, this shared framework suggests basic compatibility rather than necessary opposition. Second, an Enlightenment foundation sets PMC apart from other perspectives that might advocate peace based on the authority of religious doctrine rather than rational critique. This distinction is useful when contrasting PMC with other so-called 'peacemakers', such as the 'Religious Right' or 'Christian Coalition'. Third, the Enlightenment tradition suggests a line of empirical enquiry and action for many PMC scholars who have been influenced by it. Finally, by recognizing the overtones of the Enlightenment tradition underlying PMC, we can more easily avoid critics' reduction of it to little more than spiritualism, anti-rationalism or relativism.

We begin our responses to the criticisms by first examining the Marxian connection. We pay more attention to this criticism not necessarily because it is the most serious, but rather because addressing the underlying issues provides an opportunity to display fundamental – but not immediately obvious – features of PMC in a way that both illustrates the perspective and highlights similarities and differences among PMC adherents. Other criticisms can be managed more directly and are thus more parsimonious. We address the criticisms of 'intellectual chaos' and 'conservatism' in separate sections on PMC as metaphor and social praxis in order to integrate and build on ideas presented in the following section.

The Marxian/radical syndrome (redux)

Because so many peacemaking scholars are associated with Marxian or conflict-oriented theories, the criticism that these perspectives are incompatible with and even subvert the PMC position might seem intellectually devastating. However, there are fundamental congruences between Marxism and PMC. The integrative power between Marxist and more humanistic or spiritual philosophies has been illustrated by Arrigo's (2000) development of Marxian social justice theory, Anderson's (1989, 1991, 2000) attempts to unify Marx, Gandhi and other humanistic scholars, and Quinney's (1988a,c) replacement of western thought with eastern philosophy. Anderson (1991) has offered a compelling argument that the core of Marxian praxis is grounded in a humanistic framework that, like peacemaking criminology, espouses a peace-based culture and society.

In addition to shared humanism, the PMC and Marxian perspectives share at least four common features: partial grounding in

Enlightenment principles; a belief in the possibility of transcendent values, a view of human nature as malleable and containing potential for 'good', and a commitment to emancipatory social action, or praxis.

The Enlightenment background

Both Marxian/radical and peacemaking traditions are shaped by Enlightenment principles. Among these are the belief in the power of reason; the potential for the accumulation and application of knowledge to contribute to theoretical understanding; the belief in the value of rational control, technological enhancement and mass communication; an adherence to established norms of testing validity claims; acceptance of the view of the possibility of establishing transcendent value premises; and belief in the possibility of progressive social change through human intervention.

However, these Enlightenment features are not shared with equal enthusiasm by PMC scholars influenced by Romanticism. Quinney (1991:3), for example, has challenged the 'Western rational mode' of knowing as conditional and incomplete, and Pepinsky (1988) has challenged the utility of positivism in criminological research. Others (e.g. Tifft, 1979; Tifft and Sullivan, 1980; Pepinsky, 1995) tend to emphasize decentralization and the role of the passionate individual in creating social order. Further, judging from the lack of empirical analysis and assessment of tenets and claims, there would seem to be an indifference among PMC proponents to conventional empirical scholarship. However, it would be premature to assume that PMC scholars within the Romanticist tradition reject rationalism or claims testing, because the perspective is built on the power of critical thought and the value of empirical illustrations of the debilitating nature of contemporary social systems.

Transcendent values

Both PMC and Marxian perspectives are based on the premise that it is possible to establish a set of fairly immutable core values on which to ground behaviour and social action. Quinney (1998) has argued that, at root, criminology is a moral philosophy. The goal for Quinney and others thus becomes substituting the existing philosophy that guides criminal justice theory and practice, and which fails to provide adequate ethical guidelines for research or social action, with one that is more responsive. Like PMC advocates, Marx proceeds from an unexplicated, but none the less visible, value system that includes an a priori Kantian-like categorical imperative similar to the fundamental PMC premise: oppression is wrong. Derived from Hegel's theory of Objective Spirit reinterpreted through a materialistic framework, Marx's condemnation of oppressive social arrangements and corresponding exhortation to struggle for alternatives aims to reduce or eliminate unnecessary forms of social domination and control. In part deontological, and in part constructionist, Marxian and PMC perspectives both formulate precepts for action and interaction that recognize the fundamental moral imperative of 'doing good'. Yet, both acknowledge the socially contingent nature of dominant value systems that subtly facilitate conflict by reinforcing the ideological edifice of dominant social relations while obscuring alternative value precepts that would enhance, rather than subvert, a peaceful society.

Human nature

Another way to examine the relationship between Marxian-informed and peacemaking perspectives lies in teasing out their respective views of human nature. 'Human nature' is an ambiguous concept that risks debates over whether behaviour and 'urges' are socially constructed and contextual, or instead essentialist and hard-wired into us. Here, we use the term 'human nature' heuristically (and cautiously) to describe how each perspective begins from, builds upon and seeks to nurture a social order based on a similar vision of humanity. Each presupposes that developing to the fullest our individual and social potential is a fundamental condition of our species. Both perspectives see an innate dignity in our species, and protecting and enhancing that dignity is an integral part of each.

Peacemaking criminology implicitly rejects the premise that we, as a species, are innately violent and committed to self-interest (Gil, 1999). The destructive behaviours and debilitating social structures that often characterize our culture result from a variety of factors. These include constraining modes of knowing, ideological systems that maintain non-coercive conceptual machinery for maintaining an oppressive social order, social institutions that create and reinforce destructive and unjust social relations, and forms of interaction that perpetuate individual pain and suffering resulting from power inequities and inegalitarian social arrangements. Both Marxian/Conflict and PMC perspectives see us not so much in struggle with our own nature as we are with the social forces that suppress human potential.

Although Marx never directly addressed human nature, there is in his writings an implicit view of it based on a distinction between 'animal nature' and 'species nature' (Marx, 1975:277). The former we share with other animals, but the latter is exclusive to our species, and begins when we organize to produce our means of subsistence (Marx, 1974:42). The justification for the emancipatory potential of a Marxian perspective draws on this distinction. While people may as a species share innate characteristics, they also possess a socially contingent nature that depends on the material conditions that shape and are shaped by how people create and express their life (ibid.). As a consequence, material conditions may either constrain or facilitate attempts to develop our full species potential. This is significant for two reasons. First, it promotes the view that human nature is malleable and socially contingent. Second, it follows from this that predatory crime is not an inevitable consequence of 'human nature'.

This underlying non-essentialist ethos in Marx's early writing is not only consistent with, but the basis for, the humanistic development of peacemaking criminology. As Wozniak (2000) has argued in illustrating Erich Fromm's relevance for PMC, a humanistic-based perspective can become a powerful tool in 'sensitizing criminologists to the ways ways that alienation penetrates the fabric of macro-level social institutions and, on the micro-level, the lives and minds of individual actors'. Anderson (2000), too, cogently illustrates the humanistic, non-violent underpinnings of Marxian-informed theory and practice by integrating Marx, critical theory, and Fromm to develop the peacemaking potential of Marx's ideas. This provides the foundation of the PMC project as one of actualizing Marx's 'species being':

> On the broadest level, then, peacemaking criminology offers us a view of life in which, negatively, we seek to put an end to violence, to those acts that deny our person's validity, that dismiss who we are, that keep us from finding, as Kierkegaard might say 'that self which one truly is'.
>
> (Sullivan, email communication, 2 December 1999)

Praxis

Finally, both Marxian and peacemaking perspectives view the human actor as the fundamental agent in both social control and social change. For both, existing social arrangements and accompanying ideology constrain our ability to recognize, articulate and act upon the sources of unnecessary social domination. For Marx, through our work on our 'objective world', we duplicate ourselves in consciousness and in the 'reality' of the social structures, institutions and forms of interaction we create (Marx, 1975:277).

Because this also reproduces the conditions that restrict realization of our full species potential and objectifies and degrades our species life, social action includes the inter-related tasks of transforming both consciousness and social structure. Peacemaking criminology also emphasizes the role of human agency in the individual and social transformative process. However, unlike the Marxian perspective, which focuses strongly on the need to change structural arrangements as the primary form of praxis, many peacemakers adopt a more idealist approach, and tend to view transforming individual consciousness and existence as the first necessary step toward changing structure. For some, altering the social structure begins with a spiritual transformation of the human psyche, which will direct our subsequent action: 'When our hearts are filled with love and our minds with willingness to serve, we will know what has to be done and how it is to be done. Such is the basis of a *nonviolent criminology*' (Quinney, 1991:12, emphasis in original).

Other PMC scholars, however, emphasize a more structural view. In summarizing the foundations of PMC, Mika provided a succinct summary of the integrated necessity for examining social structure while simultaneously expanding conscious understanding of the peacemaking goal and ways to attain it:

So we have said, I think, that: 1) Peacemaking criminology is premised on developing an understanding of the social bases of structural and interpersonal violence and their engine power in its coat of many colors that both creates and perpetuates the harms in contemporary life that undergird human interactions and social arrangements. We have also said, I think, that: 2) Peacemaking criminology is equally premised on developing an understanding of peace, on finding in our collective response to harms a justice that is participatory and inclusive, attentive to the root causes of harms and their prevention, driven by the satisfaction of needs and achievement of equal well-being.

(Mika, 1999)

Despite congruences, there are, of course, substantial differences between Marxian and peacemaking perspectives. By identifying similarities, we do not minimize difference, especially at the theoretical level. For example, few peacemaking scholars have any interest in such fundamental Marxist theoretical issues as emphasis on the commodity relations of capitalism, the theory of surplus, the labour theory of value, necessity of class struggle, or the tendential decline in the rate of profit. Yet, substantial theoretical differences should not obscure common themes that overlap in each perspective, illustrating that the two are not only compatible, but also converge on many fundamental points.

The functionalist syndrome (redux)

The criticism that the peacemaking perspective is inherently conservative because it shares the functionalist core assumption that societies are based on consensus reflects at least three errors. The first is a fatal false analogy: that two perspectives employ similar concepts does not make them homologous such that they share similar domain assumptions or premises. To suggest that functionalists and PMC adherents employ 'harmony' or 'consensus similarly confuses functionalism's assumptive concept with PMC's prescriptive use of the term as both an ideal state and a form of transformative praxis. Second, functionalism, a macro-theory for understanding social structure, de-emphasises micro-analytical issues and the significance of the human agent in creating, maintaining, and changing the social order' (Wallace and Wolff, 1999). The PMC perspective, by contrast, combines macro–micro analysis by focusing on the structural factors that contribute to crime and the conditions that facilitate it, and on how oppressive conditions are recreated through language, status-based interaction and ideology. More importantly, PMC emphasizes the necessity of bottom-to-top social change and sees individual praxis as one means by which to shape a more harmonious, less violent world.

Finally, despite the iterative power of the 'functionalism is conservative!' mantra, nothing inherent in either the background or domain assumptions of functionalism requires such an immutable conclusion. In attempting to develop a neo-functionalist theory that overcomes the criticism of conservatism, Alexander (1998) identifies several congruences between neo-functionalism and neo-Marxism. He argues that functionalism can readily be reformulated to develop its conflict and critical potential. In fact, a cogent argument could be made that functionalism is consistent with a radical/humanist perspective:

> If there is some wisdom in the saying, 'You have to know the system to beat the system,' then functionalism can help those who are

dedicated to radical social change to a fuller understanding of how the system operates.

(Wallace and Wolf, 1999:65)

The (in)credibility syndrome (redux)

Some critics contend that peacemaking criminology lacks credibility not only because it is not 'science', but also because it offers nothing that religious groups had not offered earlier: long before the peacemaking criminology label was adopted by Pepinsky, Quinney and others, the in-prison religious programmes and the many prison ministries run by churches and lay groups were practising peacemaking; they have long applied the tenets of love and peaceful reformation of offenders by persuading them toward a religious commitment and lifestyle incompatible with committing crime and causing suffering (Akers, 1997:183).

The judgement that peacemaking criminology represents little more than a secular repackaging of religion is unconvincing. Although PMC principles and programmes dovetail nicely with the agendas of many religious organizations, at least three characteristics set them apart. First, unlike most religious organizations such as prison ministries and similar groups that use carceral institutions as recruiting grounds (e.g. Colson, 1979), PMC strategies do not promote acceptance of a formal doctrine, but rather advocate humanism as a form of social change. Second, religious organizations tend to have a narrower action focus, one that rarely extends to broad social issues. Third, PMC has a wider range of actions on more levels. Finally, religious factions attempt to establish and maintain peace among their members, but in doing so tend to promote out-group/in-group dichotomies.

A more devastating criticism of PMC lies in the accusation that it is unamenable to empirical assessment. Defence of empirical credibility might strike especially those PMC proponents influenced by Romanticism as unnecessary, even anathema, because it saps energy that could be invested in promoting the concept of peace. However, because the perspective is being pursued by academics who try to persuade other academics of the viability of the perspective, we offer several reasons why peacemaking advocates should encourage empirical assessment of peacemaking principles and programmes. First, peacemaking is presented as an intellectual position; therefore, rigorous scholarship would promote, not hinder, its development. Second, new scholars accepting academic positions where tenure requires publication may be discouraged from pursuing a line of enquiry that is seen as neither rigorous nor intellectual, but instead is viewed as a conversation among co-ideologues. Third, supporting evidence is useful when making claims. Therefore, substantiating that a peacemaking alternative is 'better' than the present model requires more than prophetic rhetoric, sermonizing or homilies. Credibility depends on evidence. Fourth, policy formulation and implementation require evidence to answer the question: 'What works?'

Critics correctly adduce the difficulty of operationally conceptualizing peace. However, conceptualizing the concept of 'peace' is no more difficult than epidemiologists' attempts to operationalize 'health' when alleviating suffering by identifying symptoms and their hypothesized source. Peacemakers might argue that their goal is not to engage in research or test hypotheses, but rather to transform the world through social action. That these advocates dismiss the need for conventional research does not disposit of such a possibility. In fact, the utility of peacemaking criminology is no less testable than the tenets of any other criminology perspective, such as symbolic interaction, labelling theory or rational choice models. If, for example, we posit a relationship between social inequality and crime, a reasonable hypothesis, then testability becomes easier. If we posit that, to reduce crime, criminal justice agencies should implement policies or programmes associated with PMC such as education, victim–offender reconciliation, restorative justice practices or conflict mediation, then we can readily test the outcome with such conventional quantitative or qualitative methods as comparative analysis or experiments. We could also take a random sample of communities that implement restorative justice in a similar fashion and compare those with demographically similar communities that do not.

Identifying and testing factors that are associated with peace is equally possible. Do social responses to crime that are less punitive than incarceration lead to such possible outcomes as reduced recidivism, less serious offending or other measurable consequences? Do programmes built around social responsiveness have the expected consequence of reducing suffering? Does reduced suffering lead to reduced crime? Does the reduction of racism or sexism in a community or within experimental groups lead to reduced crime or recidivism? Does implementation of empathy therapy rather than obedience training have a similar outcome?

Quinney (2000:21), often considered the most spiritual of peacemaking scholars, has observed that 'What is important in the study of crime is everything that happens before the crime occurs'. Despite the vagueness of the observation, it none the less grounded in a domain assumption that a discernible set of factors generates a particular outcome, and that by altering those factors we alter the outcome. Whether the precedents of crime are grounded in social structure or human agency, and whether reshaping those precedents by reducing shame, suffering or unfairness, is irrelevant. What matters is that the action-oriented philosophy of peacemaking criminology generates a number of testable claims. For this reason, the perspective clearly has the potential to be more than 'a vague utopian vision' of little explanatory use for understanding or fighting crime.

Such a perspective contains rich possibilities for understanding the aetiology of crime and identifying remedies that are testable through either the canons of normal science or Deweyian pragmatism. The intent of this section has not been to overcome the criticisms we identify, but rather to suggest directions for resolving them. Even if such criticisms are resolved, however, peacemaking criminology still faces the perception that it is excessively ideological and therefore cannot appeal to mainstream scholars or practitioners. The final question remains: 'So what?'

Peacemaking as criminal justice praxis

We have so far argued that peacemaking criminology is consistent with Marxian/radical theory, that it bears no resemblance to functionalism, and that it is fully amenable to empirical evaluation and critical assessment. In this section, we address the two remaining criticisms by illustrating how, through the variety of ways in which it is being implemented, PMC is neither conservative nor chaotic. By identifying ways in which it has been implemented, we address the 'chaos syndrome' by suggesting that critics and advocates alike should pay more attention to practitioners who, while not as visible as some of the high-profile advocates, are more deserving of attention as exemplars who implement PMC principles.

If the peacemaking perspective is to be more than merely a rallying mantra, then it should have direct policy implications for the criminal justice system, or at least peripheral implications for societal change that would bring the system more in line with the vision of peace and love. Some critics suggest that peacemaking criminologists, while effusive about the good, the true and the beautiful, are too muddle-minded to offer anything of policy significance (Akers, 1997:183). If correct, this criticism would be fatal. Fortunately, as the chapters in this volume and elsewhere and various demonstration projects attest, this criticism is not sustainable. To compartmentalize PMC into the standard criminal justice components of police, courts and corrections does violence to both to the perspective and its application. In practice, peacemaking efforts are geared toward breaking down the conceptual barriers that narrow our thinking and to expanding our thinking to see criminal justice agencies as interconnected with and grounded in broader social processes. Fuller's (1998) fourfold typology suggests several levels on which peacemaking criminology could be or has been implemented.

The broadest level involves organization around international issues that can be addressed locally. The second, institutional, level includes focusing on governmental agencies (especially the criminal justice system), political or social structures or embedded cultural practices (such as racism or sexism). Third, interpersonal action invites assessing and changing how people interact with one another in ways that enhance what Habermas (1981) recognized as the intersubjective forms of domination that repress realization of individual and group potential. Finally, the intrapersonal level is a call for individual transformation and individual self-actualization.

International/global action

Some PMC advocates begin with a macro-level analysis that requires fundamental changes in social structure as a way of establishing the foundations for creating a peaceful social order. Following the adage that 'none can be free until all are free', a balanced and harmonious existence at the micro-level cannot occur without recognizing the origins of socially/ structurally induced violence (Gil, 1999). On the global level, peace-making criminologists offer a vision of an interconnectedness between all things, similar to the Marxian doctrine of internal relations. This requires making governments more responsive to their own people as well as people affected by their policies, and to oppose war or other means of violence as a way to pursue social justice (Cullen, 1999). The goal, as Elias (1991) argues, is to work for peace by promoting human rights both on the streets and among nations. One way to do this between conflicting political groups is by recognizing that all parties share an equitable status in the process, identifying common ideological ground on which to build a lasting commitment to peace, and implementing future conflict resolution mechanisms (Currie and MacLean, 1995:100).

Institutional/systemic action

At the institutional level, peacemaking challenges unresponsive and repressive systems of government, economic systems and religious systems. By examining how institutions have developed and how they implement rules and policies and create the ideological and related apparatus necessary for control, action can take many trajectories. Groups working to reform the criminal justice system, such as prison reform and anti-capital-punishment organizations, community/police neighbourhood councils, and similar collectives provide one line of direct action. Caulfield (1999) nicely demonstrates the variegated peacemaking intersections between feminism, the military and criminal justice for research and policy. Grassroots projects also provide a short-term strategy for promoting social justice, as Barak (1991) illustrated in his study of a community-based homeless shelter.

Institutional action can occur within the criminal justice system in many ways. In law enforcement agencies, community policy, enhanced informal dispute resolution and police/community involvement are a few viable options. For example, although aware of political, practitioner and other barriers, Volpe (1991) suggests police/citizen mediation programmes as one way of implementing peacemaking practices in the criminal justice system. This, she argues, would shift the emphasis from an adversarial process to one of conflict resolution between disputants. At the judicial level, peacemaking criminology offers a way to move from the current punitive model of retributive justice to one based on responsiveness to the needs of society, the victim and the offender. Although some peacemakers reject the concept of punishment and confinement, most do not, and neither concept is incompatible with PMC. The goal is to balance the needs of all parties rather than exact a 'just measure of pain'. Prison-oriented peacemaking activity includes working for the attrition of prisons (Knopp, 1991), 'Alternative to Violence Projects' in which volunteer facilitators enter prisons to conduct workshops on restoration, healing and emphasizing individual responsibility (Bitel, 1998), or developing peace-oriented self-help or 'healing' programmes that teach non-violence (Rucker, 1991).

Community-oriented examples of a peacemaking process are reflected in neighbourhood associations, 'peacemaking courts' of Native Americans such as the Navajo (Pepinsky, 1998a:3) or other indigenous societies (Melton, 1995; Pranis, 1997; Tomaszewski, 1997). Fuller (1998) develops a list of additional social/institutional level targets for policy, including drug legalization, opposition to capital punishment, increased emphasis on rehabilitation of offenders, expansion of community policing, aggressive gun control, implementing peacemaking programmes for youth, especially as a way of dealing with gang culture, and implementing peacemaking alternatives in the court system.

Interpersonal/intrapersonal action

The third and fourth levels of Fuller's (1998) action typology focus on individuals as they interact with others and as they engage in their own personal development. At the interpersonal level, peacemaking criminology invites reflection on the ways in which power asymmetries are recreated and maintained in every social encounter. Once recognized, the goal is to change attitudes about and ways of social interaction. At this level, PMC 'has to do with a way of life and a choice to live a certain way with and among others, a way that refuses to seek and exercise power and that means ultimately redeeming our words and selves out of the marketplace' (Sullivan, 1999, personal communication).

Finally, the intrapersonal level refers to how we treat ourselves and invites personal transformation. Knopp (1991:184) argues that the first step in social change is consciousness raising, or 'seeing the need for the new'. This requires 'learning how to organize and construct the new', which she sees as a new restorative justice model, especially in crimes of sexual aggression and violence. Growth on the intrapersonal level requires that we be gentle and forgiving, and learn how to make peace with ourselves (Fuller, 1998:41).

Activity on these four levels overlaps and builds on the others. One effective way to integrate them is through education, especially the promotion of holistic peace education (Mackey, 1998) or justice literacy (Sanzen, 1991; Brush, Caulfield and Snyder-Joy, 1998; McEvoy and Mika, 1998; Sullivan, Tifft and Cordella, 1998). Education programmes promote individual growth while raising consciousness that alters behaviours and suggesting ways to engage in political action. A second way to integrate peacemaking in criminal justice, and one that is beginning to receive attention by mainstream practitioners (Boyes-Watson, 1999), is by developing programmes based on restorative justice. As Sullivan and Tifft (1998) remind us, restorative justice is intertwined with all levels of existence, including the workplace, home and in interpersonal communication. This suggests that restorative justice transcends the reactive component of the criminal justice system, making it a powerful integrative approach (Bazemore, 1998).

We have argued that, although peacemaking criminology has not yet overcome many of the problems that keep it out of the mainstream, many of the criticisms either lack foundation or can be successfully addressed. We also identified several ways system. However, this still has not brought us to a definition or summary of the perspective. That we attempt in the next section.

Peacemaking as metaphor

Many of the definitional and other problems of peacemaking criminology dissolve if, rather than demand a clearly focused definition, we instead see the peacemaking perspective as a metaphor that juxtaposes Pepinsky's (1998a) imagery of war, violence and conflict against that of harmony, reparation and healing. When understood as a cognitive mapping device, the perspective becomes a lens through which to reframe and suggest alternatives to existing responses to social offence and control.

Different metaphors produce different sets of images through which to view, interpret, and act upon our world. Metaphors provide icons and mapping techniques for interpreting and acting upon the social terrain. Metaphors also allow us to examine and discuss our objects from several perspectives, employing various sets of images. This expands our concrete knowledge of, as well as our insight into, the topic of choice. By replacing the metaphor of war with that of peace, we redirect our gaze to an alternative recoding of aspects of social existence into a more fruitful set of images. To paraphrase Brown's (1977:178) observation in a related context, the choice is not between scientific rigour and peacemaking criminology, but between more or less fruitful metaphors, and between rejecting metaphors of violence or being their victims.

Like all critical metaphors, that of peacemaking directs attention to symbols of oppression and suggests strategies for reconceptualizing crime and social control and their relationship to our fundamental social existence. As metaphor, even the hyperbole of some of the more extreme commentators is more easily seen as bathos, a rhetorical trope by which mundane discourse is exaggerated to produce richer images of analytical significance. As a metaphor, peacemaking criminology is both a sensitizing concept and a set of heuristic images that become transformative elements in a dialectical process of changing both individual consciousness and the social conditions that breed unnecessary forms of social domination. As metaphor, peacemaking criminology may best be seen as a means for coalition building. It cuts across ideological boundaries by suggesting forms of praxis that range from something as simple as creating new forms of consciousness at one end to more idealistic calls for fundamental social, political and cultural changes at the other.

Finally, the metaphor of 'peacemaking' merges the Romantic and Enlightenment intellectual traditions into a dialectical blend of science and spirit. By recognizing the power of the metaphor to unify two ways of viewing, thinking about and acting upon our existence and our social world, it becomes easier to understand that the two traditions are not in opposition, but supplement each other. Our own exploration of peace-making criminology led us to three conclusions that, for us, helped clarify the perspective. First, PMC constitutes a paradigm shift, or a new direction for developing theories, methods, concepts and forms of action for reducing crime. Second, PMC offers a redemptive rejuvenation for criminal justice practitioners, scholars, and offenders. Finally, the perspective challenges our thinking not only about crime, but about the fundamental foundations of our social existence.

Conclusion

Our final assessment of peacemaking criminology reflects not so much a conclusion, but rather a beginning, a redemptive call to action. Ultimately, the value of peacemaking, whether grounded in criminology or some other enterprise, lies in the degree to which individuals can transform themselves, their interactions and their social institutions away from a violent and hostile environment and toward one that is more conducive to fulfilling the 'species being' of which Marx spoke. As a consequence, the criticisms that PMC is utopian, idealistic and ambitious remain valid. However, these should be considered advantages rather than weaknesses. Peacemaking is nothing less than an integrative new beginning. The metaphor of peace guides the interplay between self-transformation and broader social change, and provides a powerful weapon of critique in doing battle against violent metaphors and actions.

Note

* We are indebted to Kevin Anderson, Jim Edwards, Kieran McEvoy, Harry Mika, Richard Quinney, Dennis Sullivan and Larry Tifft for sharing their insights and stimulating our thinking. We also thank colleagues and others at the 1999 American Society of Criminology annual meetings in Toronto for tolerating our often-persistent questions about peacemaking.

References

Akers, R.L. (1997) *Criminological Theories: Introduction and Evaluation*. Los Angeles: Roxbury Publishing.
Alexander, J.C. (1998) *Neofunctionalism and After*. Malden, MA: Blackwell.

Anderson, K. (1989) 'Preliminary Exploration of the Dunayevskaya–Marcuse Dialogue, 1954–79', *Quarterly Journal of Ideology* 13 (4), 21–33.

Anderson, K. (1991) 'Perspectives from Marxian and Gandhian Humanism', in H.E. Pepinsky and R. Quinney (eds), *Criminology as Peacemaking*. Bloomington, IN: Indiana University Press, 14–29.

Anderson, K. (2000) 'Erich Fromm and the Frankfurt School Critique of Criminal Justice', in K. Anderson and R. Quinney (eds) *Erich Fromm and Critical Criminology: Beyond the Punitive Society*. Urbana, IL: University of Illinois Press, 83–117.

Arrigo, B. (1999) 'Martial Metaphors and Medical Justice: Implications for Law, Crime, and Deviance', *Journal of Political and Military Sociology* 2 (Winter), 307–22.

Arrigo, B.A. (2000) 'Social Justice and Critical Criminology: On Integrating Knowledge', *Contemporary Justice Review* 3 (1), 7–36.

Barak, G. (1991) 'Homelessness and the Case for Community-Based Initiatives: The Emergence of a Model Shelter as a Short-Term Response to the Deepening Crisis in Housing', in H. Pepinsky and R. Quinney (eds) *Criminology as Peacemaking*. Bloomington, IN: Indiana University Press, 47–68.

Bazemore, G. (1998) 'Crime Victims and Restorative Justice in Juvenile Courts: Judges as Obstacle or Leader?', *Western Criminology Review* 1 (1) [Online].

Beirne, P. and J. Messerschmidt (1995) *Criminology*. New York: Harcourt Brace.

Bitel, M. (1998) 'The Alternatives to Violence Project (AVP)', *Humanity and Society* 22 (February), 123–6.

Bohm, R.M. (1997) *A Primer on Crime and Delinquency*. New York: Wadsworth.

Boyes-Watson, C. (1999) 'In the Belly of the Beast? Exploring the Dilemmas of State-Sponsored Restorative Justice', *Contemporary Justice Review* 2 (3), 261–81.

Braithwaite, J. (1989) *Crime, Shame and Reintegration*. Cambridge: Cambridge University Press.

Brown, R.H. (1977) *A Poetic for Sociology: Toward a Logic of Discovery for the Human Sciences*. New York: Cambridge University Press.

Brush, P.S., S.L. Caulfield and Z.K. Snyder-Joy (1998) 'Seeking a Social Justice-Oriented Classroom: The Role of Curriculum Transformation and the Importance of Difference', *Criminal Justice Review* 1 (2/3), 297–321.

Caulfield, S. (1999) 'Transforming the Criminological Dialogue: A Feminist Perspective on the Impact of Militarism', *Journal of Political and Military Sociology* 2 (Winter), 291–306.

Chambliss, W.J. and R.B. Seidman (1971) *Law, Order, and Power*. Reading, MA: Addison-Wesley.

Colson, C.W. (1979) *Life Sentence*. Lincoln, VA: Chosen Books.

Cullen, P.P. (1999) 'Coalitions Working for Social Justice Transnational Non-Governmental Organizations and International Governance', *Contemporary Justice Review* 2 (2), 159–77.

Curle, A. (1971) *Making Peace*. London: Tavistock.

Currie, D.H. and B.D. MacLean (1995) 'Critical Reflections on the Peace Process in Northern Ireland: Implications for "Peacethinking Criminology"', *Humanity and Society* 19 (August), 99–108.

Dahrendorf, R. (1958) 'Out of Utopia: Toward a Reorientation of Sociological Analysis', *American Journal of Sociology* 64 (September), 115–27.

Durkheim, E. (1951) *Suicide*. Glencoe, IL: The Free Press.

Elias, R. (1991) 'Crime Control as Human Rights Enforcement', in H. Pepinsky and R. Quinney (eds) *Criminology as Peacemaking*. Bloomington, IN: Indiana University Press, 251–62.

Fallding, H. (1972) 'Only One Sociology', *British Journal of Sociology* 23 (March), 93–101.

Friedrichs, D.O. (1980) 'Radical Criminology in the United States: An Interpretive Understanding', in J. Inciardi (ed) *Radical Criminology: The Coming Crisis*. Beverly Hills, CA: Sage, 35–60.

Fuller, J.R. (1998) *Criminal Justice: A Peacemaking Perspective*. Boston, MA: Allyn and Bacon.

Gil, D.G. (1999) 'Understanding and Overcoming Social-Structural Violence', *Contemporary Justice Review*, 2 (1), 23–35.

Gilligan, J. (1997) *Violence: Reflections on a National Epidemic*. New York: Vintage Books.

Habermas, J. (1981) *The Theory of Communicative Action: Volume 1 – Reason and the Rationalization of Society*. Boston: Beacon Press.

Henry, S. (2000) 'Peacemaking Crim?' *Critical Criminology Listserv*, 20 March, available at: http://venus.soci.niu.edu/~archives/CRITCRIM/jan00/index.html.

Inciardi, J.A. (1980) *Radical Criminology: The Coming Crisis*. Beverly Hills, CA: Sage.

Knopp, F.H. (1991) 'Community Solutions to Sexual Violence: Feminist/ Abolitionist Perspectives', in H. Pepinsky and R. Quinney (eds) *Criminology as Peacemaking*. Bloomington, IN: Indiana University Press, 181–93.

Kraska, P.B. (1999) 'Militarizing Criminal Justice: Exploring the Possibilities', *Journal of Political and Military Sociology* 2 (Winter), 205–15.

Levrant, S., F.T. Cullen, B. Fulton and J.F. Wozniak (1999) 'Reconsidering Restorative Justice: The Corruption of Benevolence Revisited', *Crime and Delinquency* 45, 3–27.

Mackey, V. (1998) 'Justice Literacy's Roots in Story', *Contemporary Justice Review* 1 (2/3), 261–76.

Marx, K. (1974) *The German Ideology*. New York: International Publishers.

Marx, K. and F. Engels (1975) *Karl Marx/Frederick Engels Collected Works, Volume 3: Marx and Engels, 1843–1844*. New York: International Publishers.

Mathiesen, T. (1998) 'Towards the 21st Century – Abolition, an Impossible Dream?', *Humanity and Society* 22 (February), 4–22.

McEvoy, K. (2003) 'Beyond the Metaphor: Political Violence, Human Rights and "New" Peacemaking Criminology', *Theoretical Criminology*, Summer, 7, 3, (in press).

McEvoy, K. and B. Gormally (1997) ' "Seeing" is Believing: Positivist Terrorology, Peacemaking Criminology, and the Northern Ireland Peace Process', *Critical Criminology: An International Journal* 8 (Spring), 9–30.

McEvoy, K. and H. Mika (1998) 'Justice Literacy in Divided Societies', *Contemporary Justice Review* 1 (2/3), 323–46.

Melton, A.P. (1995) 'Indigenous Justice Systems and Tribal Society', *Judicature*, 79 (December), 126–33.

Mika, H. (1987) 'Mediating Neighborhood Conflict: Conceptual and Strategic Considerations', *Negotiation Journal* 3, 397–410.

Mika, H. (1992) 'Mediation Interventions and Restorative Justice: Responding to the Astructural Bias', in H. Messmer and H. Otto (eds) *Restorative Justice on Trial: Pitfalls and Potentials of Victim–Offender Mediation. International Research Perspectives.* Dordrecht, The Netherlands: Kluwer, 559–67.

Mika, H. (1999) 'Discussant Comments: "Whatever Happened to Peacemaking Criminology?"', American Society of Criminology annual conference, Toronto, November, 17–20.

Mika, H. and H. Zehr (1998) 'Fundamental Concepts of Restorative Justice', *Contemporary Justice Review* 1 (1), 47–55.

Mika, H. and H. Zehr (2003) 'A Restorative Framework for Community Justice Practice', in K. McEvoy and T. Newburn (eds) *Criminology, Conflict Resolution and Restorative Justice*, 135–52. London: Macmillan – now Palgrave Macmillan.

Nietzsche, F. (1966) *Beyond Good and Evil: Prelude to a Philosophy of the Future.* New York: Vintage Books.

Parsons, T. (1937) *The Structure of Social Action.* New York: McGraw-Hill.

Pepinsky, H.E. (1979) 'Optimism and Pessimism in Criminology', *Social Problems* 27 (December), 248–51.

Pepinsky, H.E. (1988) 'Violence as Unresponsiveness: Toward a New Conception of Crime', *Justice Quarterly* 5 (December), 539–63.

Pepinsky, H.E. (1995) *Peacemaking Primer.* http://sun.soci.niu.edu/~critcrim/pepinsky/hal.primer

Pepinsky, H.E. (1998a) *Empathy Works, Obedience Doesn't.* http://sun.soci.niu.edu/~critcrim/pepinsky/peace1.html.

Pepinsky, H.E. (1998b) 'Safety from Personal Violence', *Humanity and Society* 22 (August), 240–59.

Pepinsky, H.E. and R. Quinney (1991) *Criminology as Peacemaking.* Bloomington, IN: Indiana University Press.

Pranis, K. (1997) 'Peacemaking Circles: Restorative Justice in Practice Allows Victims and Offenders to Begin Repairing the Harm', *Corrections Today* 59 (7), 72–6.

Quinney, R. (1970) *The Social Reality of Crime.* Boston, MA: Little, Brown and Company.

Quinney, R. (1974) *Critique of the Legal Order: Crime Control in Capitalist Society.* Boston, MA: Little, Brown and Company.

Quinney, R. (1977) *Class, State, and Crime: On the Theory and Practice of Criminal Justice.* New York: Longman Inc.

Quinney, R. (1988a) 'Crime, Suffering, and Service: Toward a Criminology of Peacemaking', *The Quest*, 66–75.

Quinney, R. (1988b) 'The Theory and Practice of Peacemaking in the Development of Radical Criminology', *The Critical Criminologist* 1, 5.

Quinney, R. (1988c) 'Beyond the Interpretive: The Way of Awareness', *Sociological Inquiry* 58 (Winter), 101–16.

Quinney, R. (1991) 'The Way of Peace: On Crime, Suffering, and Deviance', in H.E. Pepinsky and R. Quinney (eds) *Criminology and Peacemaking.* Bloomington, IN: Indiana University Press, 3–13.

Quinney, R. (1993) 'Once Again the Wonder', *Humanity and Society* 17 (February), 90–7.

Quinney, R. (1997) 'Criminology: The Continuing Project', in B. Maclean and D. Milovanovic (eds) *Thinking Critically about Crime*. Vancouver, Canada: Collective Press, 114–17.

Quinney, R. (1998) 'Criminology as Moral Philosophy, Criminologist as Witness', *Contemporary Justice Review* 1 (2/3), 347–64.

Quinney, R. (2000) 'Socialist Humanism and the Problem of Crime: Thinking about Erich Fromm in the Development of Critical/Peacemaking Criminology', in K. Anderson and R. Quinney (eds) *Erich Fromm and Critical Criminology: Beyond the Punitive Society*. Urbana, IL: University of Illinois Press, 21–30.

Rucker, L. (1991) 'Peacemaking in Prisons', in H.E. Pepinsky and R. Quinney (eds), *Criminology as Peacemaking*. Bloomington, IN: Indiana University Press, 172–80.

Sanzen, P.L. (1991) 'The Role of Education in Peacemaking', in H.E. Pepinsky and R. Quinney (eds) *Criminology as Peacemaking*. Bloomington, IN: Indiana University Press, 239–44.

Smith, D. Lee (1966) 'Robert King Merton: From Middle Range to Middle Road', *Catalyst* 2 (Summer), 11–40.

Sullivan, D., L. Tifft and P. Cordella (1998) *Criminal Justice Review: Special Issue:* 'Justice Literacy – What Every Student of Justice Needs to Know (and Speak Intelligently About) Before Graduation', 1 (2/3).

Szymanski, A. (1972) 'Malinowski, Marx, and Functionalism', *Insurgent Sociologist* 4 (Summer), 35–43.

Tarnas, R. (1991) *The Passion of the Western Mind. Understanding the Ideas that Have Shaped our World*. New York: Ballantine.

Taylor, I., P. Walton and J. Young (1974) *The New Criminology: For a Social Theory of Deviance*. New York: Harper and Row.

Thomas, J. and A. O'Maolchatha (1989) 'Re-Assessing the Critical Metaphor: An Optimistic Revisionist View', *Justice Quarterly* 6 (June), 101–30.

Tifft, L.L. (1979) 'The Coming Redefinitions of Crime: An Anarchist Perspective', *Social Problems* 26 (4), 392–402.

Tifft, L.L. and D. Sullivan (1980) *The Struggle to be Human: Crime, Criminology and Anarchism*. Orkney, UK: Cienfuegos.

Tomaszewski, E.A. (1997) ' "AlterNative" Approaches to Criminal Justice: John Braithwaite's Theory of Reintegrative Shaming Revisited', *Radical Criminology – An International Review* 8 (2), 105–18.

Volpe, M.R. (1991) 'Mediation in the Criminal Justice System: Process, Promises, and Problems', in H.E. Pepinsky and R. Quinney (eds) *Criminology as Peacemaking*. Bloomington, IN: Indiana University Press, 194–206.

Wallace, R.A. and A. Wolf (1999) *Contemporary Sociological Theory: Expanding the Classical Tradition*. Upper Saddle River, NJ: Prentice-Hall.

Williams, F. P. and M.D. McShane (1994) *Criminological Theory*. Englewood Cliffs, NJ: Prentice-Hall.

Wozniak, J.F. (2000) 'Alienation and Crime: Lessons from Erich Fromm', in K. Anderson and R. Quinney (eds) *Erich Fromm and Critical Criminology: Beyond the Punitive Society*. Urbana, IL: University of Illinois Press, 43–58.

6

A Restorative Framework for Community Justice Practice*

Harry Mika and Howard Zehr

Restorative justice: a somewhat worrisome road

The momentum of restorative justice in the past 20 years has been breathtaking; from a few small experiments in the mid-1970s, restorative justice has today become 'the flavour of the month' in many justice circles and is clearly gaining in international respectability.

Programme initiatives that explicitly utilize the imagery and values of restorative justice are quite diverse and can be found in the United Kingdom, North America, Western and Eastern Europe, Australia, New Zealand and Africa; interest is also developing in parts of Asia. Some programmes are state-controlled and annexed to the formal justice system; others are entirely community-based and strive to operate independently of formal justice structures, and many programmes represent a mixed model.

There is some debate about whether conceptually and pragmatically to think of restorative justice as a 'global' social movement (Braithwaite, 1996), or a convergence of the civil rights, women's, alternative dispute resolution, abolitionist and victims' social movements (Daly and Immarigeon, 1998), or in the sense of Wallace (1956), as a type of revitalization movement (Taraschi, 1998). The intellectual heritage of restorative justice is rooted in the critique of conventional justice approaches and informal justice prospects (Nader and Todd, 1978; Abel, 1982; Auerbach, 1983; Henry, 1983; Harrington, 1985; and Matthews, 1988), community mediation generally (Beer, 1986; Merry and Milner, 1995; and Pavlich, 1996), theoretical deliberations on new concepts of crime and justice (Christie, 1982, 1994; Braithwaite, 1989; Pepinsky, 1991; Pepinsky and Quinney, 1991; Bianchi, 1994; and Sullivan and Tifft, 1998), theoretical treatments of restorative and transformative justice approaches (Lederach, 1995, 1997; Morris, 1995; Zehr, 1995a; Wright, 1996; and Van Ness and Strong, 1997), and contemporary and comparative applications of restorative justice (Messmer and Otto, 1992; Consedine, 1995; Mika, 1995a; Galaway and Hudson, 1996; and Bowen and Consedine, 1999).

With the recent popularity of restorative justice comes the danger that the concept will be used so loosely and carelessly that it will be meaningless. The intuitive appeal of the term 'restorative' is the root of both its popularity and its potential misuse. Even worse, restorative justice may be simply a cover for – even an extension of – non-restorative and conventional punitive practices.

As in all social interventions, even the best-laid plans may result in unanticipated outcomes, where reform is subverted. The works of Takagi (1975), Rothman (1980), Cullen and Gilbert (1982), Zehr (1995b) and others suggest that within the hierarchical and coercive structures of criminal justice, alternative sanctions may result in something not only different from intended but worse than what they were designed to fix. Determinate sentences in the name of just deserts were instituted as an alternative to abusive and debilitating indeterminate sentences justified as rehabilitation. In practice, they have made the system more punitive. Today many worry that so-called intermediate punishments such as house arrest, electronic monitoring and even community service offer new technologies of punishment that will widen, deepen and strengthen the net of social control (Cohen, 1983, 1985). Determinate sentences have flourished in the US 'war on drugs', resulting in very high and decidedly disproportionate incarceration of African American males, and disenfranchisement of their communities generally (Mauer and Huling, 1995; Mauer, 1999). This could also be the fate of restorative justice initiatives which operate within the framework of criminal law, as not only a corruption of benevolence (Levrant et al., 1999) but so distorted as to offer new, more invasive, forms of punishment and control (Matthews, 1988).

Already in 1987, researchers on British mediation and 'reparation' programmes warned that such cooptation might already be under way (Davis, Boucherat and Watson, 1987). They identified the primary source of this subversion as a conflict between values in which retributive, offender-oriented goals overwhelm and subvert reparatively oriented programmes that attempt to operate within criminal justice parameters.

For example, restorative justice programmes claim to incorporate equally the needs and perspectives of both offenders and victims.

However, the conventional justice process defines crime, its impacts and salience, and professional justice roles by reference exclusively to offending and offenders. Since most restorative justice programmes must function within this criminal justice framework, they are easily distorted into offender-oriented programmes. Such programmes come to be used primarily to help reform offenders, to keep them from incarceration or, on the other hand, to punish them by forcing them to pay for their crimes or take verbal abuse from victims. Either way, victims may be used for others' purposes; empowering and interpersonal potentials for victims are muted or lost. In the USA, despite thousands of victim organizations and tens of thousands of victim statutes, the 'victim movement' is littered with such failed promises (Elias, 1990, 1993). There is ample evidence that victims elsewhere have likewise been betrayed (Mawby and Walklake, 1994; Wright, 1996).

Where restorative justice practice and programmes become highly dependent upon working relationships with conventional justice organizations (as a primary source of referrals, for example), what might be gained in ease of programme development and credibility may be quickly sacrificed where such a close alliance will circumscribe and restrict who has access to restorative justice. It is certainly the case in the USA that, given its historically low clearance rates of crime generally, and the reluctance of about half of all victims of violence to report crimes to the police, conventional justice programmes, in the very best of circumstances, could only refer a subset of victims and offenders to restorative justice initiatives.

Similarly, restitution, one possible outcome of restorative justice processes, may come to be viewed as punishment or as a way to reduce imprisonment rather than an opportunity to make things right for victims and to encourage offenders to take responsibility. The focus of dialogue or mediation may be transformed from empowerment and personalization into a means to secure restitution or force a confrontation to teach offenders a lesson. Face-to-face dialogue may be replaced by routinized settlement-driven shuttle diplomacy by the mediator. Success may be measured by restitution statistics, or cases deferred from jail, or by settlement rates. All of these represent subtle perversions of restorative concepts.

Often, however, the subversion is less subtle. Existing programmes are renamed or new programmes are created with restorative justice nomenclature, but underlying principles remain unexamined and unaltered; in reality, little has changed. Judges wash their hands, concluding that restorative justice represents no improvement. Victims are discouraged, feeling ignored and misused once again. Offenders are punished rather than encouraged to take responsibility and rejoin the community. Communities participate in name only, content to ignore victims and exile offenders.

A core assumption in the following pages is that if restorative justice is to be true to its potential and vision, articulation of values and principles is crucial. Further, appropriate new measures to gauge the authenticity and impact of restorative justice must be developed. Even lacking consensus on such weighty matters, dialogue and collaboration among the victim, offender, their communities, and justice professions are needed. This chapter attempts to identify fundamental principles of restorative justice, and to explore their primary implications for such critical dialogue.

The devil is in the details: defining restorative justice

Formulating a definition of restorative justice is challenging. While numerous efforts have been made, no single generally agreed-upon formulation has emerged. Nevertheless, there is often a general consistency and pattern in the core values and outlines that are proposed as restorative. Rather than a strict and rigid definition, it may be more useful to articulate basic principles and their implications for implementation. In doing so, the goal here is to make values explicit, encourage practitioners to examine some of the implications of their work, reduce the tendency towards the dilution of language and values, and provide benchmarks for evaluation.

Restorative justice constitutes a bold response to the conventional and punitive justice reflexes of contemporary societies. Consequently, it often includes a formidable critique of the state as well. In practice, though, restorative justice often operates within the general parameters of the state administration of justice. In reality, restorative justice represents a continuum of possibilities: (1) programmes that are fully restorative (meeting all the essential criteria of restorative justice); (2) programmes that are partially restorative, holding to important values shared by restorative justice (e.g. victim impact) and therefore having the potential to play an important role within a larger restorative framework; (3) programmes that are not inherently restorative in nature, but seemingly could be redesigned and redefined to 'fit' within its basic principles (e.g. community service); and finally (4) programmes that are incompatible with restorative justice. In contemporary industrial societies, many different justice responses could be plotted along the continuum of restorative justice: selected programme venues might include victim–offender mediation, community safety partnerships, victim services (support, advocacy, intervention, control), crime prevention, community (neighbourhood) mediation, rehabilitation programmes for offenders, family group conferencing, victim–offender community meetings, diversion, reintegration, re-entry and aftercare, basic habilitation for offenders (literacy, substance abuse treatment, employment), community service and reparations community conferencing and peacemaking circles.

In addition, restorative justice programmes can be distinguished by their locations relative to bases of power and control. Once again, restorative justice programmes in practice can be arranged along a continuum, from programmes that are community-based, where the responsibility, resources and control of services are vested in the local community and its citizens, to those programmes that are promulgated, underwritten and controlled by the state. Many restorative justice programmes gravitate to the middle, indicating significant relationships and collaborations between community initiatives and government, such as referral relationships, financial support and the like.

The underlying understanding of restorative justice reflected in the principles that follow might be summarized by two basic concepts: restorative justice is *harm-focused*, and it promotes the *engagement* of an enlarged set of stakeholders. A definition of restorative justice should flow from these two concepts.

Tony Marshall's (1996) restorative justice definition, as 'a process whereby all the parties with a stake in a particular offence come together to resolve collectively how to deal with the aftermath of the offence and its implications for the future', captures this core idea of restorative justice practice as a collaborative process to resolve harms. Despite the seductiveness of his succinct definition, however, we feel it is important to be more explicit about the elemental features of a restorative approach and acknowledge that direct encounters are not always practical or appropriate.

Put simply, restorative justice views crime first of all as harm done to people and communities. This has a number of implications, several of which should be highlighted here. A harm focus implies a central concern for victims' needs and roles. Restorative justice, then, begins with a concern for victims and how to meet their needs, for repairing the harm as much as possible, both concretely and symbolically. Second, harms are not only individual, but affect the community as well. Hence a focus on harm also implies an emphasis on offender accountability and responsibility to individuals and to their communities: it requires, for example, that offenders should be encouraged to understand and, as far as possible, should take steps to make right that harm. Third, a harm focus reminds us that harms to the offender which may have contributed to and/or resulted from the wrong must be taken into account as well. The essence of crime, then, is the harm that it represents, and that harm has three dimensions: to victims, to communities, and to offenders.

This leads to the second foundational concept of restorative justice: the idea and ideal of engagement. In restorative justice, the primary parties affected by crime – victims, offenders, members of the community – are treated as key stakeholders, vested by virtue of their ownership of conflict (Christie, 1977), and are thus offered significant roles in the justice process. They need to be given information about each other and to be involved in deciding what justice in a particular case requires. In some circumstances, this may mean actual dialogue between these parties, as happens in victim/offender mediation or family group conferences, to come to a consensus about what should be done. In others cases it may involve indirect exchange or the use of surrogates. Community roles, including responding to the needs of victims and facilitating the reintegration of offenders (Makkai and Braithwaite, 1994) suggest fundamentally new terms of responding to the impact of local harms. In any event, engagement implies involvement of an enlarged circle of parties as compared to the traditional justice process. Perhaps it goes without saying that a threshold requirement for greater levels of participation and engagement is increasing the transparency of the justice process itself. In many venues, lack of transparency is a significant obstacle to the practice of restorative justice, and the experience of justice generally.

Simply put, in the language of the following principles, restorative justice treats crime as fundamentally a violation of people and interpersonal relationships, the impact of crime as violations of people that create needs, obligations and liabilities, and the appropriate (restorative) justice response to engage victims, offenders and their communities to put right the wrongs. Restorative justice describes interrelated dimensions of practice and outcomes, beginning with core values and principles, which are articulated into processes and techniques, fashioned into programmes and organizations, and resulting in the 'just community'. Restorative justice is a framework within which multiple aims of justice – victim service and support *and* offender rehabilitation and integration *and* community safety and crime control/prevention *and* community empowerment and resourcing – become articulated in practice.

Principles of restorative justice

Before proposing principles of restorative justice, several limitations and qualifications must be noted. First, it is unlikely that any restorative justice practice will incorporate all the following elements. Further, the critical mass of these elements that would absolutely distinguish between retributive and restorative justice practice seem very difficult to specify. Second, these elements are not static, but are rather dynamic in response to changing needs, changing relationships and cultural values. Third, there may be an overemphasis here of victim *and* offender. Opportunities to enhance community safety, for example, do not need inevitably to involve specific offenders in order to reduce the possibility of future harms. Further, there is no suggestion here that if an offender is absent (who is not found or who refuses to participate) a victim should have no recourse to restorative justice generally, and community support specifically.

A fourth limitation is the lexicon of restorative justice itself a matter. From time to time and place to place, certain language conventions become themselves barriers to shared meanings and understanding. For example, the terminology 'victim' suggests to some dependence, resignation, and lack of capacity and competence, the very antithesis of support and advocacy by those who bear the harms of crime. The preference in some places might be to refer to such persons as, for example, 'survivors'. For some, there is an aversion to the concept of 'offender' where it might include persons who break laws, whose actions are criminalized as a strategy for denying the political nature of behaviours that are intended as anti-state actions. 'Combatants', and 'politically motivated' are felt to be more accurate representations in such circumstances. Similarly, the terms 'offender' and 'crime' presuppose that the actions and reactions of those oppressed politically and economically merit punitive intervention, and the conditions that beget such actions or 'crimes' in the first place will not be subject to scrutiny. The idea of 'community' is notoriously difficult to define, and at its worst, may conjure up romantic ideas of a place or a people that do not appear to have much basis in reality. 'Restoration', it is said, may be impossibly ambitious for some bereaved, who might eventually be reconciled to their loss, but never again be whole or restored. Restoration also suggests a return to an earlier state, whereas the real need is for transformation in the present (Morris, 1995). The conventional language of this definition is encumbered and limited by difficulties such as these.

A fifth qualification is the variable role of community *vis-à-vis* the state and statutory organizations. In some venues, restorative justice might involve programmes and processes of recouping the exercise of appropriate, local justice where the state is deemed illegitimate, or even where other local control (e.g. paramilitary policing) is rejected. In these circumstances, collaborations of community-based justice initiatives with the state and statutory organizations may become quite risky, and would themselves be part of longer-term social and political transitions and transformations to peace. In both South Africa and Northern Ireland, significant political capital has been invested in 'justice wars' involving contested ownership of community justice and restorative justice values and practices.

An obvious sixth limitation is that the effort here at formulating restorative justice principles is surely shaped by the US experience. While the authors are well versed in restorative justice practices elsewhere, the limitations of any 'North American model' of alternative justice is acknowledged (Mika, 1995b). For example, the popular US nomenclature '*balanced* and restorative justice' seeks to promote victim needs and interests in particular, a North American ideal given a widely held perception that conventional justice is skewed towards offenders. Empirically, expenditures of public resources for victim support *are* minuscule compared to investments in corrections. But in other places, where it is perceived that justice caters to victims at the expense of offender rehabilitation, or where local communities are literally at war with the state, or where statutory organizations cannibalize community organizations and justice initiatives, dramatically different ideas about 'balance' might emerge.

Finally, proposing this definition in the first place is a profoundly reflexive and sobering exercise for the authors, who in the process of articulating values and principles and reflecting on their shortcomings and limitations, are forced to consider how fundamentally uneven and deficient much North American restorative justice practice may be at the present time.

The following elements seek to address the critical components of one vision of restorative justice practice. Organizationally, the definition is composed of three major headings that define crime, obligations and liabilities, and justice practice. Under each of the headings, a number of secondary and tertiary points specify and elaborate on these general themes.

Crime is fundamentally a violation of people and interpersonal relationships

Victims and the community have been harmed and are in need of restoration

- The primary victims are those most directly affected by the offence, but others, such as family members of victims and offenders, witnesses and members of the affected community, are also victims.
- The relationships affected (and reflected) by crime must be addressed.
- Restoration is a continuum of responses to the range of needs and harms experienced by victims, offenders and the community.

Victims, offenders and the affected communities are the key stakeholders in justice

- A restorative justice process maximizes the input and participation of these parties – but especially primary victims as well as offenders – in the search for restoration, healing, responsibility and prevention.
- The roles of these parties will vary according to the nature of the offence as well as the capacities and preferences of the parties.
- The state has circumscribed roles, such as investigating facts, facilitating processes and ensuring safety, but the state is not a primary victim.

Violations create obligations and liabilities

Offenders' obligations are to make things right as much as possible

- Since the primary obligation is to victims, a restorative justice process empowers victims to effectively participate in defining obligations.
- Offenders are provided opportunities and encouragement to understand the harm they have caused to victims and the community and to develop plans for taking appropriate responsibility.
- Voluntary participation by offenders is maximized; coercion and exclusion are minimized. However, offenders may be required to accept their obligations if they do not do so voluntarily.
- Obligations that follow from the harm inflicted by crime should be related to making things right.
- Obligations may be experienced as difficult, even painful, but are not intended as pain, vengeance or revenge.
- Obligations to victims such as restitution take priority over other sanctions and obligations to the state such as fines.

- Offenders have an obligation to be active participants in addressing their own needs.

The community's obligations are to victims and to offenders and for the general welfare of its members

- The community has a responsibility to support and help victims of crime to meet their needs.
- The community bears a responsibility for the welfare of its members and the social conditions and relationships which promote both crime and community peace.
- The community has responsibilities to support efforts to integrate offenders into the community, to be actively involved in the definitions of offender obligations and to ensure opportunities for offenders to make amends.

Restorative justice seeks to heal and put right the wrongs

The needs of victims for information, validation, vindication, restitution, testimony, safety and support are the starting-points of justice

- The safety of victims is an immediate priority.
- The justice process provides a framework that promotes the work of recovery and healing that is ultimately the domain of the individual victim.
- Victims are empowered by maximizing their input and participation in determining needs and outcomes.
- Offenders are involved in repair of the harm as far as possible.

The process of justice maximizes opportunities for exchange of information, participation, dialogue and mutual consent between victim and offender

- Face-to-face encounters are appropriate in some instances while alternative forms of exchange are more appropriate in others.
- Victims have the principal role in defining and directing the terms and conditions of the exchange.
- Mutual agreement takes precedence over imposed outcomes.
- Opportunities are provided for remorse, forgiveness and reconciliation.

Offenders' needs and competencies are addressed

- Recognizing that offenders themselves have often been harmed, healing and integration of offenders into the community are emphasized.
- Offenders are supported and treated respectfully in the justice process.
- Removal from the community and severe restriction of offenders is limited to the minimum necessary.
- Justice values personal change above compliant behaviour.

The justice process belongs to the community

- Community members are actively involved in doing justice.
- The justice process draws from community resources and, in turn, contributes to the building and strengthening of the community.
- The justice process attempts to promote changes in the community to both prevent similar harms from happening to others, and to foster early intervention to address the needs of victims and the accountability of offenders.

Justice is mindful of the outcomes, intended and unintended, of its responses to crime and victimization

- Justice monitors and encourages follow-through since healing, recovery, accountability and change are maximized when agreements are kept.
- Fairness is ensured, not by uniformity of outcomes, but through provision of necessary support and opportunities to all parties and avoidance of discrimination based on ethnicity, class and sex.
- Outcomes which are predominantly deterrent or incapacitative should be implemented as a last resort, involving the least restrictive intervention while seeking restoration of the parties involved.
- Unintended consequences such as the cooptation of restorative processes for coercive or punitive ends, undue offender orientation, or the expansion of social control, are resisted.

Restorative justice: signposts and the road ahead

Ultimately, any definition of a concept contains the seeds of the values to which it subscribes. In particular, the foregoing formulation seeks to be unambiguous in this regard. For example, this is a community-oriented perspective, quite different in fundamental respects from other contemporary visions of restorative justice in the USA that use as their basic framework a top-down dissemination, promotion and practice of justice by the state. In the main, this definition can only be a preliminary guideline that must be adapted to the needs and resources of a time and a place. It seeks to be malleable enough to embrace a formulation and balance of its core values and principles that are rooted in the realities of particular circumstances and applications. Ten simple benchmarks flow generally from the definition that may be used to guide value-based justice work within a restorative framework, where restorative justice practice would:

- focus on the harms of wrongdoing more than the rules that have been broken;
- show equal concern and commitment to victims and offenders, involving both in the process of justice;
- work toward the restoration of victims, empowering them and responding to their needs as they see them;
- support offenders while encouraging them to understand, accept and carry out their obligations;
- recognize that while obligations may be difficult for offenders, they should not be intended as harms and they must be achievable;
- provide opportunities for dialogue, direct or indirect, between victims and offenders as appropriate;
- involve and empower the affected community through the justice process, and increase its capacity to recognize and respond to community bases of crime;
- encourage collaboration and reintegration rather than coercion and isolation;
- give attention to the unintended consequences of our actions and programmes;
- and show respect to all parties, including victims, offenders and justice colleagues.

However, regardless of how marvellously skilled, highly motivated and well intentioned practitioners might be, desired justice outcomes can remain slippery and elusive. Often, the pivotal factor that promises to enhance the viability, sustainability and performance of restorative justice programmes the most is the ability and willingness of practitioners to remain reflective about their work. The role of these practitioners is to promote a double standard of justice practice: where the state justice monopoly is very seldom called to task for its performance and excesses, restorative justice practitioners will insist upon critique of their own works. To this end, a series of pragmatic questions or probes is proposed for selected themes. These will tend to accentuate differences between conventional and restorative justice practice, pushing the 'envelope' of the latter to stimulate its salience and vitality.

Values and philosophy

There is little question that justice practitioners will have great difficulty in making sense of their work to others if they have not first made sense of their work to themselves. In other words, have the values and philosophy of local justice practice been articulated? Is there a reasonable continuity and consistency between such values and justice practices? For example, does a justice programme subscribe to a statement of mission that carefully stakes out what the programme is for? What it is against? How does an alternative justice programme and practice stay true to this course, irrespective of which way the political winds are blowing?

Risks

To be taken seriously, restorative justice programmes must be doing serious work. Too often, alternative justice programmes take few risks, and target relatively minor conflict and crime. It is not surprising, then, that some of these programmes exist only on the periphery of community justice practice, and are marginalized by their relatively insignificant contributions to peacebuilding. To mitigate this outcome, restorative justice programmes must creatively embrace the realities of conflict in their midst. What types of conflict, and profiles of offenders and victims, are included in justice practice? Who is excluded? Does justice work respond to community needs? Is there *proof* that restorative justice practice is animated by such needs? Does restorative justice practice include addressing interpersonal violence, and particular classes of victims affected by such violence (women, youth, the poor)? In what vital respects are restorative justice and offender rehabilitation related and interdependent? What impacts do community goals and needs, such as safety, and harm prevention and control, have on the restorative justice agenda?

State justice context

Unquestionably, a significant challenge to the practice of restorative justice on the ground in industrialized democracies is the pervasive state criminal justice context. What is the relationship of local communities (e.g. their needs) to the conventional state justice (statutory) apparatus?

In practice, how do alternative justice programmes 'fit' into the continuum of local justice services? What are the levels of legitimacy, credibility, and impact of restorative justice programmes among statutory organizations? Are restorative justice practitioners deemed to be significant and influential 'players' in local community justice? What is the nature of their relationships with statutory organizations? Is the door open for such possibilities? Are alternative values and practices subverted in the state justice context? If so, is this necessarily the outcome?

Social justice

Restorative justice advocates a quantum leap in understanding conflict as something not residing in the moral fibre of individuals, nor in their poor decisions, nor in their diseased minds or bodies. Rather, conflict is treated as social and relational in nature. The sources of conflict extend to the community and the state, beyond the limited venue of crime and delinquency, to broader social conflict. Accordingly, restorative justice practice must address social justice issues. What, then, is the relationship of alternative justice practice, in the crime and delinquency arenas, to social justice concerns? What is the fundamental perception of conflict? Does it have a broader context than the law, and if so, is the practice of justice responsive to *these* sources of conflict? Is there in practice a conception of justice that includes community obligations, and state obligations, to offenders and victims? In justice practice, is the social marginalization of victims and offenders recognized? Is it addressed? Is the practice of restorative justice itself involved in processes that continue to marginalize the roles of victims, offenders and local communities?

Vestiture

Some of the most critical issues in distinguishing between conventional and alternative (restorative) practices of justice are centred on the idea of ownership. For example, is justice to remain a state monopoly, or should local communities control it, animated by the needs of victims and offenders who are members of these local communities? Relative to the control of justice, what is the role of restorative justice practitioners? Do *they* seek to practise a monopoly of justice as well? Is a basic value of restorative justice practice that groups in the community are capable of 'finding justice'? Are justice practitioners willing or even anxious to play a facilitative role, by advocating, resourcing and empowering local communities to develop programmes appropriate to their time and place? Do justice practitioners, in the main, trust people who are not justice 'professionals', to know their minds, to articulate their needs, and to assist practitioners to do responsive, responsible, and relevant justice work? To whom are restorative justice practitioners accountable? To the communities where they practice? Do local communities 'buy into' and support restorative justice practices? Is the work of restorative justice practitioners transparent, readily available to critique and change? Has alternative justice work become too 'dear' to its practitioners, or does such work remain open to, and even dependent upon, partnership with other community groups?

These dimensions of ownership reveal justice practice to its very core as an affirmation of justice imperialism, or a deliberate rejection of justice imperialism. The question is *whose* model of justice is being practised. To what extent do local knowledge and local needs shape restorative justice practice? In other words, how relevant are such programmes to this time and place? Or are indigenous practices, developments and expertise ignored for newer, exotic flavours (e.g. developed for North American appetites)? Simply, the practice of restorative justice reveals who is trusted.

Vision of community

Finally, two intriguing proposals. First, consider the distinct possibility that the sheer quantity of state justice – laws, enforcement, courts, corrections – and the historical momentum to codify 'right relationships' in the criminal law have virtually nothing to do with reducing the levels of social conflict, peacebuilding, and experiencing justice on the ground. Rather, is contemporary state justice a better barometer (or even a cause?) of the increasing levels of community conflict and divisiveness? Has the historical growth of state justice been accelerated through the systematic destabilization of local community's capacity to find and create justice? As Diamond (1971) posed the question, is it really 'law *and* order', or 'law *versus* order'? A second possibility (Auerbach, 1983) is that the law and the state justice apparatus to manage it rise and become a monopoly as affiliations to community decline. Does state growth beget community decline (Nisbet, 1953)? Is state justice antithetical to community peace? And perhaps the most significant acid test, is it even possible to succeed in restorative justice practice without a strong affiliation and vision of community?

These questions, directed to critical and self-aware practitioners, beg for fundamental rethinking and reordering of justice priorities among at least the themes of values and philosophy, risks, the state justice context, social justice, ownership and the vision of community. The process of critique is itself fraught with risks and uncertainties, as the state and local communities forge what are perhaps new relationships, and practitioners explore for themselves facilitative, responsive and effective roles. Restorative justice may be a suitable, potent framework with which to chart this uncertain road ahead.

Note

* Elements of this chapter were first outlined in previous publications (Zehr and Mika, 1998; Mika, 1999) and are used here with permission.

References

Abel, R. (ed.) (1982) *The Politics of Informal Justice. Volumes 1 & 2*. New York: Academic Press.
Auerbach, J. (1983) *Justice Without Law? Resolving Disputes Without Lawyers*. New York: Oxford University Press.
Beer, J. (1986) *Peacemaking in Your Neighborhood*. Philadelphia: New Society Publishers.
Bianchi, H. (1994) *Justice as Sanctuary: Toward a New System of Crime Control*. Bloomington, IN: Indiana University Press.
Bowen, H. and J. Consedine (1999) *Restorative Justice: Contemporary Themes and Practice*. Lyttleton, New Zealand: Ploughshares.
Braithwaite, J. (1989) *Crime, Shame and Reintegration*. London: Cambridge University Press.
Braithwaite, J. (1996) *Restorative Justice and a Better Future*. Dorothy J. Killam Memorial Lecture, Dalhousie University, Halifax, Nova Scotia.
Christie, N. (1977) 'Crime as Property', *British Journal of Criminology* 17, 1–14.
Christie, N. (1982) *Limits to Pain*. Oxford: Martin Robertson.
Christie, N. (1994) *Crime Control as Industry: Towards Gulags, Western Style*. London: Routledge.
Cohen, S. (1983) 'Social Control Talk: Telling Stories About Correctional Change', in D. Garland and P. Young (eds) *The Power to Punish: Contemporary Penalty and Social Analysis*. New Jersey: Humanities Press, 101–29.
Cohen, S. (1985) *Visions of Social Control: Crime, Punishment, and Classification*. Cambridge: Polity Press.
Consedine, J. (1995) *Restorative Justice: Healing the Effects of Crime*. Lyttleton, New Zealand: Ploughshares.
Cullen, F. and K. Gilbert (1982) *Reaffirming Rehabilitation*. Cincinnati: Anderson.
Daly, K. and R. Immarigeon (1998) 'The Past, Present, and Future of Restorative Justice: Some Critical Reflections', *Contemporary Justice Review* 1, 21–45.
Davis, G., J. Boucherat and D. Watson (1987) 'A Preliminary Study of Victim/Offender Mediation and Reparation Schemes in England and Wales', *Research and Planning Unit Paper 42*. London: Home Office.

Diamond, S. (1971) 'The Rule of Law Versus the Order of Custom', in R. Wolf (ed.) *The rule of law.* New York: Simon and Schuster, 115–44.

Elias, R. (1990) *The Politics of Victimization: Victims, Victimology and Human Rights.* New York: Oxford University Press.

Elias, R. (1993) *Victim Still: The Political Manipulation of Crime Victims.* Newberry Park: Sage.

Galaway, B. and J. Hudson (eds) (1996) *Restorative Justice: International Perspectives.* Monsey, NY: Criminal Justice Press.

Harrington, C. (1985) *Shadow Justice: The Ideology and Institutionalization of Alternatives to the Court.* Westport, CT: Greenwood.

Henry, S. (1983) *Private Justice: Towards Integrated Theorizing in the Sociology of Law.* London: Routledge & Kegan Paul.

Lederach, J.P. (1995). *Preparing for Peace: Conflict Transformation Across Cultures.* Syracuse: Syracuse University Press.

Lederach, J.P. (1997) *Building Peace: Sustainable Reconciliation in Divided Societies.* Washington, DC: US Institute of Peace Press.

Levrant, S., F. Cullen, B. Fulton and J. Wozniak (1999) 'Reconsidering Restorative Justice: The Corruption of Benevolence Revisited?', *Crime and Delinquency* 45, 3–27.

Makkai, T. and J. Braithwaite (1994). 'Reintegrative Shaming and Compliance with Regulatory Standards', *Criminology* 32, 361–85.

Marshall, T. (1996) 'The Evolution of Restorative Justice in Britain', Unpublished Manuscript. European Committee of Experts on Mediation in Penal Matters.

Matthews, R. (1988) *Informal Justice?* London: Sage.

Mauer, M. (1999) *Race to Incarcerate.* New York: The New Press.

Mauer, M. and T. Huling (1995) *Young Black Men and the Criminal Justice System: Five Years Later.* Washington, DC: The Sentencing Project.

Mawby, R.I. and S. Walklate (1994) *Critical Victimology: International Perspectives.* London: Sage.

Merry, S. and N. Milner (eds) (1995) *The Possibility of Popular Justice: A Case Study of Community Mediation in the United States.* Ann Arbor, MI: University of Michigan Press.

Messmer, H. and H.-U. Otto (eds) (1992) *Restorative Justice on Trial: Pitfalls and Potentials of Victim Offender Mediation – International Research Perspectives.* Dordrecht: Kluwer.

Mika, H. (ed.) (1995a) 'Victim and Offender Mediation: International Perspectives on Theory, Research, and Practice', *Special Issue of Mediation Quarterly* 12, 199–297.

Mika, H. (1995b) 'On Limits and Needs: A Justice Agenda', *Mediation Quarterly* 12, 293–97.

Mika, H. (1999) 'A Restorative Framework of Community Justice Practice: The Critical Road Ahead', *Reflections on Restorative Justice in the Community.* Belfast: NIACRO.

Morris, R. (1995) *Penal Abolition: the Tactical Choice.* Toronto: Canadian Scholars Press.

Nader, L. and H. Todd (eds) (1978) *The Disputing Process in Ten Societies.* New York: Columbia University Press.

Nisbet, R. (1953) *The Quest for Community: A Study in the Ethics of Order and Freedom.* New York: Oxford University Press.

Pavlich, G. (1996) *Justice Fragmented: Mediating Community Disputes Under Post-Modern Conditions*. London: Routledge.

Pepinsky, H. (1991) *The Geometry of Violence and Democracy*. Bloomington, IN: Indiana University Press.

Pepinsky, H. and R. Quinney (eds) (1991) *Criminology as Peacemaking*. Bloomington, IN: Indiana University Press.

Rothman, D. (1980) *Conscience and Convenience: The Asylum and its Alternatives in Progressive America*. Boston, MA: Little, Brown.

Sullivan, D. and L. Tifft (1998) 'Criminology as Peacemaking: A Peace-oriented Perspective on Crime, Punishment and Justice That Takes Into Account the Needs of All', *The Justice Professional* 11, 5–34.

Takagi, P. (1975) 'The Walnut Street Jail: A Penal Reform to Centralize the Powers of the State', *Federal Probation* 39, 18–25.

Taraschi, S.G. (1998) 'Peacemaking Criminology and Aboriginal Justice Initiatives as a Revitalization of Justice', *Contemporary Justice Review* 1, 103–21.

Van Ness, D. and K. Heetderks Strong (1997) *Restoring Justice*. Cincinnati: Anderson.

Wallace, A.F.C. (1956) 'Revitalization Movements', *American Anthropologist* 58, 264–81.

Wright, M. (1996) *Justice for Victims and Offenders: A Restorative Response to Crime*, 2nd edn. Winchester, UK: Waterside Press.

Zehr, H. (1995a) *Changing Lenses*. Scottdale, PA: Herald Press.

Zehr, H. (1995b) 'Justice Paradigm Shift? Values and Visions in the Reform Process', *Mediation Quarterly* 12, 207–16.

Zehr, H. and H. Mika (1998) 'Fundamental Concepts of Restorative Justice', *Contemporary Justice Review* 1, 47–55.

7

Cross-cultural Issues in Informal Juvenile Processes: Applying Urban Models to Rural Alaska Native Villages

Lisa Rieger

Introduction

In the burgeoning area of restorative justice, alternatives to court processes such as youth court are often included as part of the restorative justice arena. However, the traditional youth court structure is remote from the reintegrative and balancing aspects of mediation and arbitration, peace-making, family group conferencing and other examples of restorative justice now being explored globally (Galaway and Hudson, 1996). Lumped with the other alternatives to court, youth court programmes are increasingly popular with politicians who are attracted to blueprints for propagation across constituencies. In contrast, the ambiguities and inconsistencies of restorative justice processes are less attractive to politicians and policy makers in the USA. This chapter explains the basic structure of teen courts, explores the theoretical perspectives that articulate teen courts as an aspect of current legal movements, and then applies these in the Alaska context. Starting with the outline of Alaska's governmental organization and an overview of how Alaska Native villages fit into the state and federal structure, the chapter points out the uncertain options that currently allow local, culturally sensitive justice in Alaska Native villages to interface with state institutions. The Alaskan experience thus presents both an example of and a challenge to restorative justice experience.

Teen, youth or peer courts

Teen, youth or peer courts started in the USA in the early 1980s as an alternative for minor juvenile offenders whose behaviour did not ordinarily institute juvenile justice response. Thus youth courts around the country constitute a diversion from the main juvenile justice system. Teen courts quickly became popular and were estimated at 250 nationwide in 1995 (Godwin, 1996). They are housed in a variety of institutions, including juvenile courts, law enforcement agencies, private, non-profit organizations and schools. Most teen courts require guilty pleas before an offender can appear, but some engage in determining guilt. There are several models of teen courts. Some use teen prosecutors and defenders to argue mitigation and aggravation before a teen judge; others use teen prosecutors and defenders to argue sentence before a teen jury; and others use teen prosecutors and defenders to argue sentence before a juvenile court judge. The last model uses the teen jury to ask the defendant questions directly, without prosecutors or defence attorneys, with an adult serving as guide and judge. Youth court teaches junior high and high school children how to be defence attorneys, prosecutors and judges. Students receive course work in court process and take a 'bar exam' before qualifying for handling cases. Under the supervision of attorney mentors, the students then handle minor juvenile misdemeanour cases such as petty theft, vandalism, alcohol possession, possession of marijuana and so on that, absent a previous record, are not currently subjected to formal processes in the juvenile system. These students prosecute, defend and sentence their juvenile peer offenders. Sentences usually involve community service, letters of apology and classes on petty theft. Clearly, the students implement a form of justice which parallels the juvenile justice system but is executed by peers. Some programmes require that defendants do the training and participate as lawyers or jurors as part of their 'punishment'. Thus the teen court model is the same as that of the juvenile and adult adversarial legal system, with the exception that peers do the lawyering and, in some cases, decision making regarding sentence.

Theoretical perspectives on youth courts

This growing and highly touted alternative to a juvenile justice system perceived to be failing has found homes in several different theoretical frameworks: restorative justice (Godwin, 1996); ecological development theory (Beck, 1997); managerialism (Singer, 1998); and therapeutic jurisprudence (Shiff and Wexler, 1996). These frameworks intersect in examining the purported effects that youth court is supposed to have on the offenders and other participants in the process. Because it is outside the 'system', it is supposed to be more responsive to community values and victims, less bureaucratic and more directed to rehabilitation (Godwin, 1996). However, as Singer comments, 'States have been quick to adopt teen court programs despite the fact that there is no evidence they are more effective than juvenile court' (Singer, 1998:522). And the same arguments now propounded for teen court are reminiscent of the justification for juvenile court reform at the turn of the last century (Singer, 1998). The question remains untested whether teen courts fulfil their expectations.

Beck (1997) examines the language content of teen court interactions under an ecological development theory and tests whether teen court truly fits as diversion. Ecological development theory posits that moments when someone changes his or her role or setting offer opportunities for development (Bronfenbrenner, 1979). In the case of misdemeanour by juvenile offenders, this change occurs when the juvenile commits an offence. The normative developmental result desired is rehabilitation, one that Beck finds to be well served by the teen court. He lists as advantages the fact that communication in the teen court is more open and less formal than in the juvenile court, and that peers provide input. Although he states that the peer advice is presented with 'few preconceptions as to standard issues to be dealt with under such conditions' (Beck, 1997:44), teen court training materials clearly delineate expectations and standards. Focusing on the impact on offenders, he uses both behavioural learning theory and cognitive learning theory to identify the advantages and pitfalls of peer judgement. He concludes that the teen court's function is diversionary and rehabilitative, but that the court is not a classic diversion programme because of the formality of the teen court hearing itself. His analysis reveals the schizophrenic nature of the teen court in that it functions as a formal process while claiming diversion as its goal.

Some commentators have suggested that such youth courts are indicative of the general decreasing faith in and efficacy of the juvenile justice system (Singer, 1998). Taking the managerial perspective, Singer looks at the teen court phenomenon in the context of the debate over the viability of a juvenile justice system in which there is increasing polarization in processing violent youthful offenders versus responding to property and behavioural offences. He views teen courts as a rising management tool for the behaviours no longer addressed in juvenile courts, especially in major urban areas, and a further subsystem of the juvenile justice system's 'loosely coupled systems' for handling juvenile offenders.

Closely linked with restorative justice principles is the new field of 'therapeutic jurisprudence', which grows out of mental health law and examines the therapeutic or anti-therapeutic effects of laws and legal policies. Placing itself in the tradition of sociological jurisprudence and legal realism, therapeutic jurisprudence refers to the process of applying 'social science to examine law's impact on the mental and physical health of the people it affects' (Winnick, 1997). At first, therapeutic jurisprudence examined case law, statutes and common law through this particular lens. Over the past decade, however, therapeutic jurisprudence has expanded to look at how law is applied by the actors in the legal system as well. Thus the theoretical framework has been utilized to analyse issues relating to involuntary commitments and mental patients, criminal defendants, victims, jurors, mental health professionals, personal injury plaintiffs and employees with disabilities (Wexler, 1995). More recently, some proponents have also emphasized the usefulness of comparative law in examining issues that may be more limited in the US context than in other countries. Therefore, like restorative justice, therapeutic jurisprudence takes a consequentialist approach (Winnick, 1997), and looks at the mental health impact of laws and legal process on the participants, with a normative agenda of making those participants feel better about the process.

Shiff and Wexler (1996) utilize this theoretical perspective in their analysis of youth court to determine that while it fulfils one normative agenda, it may pose problems for another. They find the following potentially positive therapeutic impacts: (1) positive peer pressure promotes taking responsibility for one's actions; (2) a socially aware jury is better able to confront a peer defendant and 'smell a lie'; (3) individualized sentencing, including requiring teen court jury duty, may show an offender the other side of miscreance; (4) defence attorneys might better understand the motivations for offenders, which will 'inoculate' them from offending themselves (Shiff and Wexler, 1996:349). On the other hand, student defence attorneys may learn to minimize offences and reject responsibility while arguing for better sentences for their peers. Thus illustrated, therapeutic jurisprudence looks at the impact of teen courts on each of the participants' development as law-abiding citizens. As with any legal programme or statutory scheme, a normative agenda can be inconsistent or conflicting. However, in extending teen court models to rural Alaska Native villages, these conflicting normative agendas become even more problematic. As a formal process mimicking the criminal justice system, teen courts are incompatible with the historically restorative nature of dispute resolution in Alaska Native villages.

Restorative justice in youth courts?

Therapeutic jurisprudence diverges from restorative justice in relation to youth courts; nothing about youth court approaches the restorative justice principles embodied in the literature (Van Ness, 1993; Bazemore and Umbreit, 1998; La Prairie, 1998). Literature from the Anchorage Youth Court states 'The court is modeled as closely as possible after the adult criminal court' (AYC, 1998). The 'restorative' aspect is supposed to lie in the power of peers judging as opposed to adults. According to students participating in the programme, this has a tremendous impact on offenders, who feel great contrition after going through the peer trial process (AYC, 1998). Of course, students participating in the programme do not know the level of shame and/or sorrow experienced by offenders who must confront probation officers at the juvenile probation office or detention centre. The claim of individualized sentencing, also a hallmark of the original juvenile courts, devolves into fairly standard lists: letters of apology, community service, restitution, service on a youth court jury or participation in the youth court process. On the other hand, the youth court process may serve a more classically reintegrative role in that offenders receive legal education. And, as mentioned above, there may even be an 'inoculating' effect on participants who are law-abiding (Schiff and Wexler, 1996). Notably absent, of course, is restorative justice's inclusion of the victim and seeking to make the victims feel whole again.[1]

Who volunteers to be part of youth court?

Youth court does not offer any protection against the systemic racism and classism that plague the US justice system. Quite often and quite naturally, it is the sons and daughters of lawyers, judges, police officers and other justice personnel who are attracted to the programme in the first place. To date, there is no information in the literature as to the demographic differences in the success and participation rates of offenders and volunteers (Nessel, 1998). Most of the anecdotal recitations of the positive impact of youth court come from volunteer 'lawyers' and 'judges', not from offenders (AYC, promotional materials). High school students who are interested in law have many venues for exercising their interest, including mock trial contests, debate and special elective courses. What is it that makes some choose the 'real-life' experience of prosecuting, defending or judging their peers? As a result of 'legal-related education' (touted as one of the primary benefits of youth court by Hunter, 1987), students involved in teen court are well indoctrinated in the adversarial legal system. In Anchorage, Alaska, three peer judges hear each case. They are each required to have completed ten trials, half as prosecutor and half as defence attorney. Before appearing in court at all, they must complete a 16-hour training course on youth court jurisdiction, procedure, evidence, advocacy and case preparation. They then must take and pass a bar exam. Monthly required meetings include 30 minutes of continuing education. This represents a significant time commitment, a luxury reserved for students who do not have after-school employment or home responsibilities. Only students who are intellectually affiliated with the adversarial legal system and economically free to do so would fulfil these requirements.[2]

Teen courts and recidivism

In spite of the broader orientation of teen courts to modify the juvenile's experience (either as explained through ecological development theory or therapeutic jurisprudence), one of the measures of the success of teen courts lies in claims of lower recidivism rates. However, current data suggest that recidivism rates are lower in youth courts than they are in juvenile courts, but these have not controlled for seriousness of offence or prior history of offender (Nessel, 1998). Where they do control for past history or seriousness of offence, they find no statistically significant difference (ibid.). As a practical matter, in both urban and rural Alaska, petty thefts and vandalism do not receive attention unless they are part of a string of more serious offences, or the juvenile is already on probation. In assessing recidivism, then, one must consider whether similar offenders would also not reappear before the probation officers who warn them. Although a national evaluation of youth courts is currently under way in the USA, there is no research comparable to the experimental design employed for Australia's Reintegrative Shaming Experiments (Sherman et al., 1998) to assess the efficacy of teen courts. Real claims of lower recidivism rates would only be justified if offenders were randomly assigned to either youth court or juvenile probation and then were prospectively followed. And further assessment would require an analysis of whether teen court has a better outcome than doing nothing at all.

State and federal promotion of teen courts in Alaska

Thus the teen court presents a contested restorative model, focused on diverting youth out of the juvenile justice system at the local level while maintaining consequences and responsibility for offending behaviour. Alaska considers teen courts to be 'restorative justice' because they are diversionary, rather than because the model reflects restorative justice principles. Given the uneven theoretical and empirical terrain, the state's promotion of youth courts as a viable alternative to juvenile court or as a remedy for its failure to respond to deviant behaviour is questionable.

The Alaskan context

Alaska has a landmass one-fifth the size of the USA and a total population of 600 000 (Alaska Labor Statistics). Largely a natural resource economy, Alaska's primary economic base is oil, timber and fish extraction, and tourism. There is little if any cash economy in most villages, with few wage-earning jobs other than governmental positions and social services providers. Alaska has a statewide police agency (the State Troopers), court system, prosecutor's and defender's offices, all of which handle cases in both urban and rural parts of the state. Alaska has three cities ranging in size from 25 000 to 75 000 to 300 000, and several regional hub communities with 3000 to 8000 people. In addition, there are 226 Alaska Native villages ranging in size from 50 to 1000 people. Most of these communities are incorporated cities with school districts under Alaska state law. Some have village police departments. Most are geographically remote, and almost all are inaccessible by road. There are 15 Native languages, loosely grouped into five main cultural and geographic areas: Tlingit, Haida and Tsimpshian Indians in southeast Alaska; Athabascan Indians in south-central and interior Alaska; Alutiiqs in the Aleutian Chain and Kodiak Island; Yupi'k Eskimos in the western and northwestern parts of the state; and Inupiaq Eskimos on the North Slope. Because of the discovery and development of oil on the North Slope in the 1960s, Alaska Native people have faced rapid integration into the cash economy. Nevertheless, village life retains much of its traditional flavour, and subsistence hunting, fishing and gathering remain strong. More recently, dancing, traditional clothing and other arts have seen a resurgence as well.

Alaska Native governance and service provision has evolved into a complex web of local, regional and statewide organizations that serve the various areas and communities of the state. Instead of the reservations typical in the continental USA, the Alaska Native community is divided into regional corporations with non-profit corporations that conduct the social services and governance functions of most tribal organizations. The state government has been consistently hostile to the political status of Alaska Native villages as tribes; in 1997, the state successfully challenged the status of these villages in the US Supreme Court (*Venetie v. State of Alaska*). However, the federal government recognizes each of 226 villages as tribal political entities with a government-to-government relationship with the federal government. This proposes a very interesting conflict between the way the state conducts business with the villages and the way the federal government does. Since large quantities of federal funds pass through state agencies, the state's historical hostility to tribal organizations undermines the ability of tribes to provide necessary services in the villages. However, in the past year the executive branch has dramatically altered its position with regard to village autonomy, and the state judiciary has also made concessions to tribal political status (*Baker v. John*).

Some villages of fewer than 500 people have both city and tribal councils, as well as school boards and regional profit and non-profit corporations that contribute to social, political and economic organization in the villages. State money goes to city government, and federal money goes to tribal government. Thus, education money which funnels through state agencies and villages must follow state department of education regulations. Similarly, if a village operates a police department through its city government, those police officers must follow state police commission guidelines and policies. On the other hand, tribal operations money goes to the tribal government from the federal government, and reports return to the federal government. Again, tribal court and tribal police money comes from the federal government, and the tribe is not answerable to state authorities. In some areas there is overlap between state and federal funding sources, as is the situation with substance abuse counselling money, which could come from both the state and federal governments. Some villages have chosen to dissolve their city governments, while others have merged the city and tribal councils and utilized both funding streams in concert. The multi-layered bureaucracy poses challenges for effective community action.

Traditional social control in Native villages

Youth courts are vibrant in Anchorage, Fairbanks, Juneau (the three largest cities), and developing in several regional hubs. However, the idea that youth court is a viable and desirable alternative to court to be attempted in small Alaska Native villages with a tradition of elder knowledge bearing is problematic. Cultural differences between indigenous social control and western legal structures pose a key thematic concern for this chapter. Since the teen court is so closely tied to the adversarial legal system, and younger generations of Alaska Natives are increasingly distant from traditional ways of life, there is a high risk of potential confrontation between teens trained to be lawyers and elders with traditional knowledge. On the other hand, teen courts will make rural Alaska youth more comfortable with the state and federal legal systems should they encounter them as offenders later in life.

Traditional models of conflict resolution vary greatly from region to region of the state. In the southeast, south-central and interior regions of the state, the primary language and culture groups are Indian, who can be very confrontational in style, or completely non-confrontational. In the northern and western regions, the primary language and culture groups are Inupiaq and Yupi'k Eskimo, whose traditional conflict resolution proceeded mainly by oblique shaming and demonstrating the right way to be (Morrow, 1994, 1996). Alaska Native people from the village experience culture shock in state and federal courts, which promote fundamentally different ways of interacting. For example, there is no word in Alaska Native languages for 'guilt', which makes understanding the language and meaning of a guilty plea or a finding of guilt after trial problematic (Morrow, 1994, 1996).[3] None of these traditional models of conflict resolution fits a model of western legal disputation, and none uses youth to correct other youth. The tradition and knowledge bearers in Alaska Native culture are the elders, as would be expected of cultures with an entirely oral tradition well into the twentieth century. Prominent figures in the community are those who pass the history on from previous culture bearers, linking people in the present to lengthy family and community identities. One Tlingit elder remembers that his uncle never told him he did anything wrong; he just showed him 'the right way to do it' (personal communication with Charles Johnson Jr). Even today, many Alaska Native people feel that their history is dying with the elders, and worry about the television that their children watch.

Options promoted by state government

As mentioned previously, state court and policing entities face significant challenges in rising to the responsibility of providing justice to rural Native villages, especially because of the state's resistance to recognizing their political autonomy. In other parts of the country, where reservations were established by treaty and tribal government has operated for over one hundred years, tribes run their own police departments, courts and corrections for all offences other than serious felonies (the federal government handles these, pursuant to statute). The state of Alaska has taken the position that the villages cannot handle any of their cases unless they use procedures authorized and supervised by the state. Three examples of these alternatives include teen courts, community courts and sentencing circles. None of these, though sponsored in some instances by the tribe, is a tribal justice entity. Cases can be heard only if the state agrees that they be heard. Participation by the parties is wholly voluntary. From the state's perspective, these options do not conflict with official positions because the villages are only acting on behalf of the state pursuant to a delegation of power.

Teen courts in the villages

Establishing a peer youth court in such villages presents another example of the problem of forcing western blueprints on to culturally, politically and geographically distinct communities. These villages are already struggling with the intersections of the western world with the traditional hunting, fishing and gathering life that is supported by the remote communities in which they live. An interesting aspect of this problematic is that the vehicle for implementing youth courts in the villages is the Alaska Native Justice Center (ANJC), an organization formed to address the inequities of the state justice system with regard to Alaska Natives. ANJC is an urban organization in Anchorage. Situated there, it can be an effective voice in state politics and policy making regarding Alaska Natives. However, with regard to what is known as 'the bush', Anchorage organizations have been singularly unwelcome.

ANJC received seed money to test the youth court model in two villages during the 1999. In the village of Tetlin, the teen court is modelled closely on the tribal court, and students who participate are expected to learn how the tribal court operates as training for service later as adults.[4] This now takes the teen court concept into the tribal court context. Since there are no advocates in most of the tribal courts, teen court in that community will mean peer judging. Issues of elders being the repository of knowledge are managed by having the adult tribal court judges mentor the youth. However, this is hardly the model outlined in the general literature. Thus, the village 'teen court' can receive financial support because it bears the necessary label, but not because it follows the spirit of peer justice.

Community courts

Previously, another alternative, entitled 'community courts', has been implemented in four other villages. Although not youth courts, these courts work with delinquent youth. More palatable to a state system that does not wish to acknowledge political sovereignty in tribal entities, these 'courts' are constituted by agreements with the State Troopers and the Division of Family and Youth Services to handle juvenile misdemeanours only. In the first two communities, the community court became defunct when its primary proponents moved on to other activities. In Togiak and Barrow, these courts are elders' courts in which the juvenile misdemeanant come before the grandparents and must account for their behaviour. The grandparents teach lessons on proper Yupi'k and Inupiaq behaviour, culture and history. Several other communities have instigated discussions with the state to create similar community courts under the auspices of small grant monies available through the Governor's Commission on Youth and Justice. Still other villages are using federal dollars supplied through Juvenile Accountability Block Grants. The agreements are with either tribal or city government. Tribal governance may maintain a role in the community courts, but the basis of jurisdiction is not politically vested in the tribe.

The community courts have the appearance of flexibility and ease in accommodating cultural difference and allowing state recognition of local activity. The statewide coordinator of these courts said, 'We don't care what form they take as long as they include fairness and accountability' (personal communication from Tom Begich, 21 June 1999). However, an examination of the requisite agreements that the villages sign in order to institute one of these courts calls into question the cross-cultural sensitivity of the state's position. These formal agreements include designated processes for arrest, referring cases, giving notice, hearing evidence and rendering decisions in a distinctly western format. As a restorative justice model, the community courts demonstrate several weaknesses and do not allow for creativity in community participation. The cases are referred by the police officers; the court must hear evidence and render decisions and then must mete out punishment of some sort. Records and notice are required. And if the state juvenile probation officer does not want to refer a case to the community court, there is no procedure for the village to claim the case (personal communication with Tom Begich, 1999).

These community courts may be the first inroad into more local juridical bases for small Alaska Native villages that do not receive adequate services from the state justice system. However, they beg the political and legal question inherent in the ability to decide and execute punishment in cases. In an era of changing political relationships in Alaska, the community court process allows the state to 'delegate' its authority to villages to decide minor juvenile misdemeanour matters. The assertion of tribal authority over tribal members, as permitted by the US Constitution and subsequent Supreme Court opinions, thus becomes mooted. This is also true of the state's promotion of circle sentencing and other alternative dispute resolution mechanisms that do not recognize the political status of Alaska Native villages as tribal governments.

Circle sentencing

Circle sentencing, a model imported from the Canadian Yukon, has appeared at several state conferences, including the Sitka Native Justice conference in 1996, the magistrates' training conference in 1998 and the Bureau of Indian Affairs Providers conference in 1998. This model uses a voluntary community group to form a sentencing circle for offenders after a plea of guilty in the Canadian provincial and territorial courts. The judge, prosecutor and defender then go to the village for sentencing. Before the circle, both the offender and the victim are required to create a safety and a healing plan and to bring it to the circle with their supporters (Crnkovich, 1993; Stuart, 1996; La Prairie, 1998). The premise of this model is that the greater the community involvement, the greater the support for both offender and victim as they attempt to restore balance in the community. While consonant with tribal social control mechanisms, these circles are not politically based; a village could choose to have a circle as the structure of its tribal court, but a village could also use the circle to bridge gaps in the community between Native and non-Native people.

For example, in a Tlingit village in southeast Alaska, the lay magistrate responded to the state court system's suggestion to use sentencing circles as a means of alternative dispute resolution in villages where offenders and victims must see each other on the street all the time and anonymity is non-existent (one Anchorage judge also employed the circle on a sentencing in October 1999). The choice of circles represented a conscious decision to use a more inclusive juridical model rather than a tribal court model that would be limited to tribal members (albeit more independent of state agencies). In soliciting the training and implementing the circles, the magistrate operated without involvement of the court system. After 20 members of the village received a week-long training in circle sentencing paid for by the tribal council, the lay magistrate began conducting circles to resolve child welfare, domestic violence and alcohol consumption cases. The circles are not recorded, the decisions are private to the circle, and the follow-up is at the discretion of the circle. Initially, the magistrate was successful in referring 15 cases to the circle. When there was a change in police personnel six months later, however, and the new police officer notified the district attorney of the circles, the state prosecutorial authority refused to agree to non-prosecution through regular channels. Thus this local legal 'self-help' ran foul of established legal structures. If the juridical base had been tribal political power, however, the district attorney would not have been able to prevent the tribal court from proceeding on cases. Now the magistrate is investigating what types of agreements are available to him to continue to conduct the circles. Unlike the community courts, these circles have not been limited to juvenile offences. Both city and tribal council officers found the circles to be beneficial and a positive force in the community. The state court system is now attempting to implement similar circles, with the assistance of the local superior court judge and the cooperation of the district attorney and public defender in another region of the state.

Seeking a viable bush justice

Why is the state promoting these teen and community courts? There have been numerous imperatives for local control in Alaska Native villages, starting soon after the Alaska Native Claims Settlement Act in 1971. Several studies of Alaska bush justice indicate that the state services do not function effectively in rural Alaska (Alaska Judicial Council, 1970; Alaska Legal Services Corporation, 1974; Angell, 1981; Alaska Federation of Natives, 1995; Alaska Natives Commission, 1994; Justice Center, 1995). For example, contrast this lack of service with the policing arrangements in the equally isolated communities of Nunavut and Northwest Territories in Canada. In nearly all of those aboriginal communities, policing services are provided by the Royal Canadian Mounted Police stationed in the village, which allows for nearly immediate emergency response (Griffiths et al., 1995). Few of the 226 Alaska Native villages have State Troopers, only 70 have Village Public Safety Officers (non-commissioned peace officers trained by the State Troopers), and fewer have city or tribal police departments. Geographic and weather limitations make it impossible at certain times of the year for the Troopers to get to villages if there is an emergency or crime. Thus law enforcement presence is minimal.

Court and attorney presence is even more minimal. The original state court system contained in its design lay magistrates for village legal presence. The number of lay magistrates has decreased dramatically over the years (from 80 per cent to 30 per cent), and the proportion of Native magistrates has decreased even more. Thus, even if cases are reported, they may require review by a magistrate or judge hundreds of miles away.

In fact, the administrator of the state court system is very concerned about what she describes to be 'boutique courts', courts that serve special subject matters or populations, because such courts undermine the strength of a unitary court system. That unitary court system may be strong from an administrative perspective, but it is ineffective from the rural point of view. People in remote communities endure telephonic appearances before distant judges who never have an opportunity to observe demeanour or make personal contact with offenders, victims or witnesses. Some areas of the state are so remote (only 47 miles from eastern Russia, for example) that the telephone connections fail. Fibre-optic cable cannot be laid across frozen tundra, so cyberspace communication cannot effectively supplement ordinary telephone communication. These factors result in village residents having little or no access to courts.

The recent report from the Governor's special Rural Governance Commission identified village public safety issues and recognition of tribal sovereignty as two of the primary problems facing Alaska Native villages and recommended that there should be local law enforcement in each village. Significantly, the report also recommended that every law enforcement officer, whether city, tribal, state or of any other designation, should be acknowledged and made part of the state public safety system (Rural Governance Commission, 1999:103). The report also urged the court system to 'encourage the use of more local/alternative dispute resolution including community courts, youth courts, tribal courts and mediation to improve the effectiveness of the justice system' (ibid.:108).

In the face of these challenges, many Alaska Native villages have begun to handle their own cases. Some have engaged in the community court model proposed by the state Division of Health and Human Services, which houses the youth corrections department. Others have created tribal courts according to models presented by the federal Bureau of Indian Affairs and Department of Justice. The southeast village described above and one Yupik community have begun to use circle sentencing. Still others use their tribal councils to resolve disputes as they arise. Amidst this range of formal and informal dispute resolution, the sovereignty issues lie relatively dormant. To the extent that they exert actual sovereignty without state interference, even if it is without actual political authority, many Alaska villages are circumventing these thorny issues. As the statewide coordinator for community courts said, 'Are any of these courts handling other types of cases? I don't know, but it's not my problem' (personal communication with Tom Begich). Thus there seems to be a mutually advantageous disregard for official state and federal court rulings and agency policies.

Conclusion

In a search for effective and politically acceptable methods of enhancing dispute resolution in Alaskan communities for juvenile delinquency, the state is turning more and more to teen courts and community courts in which the goals of rehabilitation and community involvement figure prominently. However, no efforts are being made to document whether these alternatives accomplish these goals any more effectively than what is currently in place. Associated with the obvious goals of rehabilitation and community involvement are the more covert aims of community healing and empowerment. Both state and federal governments across the USA have struggled for decades with the appropriate roles and methods for restoring health to devastated Native communities. To the extent that the teen and community courts merely supply yet another western-modelled solution to culturally diverse problems, they will probably not succeed. On the other hand, should these alternatives provide an opportunity for locally crafted and owned programmes, they may turn the tide of community dysfunction. Unfortunately, the agreements that villages must sign in order to have community courts, and the structure and process of teen courts, do not bode well. These issues also have greater implications for examining the local context of national and global trends in legal policy making and the ways in which local, diverse legal systems operate within centralized legal systems.

While much of the state literature indicates a desire to achieve 'culturally relevant' justice in the village (see, for example, Rural Governance Commission, 1999:110), the tension between a need for systemic and systematic processes undermines the ability to allow for culturally relevant justice. The wide variety of social control techniques, coupled with significant differences in acculturation, amenities and accessibility, demands a varied response to these complicated problems. The tendency in the USA is to ride enthusiastically with one or more models from one venue to the next. However, despite the imperatives coming from federal and state governments, village structures remain strong. The need for grant money to supplement the non-cash economy in the village is both real and pressing; therefore, villages will grab models if the funding streams will back them. However, what they do with those models will be uniquely their own. Ideally, cross-fertilization would occur, with the villages explaining what works for them and informing decisions made on their behalf in Washington DC. To the extent that restorative justice seeks to use traditional Native modalities to resolve disputes in non-Native settings, western legal actors could learn from village experience. Sound ethnographic research about what villages are choosing and why, which models are most effective in which contexts and what is the experience of all participants in these alternatives, needs to support policy decisions. Politically simple and catchy solutions might satisfy the voters, but will not resolve long-term difficult problems at the local level.

Notes

1. In contrast, another programme in Anchorage, entitled 'Victim Offender Mediation Program', does bring the offenders into the same room with the victims and allows them to interact. Like youth court, this is also used only for first-time offenders.
2. As such, teen court training focuses on the next generation to instil knowledge and acceptance of the adversarial legal system. It is interesting to note the seeming lack of angst with which youth court proponents pass this formalism on to the next generation. In contrast, restorative justice has experienced critiques related to becoming overly professional and absorbed by the justice system.
3. Of course, many Alaska Natives no longer speak their Native languages; for one of the languages only one speaker still lives. However, in the northern parts of the state, more children and young adults are bilingual. The 40–50-year-old generation was forbidden to speak their Native languages when they were sent to mandatory boarding school. Only those whose parents kept them home maintained their language and understanding of Native culture.
4. The tribal courts in Alaska range from panels of elected judges, to elders' panels, to single appointed judges, to village councils serving as tribal courts (see Vandercook, 1999). In some parts of the state, these tribal courts closely parallel the state and federal justice system, in part because due process requirements impose certain procedures. However, they are rarely fact-finding courts, and parties appear voluntarily before them. In small remote villages where everyone is related, there are usually few secrets, and fact finding is less important than relationship rebuilding.

References

Alaska Federation of Natives (1995) *Bush Justice: Report on the Fourth AFN Bush Justice Conference; Policing – Courts – Corrections*. Alaska Federation of Natives: Fourth AFNB Bush Justice Conference, 20–22 November.

Alaska Judicial Council (1970) *Bush Justice Conference Report*, Girdwodd Bush Justice Conference, 8–11 December.

Alaska Legal Services Corporation (1974) *Bush Justice Conference Report*, Minto Bush Justice Conference, 12 June.

Alaska Natives Commission (1994) *Final Report*. Anchorage: Alaska Natives Commission, May.

Anchorage Youth Court (1998) *Newsletter*.

Anchorage Youth Court (1999) *Qualities for Effectiveness*.

Angell, J. (1981) *Public Safety and the Justice System in Alaska Native Villages*. Anchorage: Justice Center.

Bazemore, G. and M. Umbreit (1998) *Conferences, Circles, Boards and Mediation: Restorative Justice and Citizen Involvement in Response to Youth Crime*. Washington, DC: Office of Juvenile Justice and Delinquency Prevention.

Beck, R.J. (1997) 'Communications in a Teen Court: Implications for Probation', *Federal Probation* 61, 40–48.

Bronfenbrenner, U. (1979) *The Ecology of Human Development*. Cambridge, MA: Harvard University Press.

Crnkovich, M. (1993) *Report on the Sentencing circle in Kangiqsujuaq*. Ottowa: Department of Justice.

Galaway, B. and J. Hudson (eds) (1996). *Restorative Justice: International Perspectives*. Monsey, NY: Criminal Justice Press.

Godwin, T. (1996) *Peer Justice and Youth Empowerment: An Implementation Guide for Teen Court Programs*. American Probation and Parole Association.

Griffiths, C.T., E. Zellerer, D.S. Wood and G. Saville (1995) *Crime, Law, and Justice Among Inuit in the Baffin Region*. N.W.T., Canada. Buraby BC: Criminology Research Centre, Simon Fraser University.

Hunter, R.M. (1987) 'Law-Related Education, Practice and Delinquency Theory', *International Journal of Social Education* 2, 52–64.

Justice Center (1995) *Public Safety and Policing in Alaska Native Villages*. Anchorage: Justice Center.

La Prairie, C. (1998) 'The New Justice: Some Implications for Aboriginal Communities', *Canadian Journal of Criminology* 40, 61–79.

Morrow, P. (1994) 'The Language of Justice: Central Alaskan Yup'iks and the Legal System', *Criminal Justice* (American Bar Association), 9, 2.

Morrow, P. (1996) 'Yup'ik Eskimo Agents and American Legal Agencies: Perspectives on Compliance and Resistance', *The Journal of the Royal Anthropological Institute* 2, 405–23.

Nessel, P. (1998) 'Teen Court: A National Movement', *American Bar Association Technical Assistance Bulletin* 17, 1–11. Washington, DC: Office of Juvenile Justice and Delinquency Prevention.

Rural Governance Commission (1999) *Final Report to the Governor*. Juneau, Alaska.

Sherman, L., et al. (1998) *Experiments in Restorative Policing: A Progress Report to the National Police Research Unit on the Canberra Reintegrative Shaming Experiments (RISE)*. Australia: National Police Research Unit, June.

Shiff, A. and D.B. Wexler (1996) 'Teen Court: A Therapeutic Jurisprudence Perspective', *Criminal Law Bulletin* 4, 342–57.

Singer, S.I. (1998) 'Criminal and Teen Courts as Loosely Coupled Systems of Juvenile Justice', *Wake Forest Law Review* 33, 509–32.

Stuart, B. (1996) 'Circle Sentencing in Canada: A Partnership of the Community and the Criminal Justice System', *International Journal of Comparative and Applied Criminal Justice* 20, 291–309.

Vandercook, M. (1999) *Directory of Dispute Resolution in Alaska Outside the Federal and State Courts.* Alaska Judicial Council.

Van Ness, D. (1993) 'New Wine and Old Wineskins: Four Challenges of Restorative Justice', *Criminal Law Forum* 492, 251–76.

Wexler, D.B. (1995) 'Reflections on the Scope of Therapeutic Jurisprudence', *Psychology, Public Policy and Law* 1, 220–36.

Winnick, B. (1997) 'The Jurisprudence of Therapeutic Jurisprudence', *Psychology, Public Policy and Law* 3, 184–206.

Baker v. John, 982 P.2d 738 (Alaska, 1998).

Venetie v. State of Alaska, 118 S.Ct. 948 (1998).

8

The Prospects for Restorative Youth Justice in England and Wales: A Tale of Two Acts*

Adam Crawford

Introduction

Restorative justice is not only a major development in recent criminological thinking, albeit with a long tradition in pre-modern forms of justice, but it also represents an increasingly global social movement (Braithwaite, 1998). At the heart of a restorative justice philosophy lies a concern with a particular mode of participatory and inclusive conflict resolution – its important social and cultural meaning and place – and an emphasis upon healing relationships, restoring victims, restoring offenders and restoring communities. An established definition is of a 'process whereby the parties with a stake in a particular offence come together to resolve collectively how to deal with the aftermath of the offence and its implications for the future' (Marshall, 1996:37). As such, restorative justice responds to Nils Christie's suggestion that 'the goal for crime prevention might be to re-create social conditions which make the conflicts visible and thereafter manageable' (1977:7). The involvement of the parties in the process of conflict resolution is seen by proponents to be an essential element of community membership (Wright, 1991:76–7). Disputes and crimes arise where 'normal' community controls have broken down (Abel, 1973). Consequently, the response to crime is an activity that is conducted both on behalf of the community and one which reflects a community's moral sensibilities. Conflict processing is, therefore, a highly *communal* act. It strengthens and reaffirms communal bonds. It represents not only a 'potential for activity, for participation', but also allows the parties 'opportunities for norm-clarification' (Christie, 1977:7–8).

As a mode of conflict resolution, which seeks to impart social and cultural messages and symbols, restorative justice has particular implications for responding to youth crime. Unsurprisingly, therefore, it is in the field of youth justice that notions of restoration have had greatest effect. From the groundbreaking developments in family group conferences in New Zealand, implemented through the Children, Young Persons and their Families Act 1989, a variety of restorative justice practices for young people has been spawned across the world (Bazemore and Walgrave, 1999; Morris and Maxwell, 2001).

In this chapter, I want to explore the manner in which recent developments with regard to juvenile offenders in England and Wales have been affected by notions of restorative justice and their potential implications within the current criminal justice policy context. The youth justice reforms have developed, with increasing momentum, over two distinct waves of legislation: the Crime and Disorder Act 1998 and the Youth Justice and Criminal Evidence Act 1999. My contention is that the current government has adopted an eclectic 'shot-gun' approach to the integration of restorative justice into the youth justice system, one which embodies a number of tensions and contradictions. The aims of this chapter are fourfold. First, I sketch out the immediate background to the two relevant pieces of legislation which have sought to adhere to, or at least have deployed a discourse of, a restorative justice philosophy. Second, I describe the salient pieces of the legislation and outline implementation developments to date. In so doing, I focus specifically upon the most recent introduction of referral orders and youth offender panels, by the 1999 Act, which appear to offer the most striking development in restorative justice in England and Wales. Third, I highlight some of the tensions and problematic issues likely to inform further implementation and future developments. Finally, I identify some of the principal dynamics which inform the models of restorative justice being advanced and comment upon the broader issues to which they give rise, particularly with regard to the politics of criminal justice and the place that restorative justice occupies therein.

Background to the reforms

By the mid-1990s there were about 5.5 million recorded crimes each year in England and Wales, with over one million burglaries and about 1.5 million vehicle crimes each year. The British Crime Surveys suggested that the actual level of crime was three to four times the recorded level. As a consequence, each year about 180000 young people aged 10–17 were being convicted or cautioned for offending: over 80 per cent were young men. However, contrary to political and media portrayal of ever-rising youth lawlessness (particularly in the aftermath of the murder of two-year-old Jamie Bulger by two ten-year-old boys on 12 February 1993), it is also worth noting that juvenile crime generally was declining and, in particular, so were offences by children. The number of boys aged 10–14 found guilty or cautioned per 100,000 of the population was 2926 in 1983 and 1686 in 1993 (the corresponding figures for girls were 941 and 621) (Home Office, 1994:122).

In many senses, the juvenile cautioning policy of the 1980s was one of the (largely untold) criminal justice success stories of the period. Driven largely at the local level, cautioning of juvenile offenders increased dramatically over the decade without a subsequent increase in crime. Under the Conservative government the Home Office had encouraged the increased use of cautioning with regard to young offenders through circulars 14/1985 and 59/1990 and even supported its expansion in relation to adult offenders via the latter circular. In 1971 the number of persons cautioned was 77,300. By 1993 this figure had risen to 311,300, more than a fourfold increase on the 1971 figures and nearly double the number cautioned ten years earlier. However, in 1993 the government's mood shifted dramatically away from the managerialist and pragmatic politics influenced by a 'just deserts' philosophy – as found in the Criminal Justice Act 1991 – to one of 'populist punitiveness' through increased resort to strategies of penal exclusion (Bottoms, 1995:39–41) and with an emphasis upon a rhetoric of 'prison works'. In this context, repeat cautioning of young people came to be seen as a strategy promoting lawlessness. Circular 18/1994 signalled a significant retrenchment and sought to arrest the use of repeat cautions. The use of multiple cautions, the circular declared,

> brings cautioning into disrepute; cautions should not be administered to an offender in circumstances where there can be no reasonable expectation that this will curb his offending. It is only in exceptional circumstances that more than one caution should be considered.

Consequently, by 1996 the number of offenders cautioned for all offences, excluding motoring offences, fell by 2 per cent to 286,000 whereas, previously, the numbers cautioned had increased by an average of 6 per cent per annum between 1985 and 1992.

It was against this increasingly punitive background that the Labour Party sought to dispose of its 'hostages to fortune' with regard to law and order and to articulate a 'new vision' for criminal justice – notably youth justice. In this, the subsequent proposals were heavily influenced by two specific publications: first, the findings of a Home Office research study into young people and crime (Graham and Bowling, 1995); and, second, the recommendations of the Audit Commission's Report, *Misspent Youth* (1996). Both helped to set a particular agenda premised upon certain assumptions and understandings about youth crime and the appropriateness of certain responses to it (Newburn, 1998).

In essence, Graham and Bowling's (1995) research, based upon a self-report study of 14–25-year-olds, revealed that one in two males and one in three females admitted that they had committed an offence at some time. Most young people commit only one or two minor offences but one in four males admitted to committing an offence in the previous 12-month period and a quarter of these offenders said they committed more than five offences in the year. According to the research, about 3 per cent of young offenders account for a quarter of all offences committed by juveniles. Moreover, the research suggested that young people (particularly young men) are not 'growing out of crime' in the way that it had previously been thought that they did. Despite a small sample and other methodological concerns, as well as the fact that it appeared to contradict other research findings (Hagell and Newburn, 1994), the research helped to affirm: first, the view that a small but distinct group of young offenders exists and is responsible for much crime; and second, that non-intervention from the courts and other criminal justice agencies would not result in young people merely 'growing out of crime'. Instead, the research suggested the need for intervention to encourage 'desistence' from crime by identifying risk and protective factors in child development in order to change behaviour when young people first start offending.

The timing of the Audit Commission's *Misspent Youth* report was significant in that it was published towards the end of 1996 and, hence, just before the general election campaign got into full swing in early 1997. The report concluded that about £1 billion a year was being spent on a youth justice system which was inefficient and ineffective. The Audit Commission (1996) found that the youth justice system was preoccupied with processing and administering young offenders rather than with direct work to address offending behaviour and with beneficial outcomes. The report drew heavily upon the Graham and Bowling research findings and argued that the essential problems of the system were that:

- prosecution through the courts was too slow (taking on average over four months to deal with juveniles from arrest to sentence and in some cases taking well over a year);

- cautioning became less and less effective the more often it was used with a particular offender;
- little money was being spent on changing offending behaviour and not enough was being done to address offending behaviour;
- monitoring of reoffending after different sentences and disposals was rare;
- traditional criminal justice agencies involved with young people often worked in an uncoordinated way, often with different priorities and performance targets; and
- little was being done to prevent young people from offending in the first place.

The report read as a damning indictment of the youth justice system. As such, it played into the hands of the then Labour opposition, which seized upon the report as a lever to present itself as the party of 'law and order' with radical proposals to address the concerns raised by the Audit Commission's findings.

The New Labour government which came to power in May 1997 set crime and disorder as a principal plank of public policy upon which its fortunes in office would hinge and in relation to which it should be judged. The importance for the new government of crime control and criminal justice policy had been articulated while in opposition and captured by the infamous slogan, first used by Tony Blair in an interview for BBC Radio 4 in 1993, namely: 'Tough on crime; tough on the causes of crime.' This catch-phrase evocatively suggested a break with a 'soft on crime' stance traditionally associated with Labour. Downes and Morgan (1997) note that, for a party historically tainted with many 'hostages to fortune' with regard to law and order (albeit paradoxically with a record in government which was no worse than that of the Conservative Party), this shift constituted a potential political vote-winner. Moreover, it marked a watershed in so far as it broke with the discourses associated both with the traditional Left of societal responsibility for crime and with the Right, which emphasized the purely individual responsibility for crime (Downes, 1998:192).

Once in office the Labour government set about a hasty consultation process over the summer of 1997 (Home Office, 1997a). The White Paper which was to inform and set the tone of the youth justice elements of both the Crime and Disorder Act 1998 and the Youth Justice and Criminal Evidence Act 1999 was provocatively titled 'No More Excuses'. In the light of the subsequent Crime and Disorder Bill, the Audit Commission continued its influence over juvenile justice policy with the publication of an update of its earlier report entitled *Misspent Youth '98* (Audit Commission, 1998), in which it expressed its sympathetic support for the Bill's intentions and encouraged a managerialist approach to implementation, with which the Audit Commission had become synonymous.

The two Acts, the contents of which were previewed in the *No More Excuses* White Paper, both claim to 'build on principles underlying the concept of restorative justice' (Home Office, 1997b: para. 9.21). These are defined in the White Paper as the '3Rs of restorative justice':

> *restoration*: young offenders apologising to their victims and making amends for the harm they have done;
> *reintegration*: young offenders paying their debt to society, putting their crime behind them and rejoining the law abiding community; and
> *responsibility*: young offenders – and their parents – facing the consequences of their offending behaviour and taking responsibility for preventing further offending.
>
> (Ibid.)

Let us now examine the particular forms through which the New Labour government has sought to institutionalize these principles.

The legislation

Phase one: the Crime and Disorder Act 1998

The key elements of the legislation with regard to youth justice include:

- the introduction of an overarching aim of the youth justice system: 'to prevent offending by young people' and a duty on youth justice agencies to have regard to it (s. 37);
- the abolition of *doli incapax* – the presumption that children under 14 and over ten years of age are incapable of knowing the difference between right and wrong which required the prosecution to establish that the child knew that what he or she had done was 'seriously wrong' and not merely naughty or mischievous (s. 34);
- the power for local authorities in consultation with the police to introduce a 'local child curfew' (not exceeding 90 days) for all children under the age of ten in a specified area between 9 p.m. and 6 a.m. unless accompanied by a parent or responsible adult (s. 14);
- the introduction of an 'anti-social behaviour order' (ASBO) which provides a civil remedy, for senior police officers and/or chief executives

of a council, to restrain 'anti-social behaviour' by individuals or a group (s. 1);[1]

- a requirement upon the local authority, after consultation with the chief officer of police, police authority, probation committee and health authority, to formulate and implement for each year a youth justice plan (s. 40);
- the introduction of a scheme of 'reprimands' and 'final warnings' to replace the existing cautioning system (s. 65–6);
- the introduction of new sentences of the court: 'parenting order'; 'child safety order'; 'action plan order' and 'reparation order';
- the introduction of youth offending teams (YOTs) to implement locally the above new sentences, orders and allied youth justice reforms (s. 39);
- the introduction of streamlined youth court procedures and statutory time limits; and
- the establishment of the Youth Justice Board (YJB) for England and Wales (s. 41).

The abolition of *doli incapax*, together with many of the above new orders, draws upon the 'no more excuses' theme of responsibilizing children and parents. The government had argued that the presumption was 'archaic ... illogical and unfair' and that by allowing children to evade accepting responsibility flew 'in the face of common sense' (Home Office, 1997b:6). As Gelsthorpe and Morris have argued, the 'importance of the presumption lay in its *symbolism*: it was a statement about the nature of childhood, the vulnerability of children and the appropriateness of *criminal justice sanctions* for children' (1999:213, emphasis in original). So too, its abolition was heavily symbolic with regard to its implications for the manner in which children are viewed and are to be treated through penal means by the state. As such, its abolition not only means that England and Wales has, with the age of criminal responsibility set at ten years, one of the lowest thresholds in Europe, but also further erodes the special protections historically afforded to children (Bandalli, 1998; Fionda, 1999).

The parenting order can consist of two elements. The first imposes a requirement on the parent or guardian to attend counselling or guidance sessions (for a maximum of 12 weeks), where they will receive help and support in dealing with their child. This element will normally form the core of the parenting order and must be imposed when an order is made. The second element, which is discretionary, is a requirement on the parent or guardian to exercise control over their child's behaviour.

This could include ensuring that the child gets to school every day or that he or she is home by a certain time at night. This element can last for up to 12 months (s. 8(4)(a)).

The Act paid considerable attention to infrastructure in the form of the YJB to oversee the changes to the youth justice system at the national level and the introduction of YOTs locally. The YJB, which came into effect on 30 September 1998, has been given statutory powers to provide national leadership in ensuring that the reforms are implemented. The Board (which has multi-agency membership) is charged with monitoring the operation and performance of the youth justice system, including inspection and requiring information provision. It advises the Home Secretary on standards of the work of YOTs and the juvenile secure units, monitoring performance against standards set and publishing results. It also has responsibility for identifying and disseminating good practice, by commissioning research and providing grants for developing innovative work. In all there are now some 450 new youth justice projects funded by the YJB, providing a menu of measures and interventions spawned by the Act.

YOTs are multi-agency teams charged with coordinating the provision of youth justice in the local authority area and delivering functions identified for them in local youth justice plans (s. 40). Each YOT must include: a probation officer; a local authority social worker; a police officer; a representative of the local health authority; and a person nominated by the chief education officer. As independently managed multidisciplinary teams, YOTs aim to work corporately, drawing upon their collective skills, expertise and resources to offer and provide local services – utilizing a range of local agencies and partnerships with voluntary organizations – in support of the various youth justice provisions in the Act and their delivery.

In terms of specific provisions introduced by the legislation, 'reprimands' and 'final warnings' replace cautions. The latter trigger interventions, whereas reprimands stand alone as a formal police caution.[2] Together, they act as two sequential levels of response prior to court appearance. Following one reprimand, any further offence will lead to a final warning or a charge. Any further offending following a final warning will normally result in a charge being brought. Once an offender has received either a reprimand or a final warning he or she must not be given a second except in the limited circumstances where the latest offence is not serious and more than two years have passed since the first reprimand or final warning was given (s. 65).

Police forces and youth offending teams administer the final warning scheme which, according to the government, is designed to:

> end repeat cautioning and provide a progressive and meaningful response to offending behaviour; ensure appropriate and effective action to help prevent re-offending; ensure that juveniles who do re-offend after a warning are dealt with quickly and effectively through the courts.
>
> (Home Office, 2000b: para. 1)

Reparation orders, by contrast, are sentences of the court, which involve supervised and directed reparation to victims. The Act and accompanying Guidance state that the consent of victim(s) is required before a reparation order can be made (although the final decision on whether to impose a reparation order and what form this should take remains with the court).[3] Finally, action plan orders involve an intensive three-month programme of supervised and directed activities for young offenders, which may involve restorative elements, including victim reparation.

As of 1 April 2000 every local authority area was required to have a YOT in place. As a result, there are now 155 YOTs composed of about 2500 staff from the different agencies across England and Wales. Before this, YOTs were piloted for 18 months in a small number of areas and the subject of Home Office evaluation (Hines et al., 1999). On 1 June 2000 all the youth justice activities specified within the Crime and Disorder Act 1998 came into effect. The principal restorative work that YOTs have been engaged in has been through the final warning scheme, reparation orders and action plan orders (see Dignan, 2000a). In this regard, the YJB is currently supporting some 45 'restorative justice' schemes, of which 29 are targeted at final warning stage, 18 at action plan orders, 15 at reparation orders, and 15 at other orders including supervision and custody (Young and Hoyle, 2000). As for their mode of operation, according to the national evaluators (ibid.), 29 schemes plan to offer 'victim–offender mediation', 22 'family group conferences', 20 'indirect reparation', 12 'community reparation', and seven 'victim–offender conferencing'. This reflects the diversity of ways in which and stages at which restorative notions are being introduced into the youth justice process.

In the light of the experience of the pilots, revised Guidance to the police and YOTs (Home Office, 2000a,b) has been produced in relation to the final warning scheme, which promotes the use of a 'restorative warning' or 'restorative conference' (the terms are used interchangeably). What is envisaged here is a form of 'restorative conference' which draws heavily upon the Australian experience of police-led restorative cautioning, particularly as developed in England in the Thames Valley Police Force (Pollard, 2000; Young, 2000).[4] The new Guidance declares that 'Ministers and the Youth Justice Board consider strongly that the restorative approach will make final warnings more meaningful and effective' and the revised Guidance suggests that:

> The impact of a warning on a young offender can be significantly enhanced by delivering it as part of a restorative conference involving the young offender, his or her parents, any other influential adults and, where appropriate and willing, the victim and any others affected by the offending behaviour (both within the victim group and the offender group).
>
> (Home Office, 2000a:2, para. 3)

The Guidance recognizes that local protocols will need to be established between police and YOTs to cover practice in relation to delivery of reprimands and warnings. It also suggests that a restorative justice approach will not be appropriate in all cases, and acknowledges that police forces will be at different stages in the development and use of restorative justice practices with young offenders.

The various restorative justice measures in the 1998 Act and its shotgun approach manifest a considerable tension between differing political and penological aims (Crawford, 1998, 2001; Newburn, 1998). Moreover, they place restorative justice practices within a primarily coercive framework, either as part of a sentence of the court (such as the reparation order or action plan order) or run by the police at the pre-court cautioning (final warning) phase. As such, they have received mixed reactions from commentators with regard to their potential for advancing restorative justice in England and Wales. Dignan has argued that the changes should ensure that restorative justice is 'no longer a marginal, irregular and highly localised activity' (Dignan, 1999:53). This optimistic view, however, is not shared by other commentators (Morris and Gelsthorpe, 2000).

Phase two: the Youth Justice and Criminal Evidence Act 1999

In many ways, the youth justice provisions in the Crime and Disorder Act reworked initiatives which had precursors and earlier resonances or had previously been proposed – albeit with a particular emphasis upon partnership working. – By contrast, the Youth Justice and Criminal Evidence Act 'belongs unambiguously to New Labour' (Ball, 2000:211). The 1999 Act goes much further down the restorative justice path than did the 1998 Act, in that it will result in the automatic referral of most young offenders convicted by the court for the first time to a youth offender panel (YOP). According to the Home Office, the panel

> will provide a constructive forum for the young offender to confront the consequences of the crime and agree a programme of meaningful activity to prevent any further offending ... A key strength of the panel is that it offers an appropriate forum in which to consider the views of victims. If they wish, victims may attend panel meetings to explain to the young offender how the crime has affected them. Victims may also help to determine an appropriate form of reparation for the young offender to make as part of the programme of activity.
>
> (Home Office, 1999)

The panel will seek to involve offenders, their families, their victims and youth offending team members in drawing up an agreed 'contract'. The Act also extends the statutory responsibility of YOTs to include the recruitment and training of community panel members.

The referral order

The 1999 Act introduces referral orders for offenders under 18 (s. 1) as an order available in the youth court (and adult magistrates' court).[5] Offenders appearing for the first time in the youth court, who admit their guilt, will be referred automatically to a YOP, unless the crime is serious enough to warrant custody or the court orders an absolute discharge. Hence the Act provides a mandatory order for most young offenders. There is a discretionary power for the court to make a referral order by virtue of s. 2(2) if a young person pleads guilty to one or more offences and not guilty to other associated offence(s) of which he or she is convicted.

The idea of the referral order was set out in the government's *No More Excuses* White Paper (although at that stage it did not have a name). It was proposed as part of a 'step change in the culture of the Youth Court' to be governed by the principles 'underlying the concept of restorative justice' (Home Office, 1997b:31–2). As such, the referral order represents an explicit critique of the effectiveness of the youth court. This the government spelt out in the White Paper stating that 'the purpose of the Youth Court must change from simply deciding guilt or innocence and then issuing a sentence' and that in future 'an offence should trigger a wider enquiry into the circumstances and nature of offending behaviour leading to action to change that behaviour' (Home Office, 1997b:29).

The court is required to explain to the offender 'in ordinary language' the effect of the order and the consequences that may follow failure to agree a contract with the panel or the breach of any terms of the contract (s. 3(3)). The court may determine the length of the referral order, which can last from three to 12 months, depending on the seriousness of the crime (as determined by the court) and must specify the length for which any contract will have effect. Where a referral is being ordered for two or more offences, the court will make a referral order for each offence; however, each order will be supervised by the same panel and there can only be one contract, the total duration of which will not exceed 12 months.

When a referral order is made it will constitute the entire sentence for the offence with which the court is dealing and is not to be treated as an additional sentence to run alongside others, although the referral order may be accompanied by certain ancillary orders such as orders for costs, compensation, forfeiture of items used in committing an offence, exclusion from football matches and so on (s. 4(2) and (3)).

Youth offender panels

The origins of YOPs correspond broadly to the adage 'something old, something new, something borrowed, something blue'[6] in drawing explicitly or implicitly from at least three sources. First, YOPs borrow from the experience of the Scottish Children's Hearings system, which has been in operation since 1971. The Children's Hearings act as a decriminalized form of diversion from the court in which youths and their families appear before a panel of trained lay people drawn from the local community in order to seek an extra-judicial resolution to the problem (see Hallett et al., 1998; Waterhouse et al., 1999; Whyte, 2000). The use of lay volunteers as panel members also has similarities with the Vermont Reparative Probation Programme (see Karp and Walther, 2001).

Second, panels draw – both inspiration and practice – from the experience of family group conferencing in New Zealand (Morris, Maxwell and Robertson, 1993; Morris and Maxwell, 2000, 2001) and the subsequent development of diverse models of community conferencing to be found in different Australian states and territories (Daly, 2001), as well as the theoretical literature which accompanied these developments (Braithwaite, 1989).

Finally, but no less importantly, YOPs draw upon the history of victim–offender mediation in England and Wales (Marshall and Merry, 1990; Marshall, 1999), as well as the developments of caution-plus in the 1980s – such as the Northamptonshire Diversion Units (NACRO, 1998) – and, more recently, the practice of 'restorative cautioning' by the Thames Valley Police (Young, 2000; Young and Goold, 2000). Nevertheless, the model of YOPs advanced by the 1999 Act departs, in significant ways, from all the above. YOPs constitute at least two lay community representatives, one of which will chair the panel meetings, together with one YOT member. Interestingly, the government's original intention had been that panels 'would contain a mix of youth justice practitioners – a magistrate (if possible, one of the magistrates responsible for the referral), a YOT member, and perhaps a police officer' (Home Office, 1997b:33, para. 9.35). The potentially radical involvement of community members making up the majority on YOPs did not appear as part of the original philosophy or ideology of referral orders.[7] The government appears to have opted for this approach rather late in the day and more by accident than by design. Moreover, the introduction of a significant lay element comes at a time in which lay involvement in criminal justice is increasingly questioned: the lay magistracy is being marginalized and increasingly replaced by professional stipendiary magistrates (Raine, 2001) and the jury is the subject of critique and incursion into its role and function.

It is intended that panel members constitute people who are 'properly representative of the community they intend to serve and who have the appropriate personal characteristics for the challenging task of dealing effectively with young offenders, and their victims, in a restorative justice context' (Home Office, 2000c: para. 1.4). Panel members must be 18 years of age or over, albeit above that minimum age young panel members are particularly encouraged as, according to the Guidance, they 'may be particularly well equipped to engage and communicate with young offenders, and to understand their needs and motivation' (ibid.: para. 1.16). A criminal conviction is not a bar to panel membership, where the applicant can demonstrate that he or she does not present any risk of reoffending. The recruitment criteria are to be 'based on personal qualities rather than professional qualifications'.

Contrary to the government's original intentions to include criminal justice professionals among panel members, it now suggests that such people should only be recruited 'in a personal, volunteer capacity, rather than as representatives of any group or profession' (ibid.: para. 1.19). Moreover, the Guidance goes on to state that: 'it will always be inappropriate for those involved in the youth justice system to sit as community panel members where they have been previously involved as sentencers or in a capacity in the young offender's case' (ibid.: para. 1.20). Whilst this may clarify matters for lay panel members, it is not the end of the matter *vis-à-vis* YOT panel members. As YOTs are required to have representatives from the police among their multi-agency staff, even if they are not 'otherwise involved in the case', nevertheless, a police officer may be privy to prejudicial information and facts about a young person which may affect subsequent deliberations.

Returning to the question of lay panel membership, the Guidance asserts that: 'it will be inappropriate for panel members to be involved in any case concerning a young offender who is a family member or close acquaintance' (ibid.: para. 1.21). However, it is unclear at what point 'acquaintance' presents a potential conflict of interests. Herein lies an inherent tension for panels (and local/community justice more generally), for whilst, on the one hand, the intention is for the social distance between panel members to be reduced, on the other hand, it is undesirable for justice to be compromised by prior personal relations.

Evaluation of pilots

In line with the government's commitment to 'evidence-based policy', referral orders and YOPs were introduced as pilots in 11 areas across England and Wales, prior to national roll-out in April 2002. The evaluation began alongside the initial recruitment and training of panel volunteers in April 2000. The first referral orders in the pilot areas were made in July 2000. The evaluation – conducted by a research team based at Goldsmiths College, Leeds and Kent Universities (of which the present author was a part) – explored the recruitment and training of panel members, the implementation of referral orders and their impact. Two interim reports were published during the course of the pilots (Newburn, 2001a,b), both of which influenced the development of the pilots and the revised Home Office Guidance (Home Office, 2001). The final report was published to co-incide with national roll-out. The findings of the evaluation and their implications are not considered in this chapter but are considered in detail elsewhere (Newburn, 2002; Crawford and Newburn, 2002, 2003).

Training panel members

Training is viewed as crucial both to ensure that community panel members are properly equipped for their role and as an integral part of the selection process (Home Office, 2000c: para. 2.1). The minimum training consists of eight hours' introductory training followed by 60 hours' pre-service training. This is to be supplemented by a minimum further 16 hours' training to support new panel members through their first few meetings. Panel chairs should receive a minimum additional 16 hours' training. The intention is that panel chairs eventually will be selected from established panel members with 9–18 months' experience. However, initially in the pilots, as there were no established panel members to draw upon, chairs undertook the panel 'leader' training and went straight into the role. This provoked some debate as to whether YOT members should chair initial panel meetings, allowing lay panel members time to get into their role as panel members before proceeding to the panel leader training. While the initial Guidance allowed for the possibility, the Home Office increasingly set its mind against such an approach as this would undermine the central and dominant lay involvement in YOPs. This initial training is to be supplemented by a minimum of ten hours' in-service training and a refresher course of a minimum of eight hours each successive year. Interestingly, the Guidance does not specify any minimum training for YOT panel members.

National training materials for panel members and chairs – entitled *Panel Matters* – were produced by trainers with considerable involvement in the training of lay panel members for the Scottish Children's Hearings, with input for the referral order steering group set up by the Home Office Juvenile Offenders Unit and YJB to oversee the implementation of the pilots. As a consequence, the training draws quite heavily upon the Scottish model and experience.

Panel meetings

The initial meeting of the panel must take place within 15 working days of the court hearing at which the referral order is made (this is now set out in the new National Standards for Youth Justice).[8] Panels must hold at least one interim meeting – the first such review is recommended to be held after one month, followed by at least one progress meeting for each three months of the contract. The panel should facilitate a full examination of the reasons for the offending behaviour and sign a 'contract' with the young person aimed at tackling his/her offending behaviour and preventing reoffending. If, at the end of the referral order period, the programme has been completed successfully, the conviction will be considered spent for the purposes of the Rehabilitation Act 1974.

At least one parent or guardian of children under 16 is required to attend panel hearings. The court, where it considers this appropriate, may require parents of children over 16 to attend (s. 5(2)). The failure of parents or guardians to attend without reasonable excuse may result in contempt proceedings under the Magistrates' Court Act 1980 (s. 63).

To encourage the restorative nature of the process a variety of other 'stakeholders' may be invited to attend panel meetings. Participation is strictly voluntary. Those who may attend include:

- the victim or a representative of the community at large – young victims (under 16) should be involved only with the agreement of their parents or primary carer, who should be given the opportunity to accompany them;
- a victim supporter (chosen by the victim and agreed by the panel);
- a supporter of the young person (invited by the offender with the panel's agreement);
- anyone else that the panel considers to be capable of having a 'good influence' on the offender; and
- signers and interpreters provided for any of the participants in the process who require them.

It is intended that the panel should consult the victim(s) of the young person's offending as to whether they wish to attend. Initial contact with victims should be made within five working days of the making of the order. The Guidance suggests that 'Ideally this will be carried out by the same member of the youth offending team as contacted the offender,' but then, somewhat contradictorily, goes on to add: 'All contact with the victim should be carried out with sensitivity, and by a member of the youth offending team trained in victim awareness' (para. 1.12). It is probable that the latter sentiment will prevail and YOTs will dedicate the work of victim contact to specific YOT staff – following the experience of the Crime and Disorder Act reforms this is likely to be the police members of the YOT – or contract it out to the police or Victim Support. In practice, as Dignan notes with regard to the Crime and Disorder Act reforms, this may mean that once a victim has indicated a willingness to participate, the case is then referred to another person, albeit that 'this "split" responsibility is cumbersome and is likely to be more time consuming' (Dignan, 2000a:18). The Guidance states that where there are multiple victims 'it may not be desirable or practical to involve all'. It goes on to suggest that 'priority should be given according to willingness to attend, and where harm has been most serious' (para. 3.30). Where there is no direct victim, the panel may wish to invite 'someone who can bring a victim perspective' to the meeting, 'for example a local business person or an individual who has suffered a similar offence' (para. 3.31). The intention is that panel meetings will be held in locations as close as possible to where the young person lives and from which the panel members are drawn. It is also intended that the venue should be as informal and non-institutional as possible.

The contract

The contract must always include some element of direct or indirect reparation and should also include activities to address the factors behind the offending behaviour. According to the Guidance, the programme of activities 'should be challenging but achievable' (para. 3.56). The contract is seen as a 'two way agreement', for which the young person should not be penalized as a result of the YOT's failure to make adequate provisions (para. 3.58). As a referral order is not a custodial sentence, the inclusion of electronic monitoring or any form of custody is precluded from contracts (Explanatory Notes, para. 58). Once the contract has been devised and agreed, it should be set out in writing and explained in clear language. It should be signed by both the young person and a member of the panel and a copy given to the young person.

Offenders may be referred back to court for failure to agree a contract with the panel, failure to attend meetings of the panel or breach of requirements of the contract. Where a young offender is referred back to the court by the panel the court may decide to revoke the original order and resentence. The court must take into account 'the circumstances' of the referral back to court and, if there was a contract between the young person and the panel, 'the extent' to which the young person complied with its terms (Explanatory Notes, para. 73). The young person can appeal against the resentencing to the Crown Court but it appears that the offender, the prosecutor or the panel have no right to appeal against the decision whether or not to revoke the referral order (Wonnacott, 1999:279).

Potential unintended consequences of referral orders

Despite the early stage in the implementation of referral orders, it is possible to identify a number of potential sites of conflict or unintended consequences of the introduction of referral orders alongside the plethora of other interventions that seek to introduce restorative practices into the youth justice system. A number of these ambiguities have been the subject of the evaluation research and may be addressed before national roll-out in the light of experiences in the pilot areas.[9] For, as researchers have noted, the failings of restorative justice programmes are often the product of poor implementation (Morris and Maxwell, 2000). In the implementation of restorative justice initiatives, the devil frequently lies in the detail. Other tensions stem from the eclectic nature of the referral order model, the awkward relationship between YOPs and the youth courts and the somewhat incoherent relationship between, on the one hand, the morally toned demonization of young people and expressive punitiveness and, on the other hand, the rationalistic and instrumental regime of order in which certain contemporary notions of restoration are couched. Let us now consider some of the implementation challenges which confront referral orders.

YOTs may become swamped by the workload

Managing the caseloads referred to YOPs is likely to be a difficult task at the best of times. Arranging on average three or four meetings per case (over the lifetime of a contract), which may often occur outside-of-office hours requiring the attendance of (at least) two community panel members, a professional YOT member, the young person and parent, not to mention the victim(s), supporters and any other relevant people, will not be easy. The requirement that the first meeting takes place within 15 working days of the referral order being made will add to this difficulty, particularly as the YOT staff will not be able to control the influx of new cases. The managerial demands may leave less time for the reparative elements of the process, such as victim contact, preparation, party participation and follow-up. Under such pressures, one potential consequence may be that reparation becomes 'tokenistic' or mechanical and may 'appear to both victims and offenders as ritualistic and formulaic', a danger noted by researchers evaluating the Crime and Disorder Act reforms (Dignan, 2000a:17).

Increased use of custody

If magistrates consider referral orders to lack credibility and/or resent the removal of their discretion in sentencing young people on their first appearance in court, the introduction of referral orders may result in an increased use of custody. Moreover, referral back to court, as a consequence of breach of the conditions of the contract by the young offender, may encourage greater use of custody in the belief that the young person had squandered the opportunity presented to them.

Increased or fewer 'not guilty' pleas

If young people (under advice from a solicitor) feel that they would get a less intensive sentence if they did not receive a referral order, we may see an increase in young people pleading 'not guilty'. Inversely, if young people opt for a referral order because they think they will get a lighter sentence, we may witness an increase in young people pleading 'guilty'. This would appear not to be an 'unintended consequence', strictly speaking, in that government policy both encourages and would welcome this. However, it would be a perverse effect if young people changed their plea even when potentially not guilty in a strict legal sense – they may have done something wrong but not criminal – let alone when they have done nothing wrong at all.

Over-intensive contracts

There is a realistic danger that panels, in their genuine desire to 'turn a kid's life around' and 'nip their offending in the bud' – as the government suggests (Home Office, 1997a) – or through their fear of not doing enough for the victim(s) and wider community, may produce contracts which are significantly disproportionate to the seriousness of the harm caused. Clearly, one of the roles of YOT staff on panels will be to discourage this. However, this tension may serve to pit YOT staff against lay community panel members.

Victims' interests are not served by the process

There are concerns over the extent to which the model adopted accommodates victims' interests and needs in a way that allows victims sufficient involvement and real choices as to the nature and use of their input. Unlike some schemes, victims are not signatories to the 'contracts' between the panel and young person, nor do victims have a veto power over the meeting (whether they are present or not).[10] Enough earlier restorative justice experiments have struggled to achieve significant victim participation (Morris, Maxwell and Robertson, 1993) for us to expect this to be a weighty issue. Others have seen victims' interests overridden by an offender focus which has resulted in 'the subordination of a good idea' (Davis, Boucherat and Watson, 1988). The integration of victims' perspectives within restorative justice is a major challenge for new initiatives, which need to be sensitive to the dangers of victims being used, sometimes inadvertently, in the service of offenders (Crawford, 2000) or in victims having little control over the nature, extent and use of their input, such as to potentially revictimize them.

Ultimately, the responsibility for decision making as to whether the offender should be charged, prosecuted, convicted or sentenced should not lie with the victim but with the state. Nevertheless, it is important for victims to be provided with tangible and well-informed choices and options as to the nature and extent of their involvement at various stages in the process.

Panels may become over-run by lawyers

The question of legal representation at meetings is a vexed one for panels. The Guidance appears to be assertive on this front in declaring that 'Young people will not be legally represented at a youth offender panel meeting as this could seriously hinder the process of the panel' (para. 3.32). Moreover, it goes on to assert that whilst 'it is not intended that the offender's supporter should act as a legal representative, lawyers may be present as parents, carers, supporters or victims' (para. 3.33). The intention here is that young people should be encouraged and have the opportunity to speak and take responsibility for themselves. However, concerns over how this might be interpreted in the light of Article 6(3)(c) of the European Convention on Human Rights (ECHR) have resulted in the Home Office backtracking from its original position. Instead, it would appear to have passed the responsibility to local YOTs to resolve as they have the power to decide who attends the panel meetings. This would seem to translate into a situation in which local YOT managers encourage solicitors not to attend. Refusal to allow attendance in such a situation may well fall foul of a legal challenge (particularly since the Human Rights Act came into effect in October 2000). However, the fact that legal aid is likely to be unavailable for panel hearings (which itself may the subject of future legal challenge) will mean that, for most young people, in reality, this question is likely to be less relevant.

Yet critics such as Wonnacott, who argue that the availability of legal advice and representation for all young offenders would only be 'an obstacle in the way of the exercise of arbitrary power by the panel' and nothing else (1999:284), assume two things. First, they assume that professional advice and representation is always in the interests of the parties; and second, that a rights-based approach to negotiation is desirable in all cases. The findings of years of socio-legal research into criminal justice processes do not support these assumptions (see McConville et al., 1994; Sanders and Young, 2000). It is questionable whether it is wise to involve lawyers whose traditions and organizational culture are rooted in partisan advisory and representative roles. Rights-based forms of representation may run counter to the logics of broader interest-based negotiation. Certainly, there is a need to contain some aspects of 'informal justice' – such as YOP hearings – by limiting power differentials, challenging arbitrary outcomes, rendering procedures open, accountable and contestable under the rule of law, but it is not clear that this cannot occur in interest-based and party-centred negotiations as distinct from rights-based and lawyer-centred proceedings. An emphasis upon forms of negotiation of the parties' common interests, rather than their legal entitlements as the basis for settlement, requires legal oversight. What is important, as Braithwaite (1998) has argued, is that these two polarities are kept in a tense relationship, in which one serves to correct the excesses of the other: 'a legal formalism that enables informalism while checking the excesses of informalism' (Braithwaite, 1999:106).

Panels become reformalized

Pressures for reformalization of YOPs could come from a number of directions. One might be the regular involvement of solicitors in the panel process, as discussed above; another might be the administrative demands produced by the sheer volume of panel meetings to be processed in a short space of time. In addition, there is a danger that referral orders may end up reproducing the magistrates' court not only in form and process but also in terms of the composition of lay members. The ability of YOTs to attract young people as well as representatives from a broad range of ethnic minority groups will be vital to disociate panels from the perceived inadequacies of lay involvement in the magistracy. In the longer term there remains the danger of creating quasi-professionals of community panel membership. Some of the lessons from the 1980s experiments in 'informal justice' were that programmes established in the name of 'community mediation' soon became increasingly formalized and professionalized, often under external pressures (Merry and Milner, 1993).

The cost of panels exceeds expectations

There may be a growing recognition that even though the system is based on unpaid volunteers (like the lay magistracy), it is far from cheap (bearing in mind the cost of training, advice and information providing, the slow pace at which they work and other supporting infrastructures which are required simply because they are volunteers). Moreover, if panels opt for intensive contracts, these too will be expensive to administer and support. Here, we are reminded of the tension between pressures to minimize cost and the restorative urge to incorporate the human (and for some the spiritual) dynamics in conflict negotiation which take time. In essence, one of the central appeals of panels over courts is that they should accommodate sufficient time for the parties to engage with and voice the 'things that matter' to them, as Daly notes: 'time for anger and forgiveness, and time for several justice principles – not just one – to be expressed' (2000b:45).

Potentially confused roles and responsibilities

The referral order and YOP model present a number of possible sites of tension in that they potentially confuse the roles and responsibilities of a number of key actors with implications for conflicts in implementation.

Between the court and panel

One of the key issues relates to how the magistracy will react to the reduced discretion and marginal role provided for it by the 1999 Act. Magistrates may question the transfer of significant judicial discretion away from the youth court to YOTs and the loss of authority that this implies. As Rob Allen has commented with regard to the reforms introduced by the Crime and Disorder Act 1998, 'if there is one weakness ... it relates to the extent to which magistrates have been brought on board' (Allen, 2000:22). This is particularly problematic, for, as Gelsthorpe and Morris note, referral orders do not supplant court proceedings; rather they supplement them (1999:219). Is the contract part of the sentence? This question has both philosophical and practical consequences. First, it has implications for the voluntary or coercive nature of the process, and second, it has implications for whether the panel meetings are to be the subject of Article 6 of the ECHR and within the jurisdiction of the Human Rights Act 1998. This has significant relevance for questions concerning the right of young people to have legal representation at panel hearings.

The fact that the court can annex a referral order with certain ancillary orders, such as compensation orders for costs and exclusion from football matches (s. 4(2) and (3)), may result in tangible ambiguities. First, it constrains the role of the panel, which might (or might not) wish to attach such conditions to a contract. Second, and more fundamentally, it offends the declared restorative intent of the panel process, as it imposes – through a coercive court order – something (such as compensation) which the young offender might otherwise agree to voluntarily.

As Wonnacott notes, 'If the offender has already been the passive and resentful object of a criminal order for the offence, there is plainly little scope for the processes of restorative justice thereafter' (1999:283). Moreover, it opens up the possibility of conflicting provisions in the court order and the panel contract.

The fact that the court determines the length of the contract, from the outset, without delegating a power to panels to terminate early (or extend) its duration, would seem unduly to fetter the work of panels. For example, if the young offender completes the contract early (say within the first four months of a 12-month contract) through his or her own commitment to it, the panel will still need to keep meeting and therefore may need to find additional activities for the young person to pursue. Perversely, this may penalize young people who strive to complete successfully their contract in a timely manner.

Between the YOT and community members of the panel

According to the Guidance the role of the YOT panel member is 'to advise on the potential components of the contract, the availability of suitable interventions, and to ensure proportionality' (para. 3.55). And yet, is the YOT member accountable for decisions arrived at by community panel members or are they just there to provide information? Moreover, the YOT member will often have been doing extensive work behind the scenes in advance of the panel. If the community members are to lead – through numerical domination and leadership/chair – then what is the role of the YOT member? This is different from Scottish Children's Hearings where all three members are lay people assisted by a reporter who has no decision-making role.

Between parent(s) or guardian and young person

At many panels attendance of both the young person and his/her parent(s) will be ordered by the court. Any resultant contract will have to be signed by the young person and the panel, but it is not clear that the parent(s) or guardian need to agree to, or sign, the contract even in the event that it includes activities which may require their involvement or participation. The pluralizing of responsibility (by incorporating parents into contract activities) here potentially confuses accountability. Moreover, this raises the question: if the contract imposes obligations upon the young person's parent(s), is the young person to be held accountable for the failings of others? If not, then how does a panel require (enforce!) parental compliance with the terms of the contract?

Joint decisions and negotiated 'contracts' tie the various parties into collective outcomes but often fail to identify lines of responsibility. As authority is 'shared' it becomes difficult to disentangle and can become elusive.

Principal dynamics and future questions

Managerialism and restorative justice: normative and administrative tensions

There is both an explicit and implicit managerialism at the heart of New Labour's reforms. In many ways recent policy initiatives have intensified the 'new public management' (NPM) reforms introduced under previous Conservative governments since the mid-1980s. These reforms have seen a significant restructuring of the public sector and the role of the state, as well as the introduction of a new regulatory style and managerial culture. NPM reforms represent a cluster of ideas and strategies which variously have sought to: hive off certain traditional aspects of public service delivery to the private sector; introduce private sector management methods to the public sector; flatten bureaucratic hierarchies; measure performance by results set against clear objectives; disaggregate separable functions into quasi-contractual or quasi-market forms; introduce purchaser/provider distinctions; open up provider roles to competition between agencies and private interests; and advocate a 'closeness to the customer' (see Hood, 1998). Under New Labour the managerialist urges to objective setting, performance measurement and output-fixation, notably through 'league table' comparisons, have reached a new zenith. This is particularly apparent with regard to crime control in the Crime and Disorder Act 1998 and the managerial processes introduced to implement the local crime and disorder strategies (Crawford, 1998).

Restorative justice has both normative and administrative appeals. Many of the normative appeals – that it is party-centred; relational; reintegrative and repairs the harm – may be undermined by the desired needs of efficiency and economy. Moreover, the administrative and managerialist appeals are themselves often in tension or contradictory. Bottoms (1995:24) highlights three forms of managerialism, which he refers to as: 'systemic', 'consumerist' and 'actuarial'. These may also increasingly come into conflict. As I have argued elsewhere, the 'consumerist' and 'systemic' aspects of managerialism are not always happy bedfellows (Crawford, 2001).

For restorative justice, however, the tensions between its normative and managerial objectives present striking practical concerns. For example, there is a serious question as to whether the current emphasis on speed through the system and the reduction of delay – through fast-tracking and the introduction of statutory time limits – can allow the proper development of restorative justice. Notably, there is a potential tension with victim consultation and input – which often take time if victims are not to be unduly pressurized and their needs are to be addressed sensitively. With regard to referral orders, this raises the question: will victims want to attend the first panel meeting to be held within 15 working days of first court appearance and potentially soon after the offence was committed? The early findings from research into the reparative work of YOTs sound a note of caution, in that they suggest that fast-tracking may undermine a victim-centred approach. The author of the interim Home Office report wisely noted that 'fast-tracking is best regarded as a means of achieving the aims of increasing the accountablility of offenders, reducing the risks of reoffending and meeting the needs of victims rather than as an unyielding end in its own right' (Dignan, 2000a:3). Consequently,

> Speeding up the trial process for its own sake could diminish the prospects for victims to receive direct reparation or take part in mediation. It could also make it less likely for offenders – after due deliberations as to their culpability and the most appropriate response – to be unambiguously confronted with the consequences of their actions.
>
> (Dignan, 2000b:134)

The implications of this for referral order panels are even more stark, here, than for other restorative aspects of YOTs' work. The requirement under national standards for youth offending teams that initial panels meet within 15 working days of referral orders being made could constitute precisely such an 'unyielding end in its own right' and undermine the intended victim input into the process.

More broadly, the pressure on output and outcome measurement risks marginalizing process aims that are central to restorative justice principles. Measurement fixation produces a trade-off between efficiency and a broader approach to effectiveness, based not on policies, which allow for easy quantification of results, but policies designed to foster public confidence and meet public expectations and, in the restorative justice context, meet the needs of the diverse parties.

There is also an important actuarial logic, which informs the youth justice reforms. Identifying risk factors is an important element of intensive early intervention. Assessing the young offender is a central aspect of the referral process. To this end, the YJB has commissioned the development of the ASSET tool. ASSET allows for a risk assessment profile to be developed and altered through progress reports. YOTs will be required to complete an ASSET profile, which must be updated if more than three months have elapsed (Guidance, para. 3.9). The YOT will often have a previous record of the young person, including a risk assessment and progress report, carried out in relation to a final warning.

These and analogous 'actuarial' techniques divide the youth population into statistical and behavioural categories organized around 'knowledge', 'risk' and 'probabilistic calculations' about future behaviour. With their future orientation, such techniques regulate aggregates and sub-populations at the intersection of certain categorical indicators, as part of a strategy of 'managing dangerousness'. Some commentators suggest that this 'new penology' (Feeley and Simon, 1992) focuses less on the individual's biography as an explanation for the causes of their offending, but more on assessment information about the possibilities of future conduct. Not only is the calculation of future risk an inexact science; it also has implications for the way in which systems construct their objects as 'enterprising offenders' who are enlisted by regimes of choice with incentives and disincentives as 'entrepreneurs' of their own personal development. As in other aspects of contemporary crime control, the offender is perceived as a 'rational choice actor'. This is reflected in the rationalistic construction of a progressively tiered process of response to crime: from reprimand to final warning to referral order and beyond (with little scope for going back). According to Feeley and Simon, such developments reflect the manner in which 'justice is increasingly understood not as a rational system but through the rationality of the system' (1994:178). In this context, it is argued, membership of certain risk categories becomes increasingly a defining criterion of personal identity and social organization.

This rationalization of justice and emphasis upon the enterprising offender enlisted in a regime of choice, also apparent in the centrality of the 'contract' within the referral order process and of 'agreements' within other restorative aspects of the legislation, gives rise to a number of further issues. The first is the ambiguity that lies in the coercive nature of the contractual process. Contracts and agreements appeal to a consensual ideal of mutually negotiated outcomes. Yet, as Wonnacott notes:

> Notwithstanding that the imagery is overwhelmingly consensual, in substance the contractual basis of the referral order is a sham, because

all the negotiating power is in the hands of the youth offender panel. There are two reasons for this imbalance of power. First, the offender has nothing to bargain with. Secondly, the offender is unlikely to have the resources or information to enable him to exploit whatever bargaining position he might have had to enable him to negotiate.

(1999:281)

However, this raises two issues. The first is that all restorative processes in and around criminal justice systems embody 'incentives' and subtle 'inducements' (Silbey and Merry, 1986), as well as outright 'coercive sticks' which may undermine absolutist notions of 'voluntariness'. What this demands, as Walgrave (2000) maintains, is that restorative justice must confront, acknowledge and negotiate the reality of coercive power which structures and frames criminal justice and state power therein. The second issue is that contracts (whether in business or not) invariably play upon an 'overwhelmingly consensual' imagery and yet are the products of 'power imbalances'.

There is a further tension between the managerialist urges of government and the philosophy of restorative justice. On the one hand, there is the centralist desire to control, to issue guidance, to ensure minimum standards, and to authorize, license, audit and inspect the doings of others. On the other hand, there is the fluid and creative potential of party empowerment that informs the principles of restorative justice and which demands flexibility, deliberation and adaptation to circumstances. This 'governing at a distance', whilst maintaining the reins of standardized authority and intervention, produces what I have elsewhere referred to as an ambiguous mode of governing 'at arm's length but hands on' (Crawford, 2001:63–4).

Let me conclude by highlighting some of the broader trends and wider criminological dynamics that infuse the recent legislative changes and the future questions to which these may give rise, particularly for their restorative ambitions.

Earlier and more intensive intervention: the end of 'diversion' and minimum intervention?

The changes to the cautioning system introduced by the 1998 Act through reprimands and final warnings have created a much more rigid, tiered structure of incremental (and potentially not-to-be-repeated) steps with little discretion. To use the baseball analogy deployed in the American 'three strikes legislation', the new reforms have created a framework of 'two strikes and you're in' – in court, that is! The referral order adds to this by creating a 'third strike'. There is a danger that courts will view referral orders as a 'last chance' and adopt an increasingly punitive approach to those who breach them or who are considered to have squandered their 'last chance' by appearing subsequently in court.

Not only is there the distinct possibility of significant 'net-widening' and 'mesh-thinning' (Cohen, 1985), as young people are drawn into and through the system more rapidly, but also that the increased intensiveness of response may be a hammer to crack a nut. Not only is there the question of proportionality to consider, but also there is the more fundamental issue that responses to crime – even restorative ones – should not be, or even cannot be, the appropriate site for redressing society's more structural inequalities and ills. Criminal justice, after all, is intrinsically reactive, bound up with state coercion and limited in its scope. As such, it is not the source of a society's civility. It should, however, reflect and express that civility, particularly with regard to the treatment of all those who turn to, or are caught up in, its machinations. In claiming a centrality in the construction of a just social order, restorative justice proponents (Pranis, 2001) can accord to reactions to crime an overriding position which they may not deserve.

We should not forget that social, educational, health, employment and housing policies rather than criminal justice policy (regardless of whether this is restorative or not) are the appropriate means through which to address aspects of deprivation which influence the concentration of offending behaviour and constitute the primary vehicles for the construction of a just and equal social order. To do otherwise would be to reduce inequality to something which is perceived to be a 'problem' only in so far as, if extreme enough, it is disruptive of social order or results in incidents of crime.

The criminalization of disorder: widening the reach of the criminal law?

Within the Crime and Disorder Act 1998 particularly, but also the Youth Justice and Criminal Evidence Act 1999, there is a significant criminalization of previously sub-criminal or non-criminal activities. This is to be found in the abolition of the presumption of *doli incapax*, the introduction of local evening curfews for children and of 'anti-social behaviour orders' (ASBO) as well as the increasing concern for incivilities, disorder and quasi-criminal activities in the community safety aspects of the 1998 Act (see Crawford, 1998). For example, concern has been expressed that the order is indiscriminate and sweeping, containing no requirement that the behaviour which triggers it should be serious or persistent or that it requires an actual victim; a hypothetical victim is sufficient (Gardner et al., 1998). As such, it may end up confusing the annoying or disagreeable behaviour of neighbours with criminal conduct. The consequences of an order are extensive in that it authorizes a vast array of prohibitions, which are regarded as necessary to protect the community from further anti-social behaviour by the defendant(s). Breach of an order can lead to criminal prosecution and imprisonment of up to five years. The penalty of breach does not necessarily have to be proportionate to the gravity of the underlying conduct. However, rather like the child curfews, initially they have been little used. In the first 14 months after they came into effect in April 1999, not one curfew was implemented and there were only 80 ASBOs taken out in England (*The Times*, 29 June 2000), much to the consternation of government ministers. At the Local Government Association conference in Bournemouth in June 2000, Jack Straw criticized councils for not making greater use of ASBOs. He claimed ASBOs to constitute a 'powerful weapon', which 'should be used swiftly where circumstances demand it, not just against the very hard cases of unacceptable behaviour' (*The Independent*, 29 June 2000).

Nevertheless, this widening of the reach of the criminal law and the criminalization of disorder constitutes a process of 'defining deviancy up' (Krauthammer, 1993). Here, the previously 'normal' is declared deviant and the deviant is unmasked residing within the normal. Perversely, this can have the inadvertent consequence of increasing the demand for crime control and judicial intervention. In part, this criminalization of disorder reflects a greater intolerance for certain youthful conduct – evocatively captured by the *en vogue* notion of 'zero tolerance' policing – but it also expresses a certain ambivalence in political responses to contemporary limitations of state governance.

The appeal to community participation: whose community?

Restorative justice immediately raises questions about legitimacy, as it reconfigures the notion of the 'public interest' through its appeal to a wider notion of stakeholders and to more localized normative orderings which rely upon 'private' and 'parochial' forms of social control (Crawford and Clear, 2001). Ideally, the normative order should emerge from the extended parties themselves, rather than being imposed from above. And yet this tends to presuppose a rather unproblematic consensus, without addressing the question of what the moral community *is*. The restorative justice response tends to assume organic wholeness of a given collectivity, one which accords little space to, or acknowledgement of, intra-community conflict and diversity of value systems. And yet, will victims and offenders always belong to the same moral community? Some restorative justice initiatives explicitly attempt to recognize and accommodate the cultural needs of specific parties or even cultural differences between victims and offenders. This may extend to the selection criteria for lay panel members or other parties to the dispute and/or its location and format. However, this recognition of multicultural heterogeneity raises a number of normative, as well as practical, dilemmas. For example, which cultural identities (ascriptions of difference) are sufficiently appropriate or worthy to be acknowledged and accommodated within the process of 'representation' or structure of negotiation? How inclusive can such a 'moral community' be, before it loses its capacity to induce compliance and encourage conformity?

If lay panel members are representatives of the community rather than the state, then the question is: upon what notion of representativeness does their legitimacy rest? Does it rest on the mere fact that they are not employed by the state? Moreover, there is a further troublesome contradiction in that the more attached to the community lay panel members are, the less likely they are to hold the required 'detached stance' which constitutes a central value in establishing facilitator neutrality and legitimacy. The more that facilitators or panel members represent particular interests or value systems, the greater the danger that the interests of one of the principal parties may become sidelined or lost altogether. Ironically, of course, it is exactly this pressure to provide neutral and detached facilitators that increases the likelihood of professionalization of lay panel members and the formalization of otherwise fluid and open restorative processes.

Perversely, perhaps, the expanded notion of stakeholder in restorative justice can serve to dilute the centrality of the primary parties: the victim and offender. It can hand power to parents, community members, service providers, trainers and para-professionals (potentially with their own interests to serve) which coalesce around restorative justice programmes, be they the new 'experts' in techniques of 'reintegrative shaming', 'conference facilitation' or 'mediation'. The somewhat pessimistic conclusion reached by Yngvesson, in relation to the San Francisco Community Boards, was that community empowerment may be possible only for a privileged 'internal community' of volunteers rather than the external 'community of neighbours' (1993:381).

It warrants noting that public participation and active citizenry in reactions to crime are paradoxical. They hold out the potential for a more participatory civil society and deliberative democracy. However, the dangers of 'participatory pluralism' turning into 'populism' are ever-present, particularly in times of social fragmentation and mistrust. The lessons from crime prevention research are that active citizenship, once extolled, can become difficult to control.

Welfarist civilizing mission – or a bastardized form of 'moral scolding'?

As I have argued elsewhere (Crawford, 1998), the recent reforms resonate with a form of 'communitarian moralism' which asserts the need to restore communities and their moral voices, requiring a greater emphasis upon individuals' responsibilities towards, rather than rights over, their communities (Etzioni, 1993). In the current politics of New Labour, obligations are both social and individual, and the 'prime motto' for the new politics is 'no rights without responsibilities' (Giddens, 1998:65). There is a concern that this moralism embodies particularly authoritarian notions of appropriate parenting and acceptable youthfulness, ones which may be at odds with the contemporary cosmopolitan and diverse forms of plural family life, ethnic cultural attachment, sexual orientation and youth culture. Some of the interventions introduced by the recent legislation – from the youth curfew and anti-social behaviour order to the parenting order and referral order – may criminalize 'difference' and 'difficulty', as well as pathologize certain ways of living, through programmes of activities produced in response to harms caused through offending.

There is a central paradox in the idea of imposing civility through coercion which echoes throughout current reforms, notably in the use of various curfews and court-based orders – such as the ASBO, reparation order, referral order and the parenting order – behind which stand criminal sanctions. Research suggests that strategies such as victim/offender mediation and work with parents are most effective where they are voluntary rather than compulsory. There are concerns as to the efficacy and effectiveness of such compulsory orders. This kind of intervention is less likely to be effective with uncooperative parents or young offenders.

Conclusion

The various provisions in both Acts adopt a 'shotgun' approach to restorative justice whereby notions of restoration have been fed into a variety of stages in the youth justice process, from reprimand through final warning to referral orders and beyond into reparation orders. The eclecticism of origin and penal philosophy of the influences upon the current politics of youth justice means that reforms in the name of restorative justice, such as the introduction of referral orders, offer both great potential and significant pitfalls. The reforms offer an opportunity to encourage a stronger, more active and participatory civil society by increasing public participation in the deliberative processes of youth justice. They aim to consider the impact on victims and others involved, be they family, kinship, friends or members of broader networks of interdependencies. They also endeavour to explore how communities can assist in the processes of restoration and conflict resolution. They challenge traditional state paternalism and monopoly by seeking to empower diverse stakeholders in the resolution of conflicts – most notably young people, their parents and victims of crime. Implicitly, they seek to limit the role of criminal justice professionals. Moreover, they question many of the modernist assumptions about professional expertise and specialization by breaking down institutional boundaries through partnership working, notably in the shape of YOTs. They afford the possibility to turn away from the 'populist punitiveness' of recent years. However, they may also become caught up in the logic of such punitiveness, facilitate greater and earlier intervention in the lives of young people and hence extend the net of state control.

Moreover, the pluralization of responsibility that restorative justice heralds acknowledges the limits of the sovereign state in respect of crime control and security. It introduces an acknowledgement that the causes of crime extend beyond the reach of the traditional criminal justice system. This responsibilization presents dangers of a blurring of responsibilities of the state and those of individuals – victims and offenders – as well as communities and other networks of 'care'. Such strategies of 'responsibilization' (Garland, 1996) should seek to clarify rather than confuse the distribution of responsibilities and simultaneously ensure the appropriate conditions under which the exercise of those responsibilities can be fulfilled and maximized.

The sites of ambiguity and tension which I have sought to highlight are likely to determine the manner in which the future shape and direction of restorative justice for juveniles unfolds in England and Wales. The extent to which the changes outlined in this chapter will succeed in the quest to accord to victims, young offenders, their families and other stakeholders greater agency and voice within the process of responding to acts of crime remains a central challenge for all those implementing and influencing the future direction of developments. In what ways they enable the restoration of harm to individuals and communities and the reintegration of offenders, as well as allow for restorative principles to take root at the heart of juvenile justice, remain to be seen.

Notes

* I would like to thank Gordon Bazemore, John Braithwaite, Kathy Daly, Susan Flint, Tim Newburn, Heather Strang and Richard Young for comments on earlier drafts of this chapter.
1. Local authorities and the police may apply to a magistrates' court for an ASBO for any person (or group) who has acted in an anti-social manner 'that caused or was likely to cause harassment, alarm or distress to one or more persons not of the same household' as that person. The minimum duration for an order is two years.
2. In some police areas restorative principles are being introduced as early as the reprimand stage. For example, Thames Valley Police conduct what they refer to as 'restorative conferences' (where a victim or victim representative is present) and 'restorative cautioning' (where there is no victim or representative present) in the context of a reprimand.
3. However, the experience of the pilots suggests that, in practice, this does not always occur. Dignan cites examples where victims had not been consulted or had not given their consent (2000a:15–16).
4. The practice in Thames Valley Police borrows largely from what is known as the Wagga Wagga model of police-run community conferences, named after the town in Australia where it was first implemented.
5. Now consolidated in the Powers of Criminal Courts (Sentencing) Act 2000.
6. Morris and Gelsthorpe (2000) note a similar eclecticism in the origins of the Crime and Disorder Act provisions.
7. This was changed quite late in the day, during the passage of the legislation, to a policy of 'lay community involvement' to include 'a broad cross-section of the community that has an interest in supporting young people and preventing offending' (Paul Boateng, Standing Committee E, House of Commons, 4th sitting, 15 June 1999 (afternoon), col. 76).
8. In the light of the evaluation of the pilots this time limit has been extended to 20 working days in cases involving a direct victim.
9. The legislation specifically allows for a certain degree of change in the light of experience of the pilots or following full implementation across the country. For example, if it appears that other categories of young offenders could also benefit from referral orders, s. 2(3) of the Act allows the Secretary of State to amend the categories of offenders eligible for the sentence subject to the agreement of Parliament by *affirmative resolution procedure* (this means that Parliament must discuss and approve the amendments).
10. For example, in one jurisdiction in Australia (Queensland) victims have veto power over whether a community conference is to be held. Moreover, in three Australian jurisdictions (Western Australia, Queensland and New South Wales) victims have veto power over the conference agreement or plan if they are present at the conference (Daly, 2001).

References

Abel, R. (1973) 'A Comparative Theory of Dispute Institutions in Society', *Law and Society Review* 8, 217–347.

Allen, R. (2000) 'Youth Justice: What Does the Future Hold?', *Safer Society*, July, 21–2.

Audit Commission (1996) *Misspent Youth*. London: Audit Commission.

Audit Commission (1998) *Misspent Youth '98*. London: Audit Commission.

Ball, C. (2000) 'The Youth Justice and Criminal Evidence Act 1999, Part I', *Criminal Law Review*, 211–22.

Bandalli, S. (1998) 'Abolition of the Presumption of Doli Incapax and the Criminalisation of Children', *Howard Journal* 37, 114–23.

Bazemore, G. and L. Walgrave (1999) (eds) *Restorative Juvenile Justice*. Monsey, NY: Criminal Justice Press.

Bottoms, A.E. (1995) 'The Philosophy and Politics of Punishment and Sentencing', in C. Clarkson and R. Morgan (eds) *The Politics of Sentencing Reform*. Oxford: Clarendon Press, 17–49.

Braithwaite, J. (1989) *Crime, Shame and Reintegration*. Cambridge: Cambridge University Press.

Braithwaite, J. (1998) 'Restorative Justice', in M. Tonry (ed.) *Handbook of Crime & Punishment*. New York: Oxford University Press, 323–44.

Braithwaite, J. (1999) 'Restorative Justice: Assessing Optimistic and Pessimistic Accounts', *Crime and Justice: A Review of Research* 25, 1–127.

Christie, N. (1977) 'Conflicts as Property', *British Journal of Criminology* 17 (1), 1–15.

Cohen, S. (1985) *Visions of Social Control*. Cambridge: Polity Press.

Crawford, A. (1998) 'Community Safety and the Quest for Security: Holding Back the Dynamics of Social Exclusion', *Policy Studies* 19 (3/4), 237–53.

Crawford, A. (2000) 'Salient Themes Towards a Victim Perspective and the Limitations of Restorative Justice', in A. Crawford and J.S. Goodey (eds) *Integrating a Victim Perspective within Criminal Justice*. Aldershot: Ashgate, 285–304.

Crawford, A. (2001) 'Joined-Up but Fragmented: Contradiction, Ambiguity and Ambivalence at the Heart of New Labour's "Third Way"', in R. Matthews and J. Pitts (eds) *Crime, Disorder and Community Safety: A New Agenda?* London: Routledge, 54–80.

Crawford, A. and T.R. Clear (2001) 'Community Justice: Transforming Communities Through Restorative Justice?', in G. Bazemore and M. Schiff (eds) *Restorative Community Justice*. Cincinnati: Anderson Publications, 127–49.

Crawford, A. and T. Newburn (2002) 'Recent Developments in Restorative Justice for Young People in England and Wales: Community Participation and Restoration', *British Journal of Criminology* 42 (3), 476–95.

Crawford, A. and T. Newburn (2003) *Youth Offending and Restorative Justice: Implementing Reform in Youth Justice*. Cullompton: Willan Publishing.

Daly, K. (2000) 'Revisiting the Relationship between Retributive and Restorative Justice', in H. Strang and J. Braithwaite (eds) *Restorative Justice: From Philosophy to Practice*. Aldershot: Dartmouth.

Daly, K. (2001) 'Conferencing in Australia and New Zealand: Jurisdiction Variation, Research Findings, and Future Prospects', in A. Morris and G. Maxwell (eds) *Restorative Justice for Juveniles*. Oxford: Hart Publishing.

Davis, G., J. Boucherat and D. Watson (1988) 'Reparation in the Service of Diversion: the Subordination of a Good Idea', *Howard Journal* 27, 127–34.

Dignan, J. (1999) 'The Crime and Disorder Act and the Prospects for Restorative Justice', *Criminal Law Review*, 48–60.

Dignan, J. (2000a) *Youth Justice Pilots Evaluation: Interim Report on Reparative Work and Youth Offending Teams*. London: Home Office.

Dignan, J. (2000b) 'Victim Consultation and Reparation: Preliminary Lessons from Pilot Youth Offending Teams', *Probation Journal* 47 (2), 132–5.

Downes, D. (1998) 'Toughing it Out: From Labour Opposition to Labour Government', *Policy Studies* 19 (3/4), 191–8.

Downes, D. and R. Morgan (1997) 'Dumping the Hostages to Fortune?: The Politics of Law and Order in Post-War Britain', in M. Maguire, R. Morgan and R. Reiner (eds) *The Oxford Handbook of Criminology*. Oxford: Clarendon Press, 87–134.

Etzioni, A. (1993) *The Spirit of Community*. New York: Simon & Schuster.

Feeley, M. and J. Simon (1992) 'The New Penology: Notes on the Emerging Strategy of Corrections and Its Implications', *Criminology* 30 (4), 449–74.

Feeley, M. and J. Simon (1994) 'Actuarial Justice: the Emerging New Criminal Law', in D. Nelken (ed.) *The Futures of Criminology*. London: Sage, 173–201.

Fionda, J. (1999) 'New Labour Old Hat: Youth Justice and the Crime and Disorder Act 1998', *Criminal Law Review*, 36–47.

Gardner, J., A. von Hirsch, A.T.H. Smith, R. Morgan, A. Ashworth and M. Wasik (1998) 'Clause 1 – The Hybrid Law From Hell?', *Criminal Justice Matters* 31, 25–7.

Garland, D. (1996) 'The Limits of the Sovereign State: Strategies of Crime Control in Contemporary Society', *British Journal of Criminology* 36 (4), 445–71.

Gelsthorpe, L. and A. Morris (1999) 'Much ado about nothing – a critical comment of key provisions relating to children in the Crime and Disorder Act 1998', *Child and Family Law Quarterly* 11 (1), 209–21.

Giddens, A. (1998) *The Third Way*. Cambridge: Polity Press.

Graham, J. and B. Bowling (1995) *Young People and Crime*, Research Study 145. London: Home Office.

Hagell, A. and T. Newburn (1994) *Persistent Young Offenders*. London: Policy Study Institute.

Hallett, C. and C. Murray, with J. Jamieson and B. Veitch (1998) *The Evaluation of Children's Hearings in Scotland, Volume 1*. Edinburgh: The Scottish Office Central Research Unit.

Hines, J., S. Holdaway, P. Wiles, N. Davidson, J. Dignan, R. Hammersley and P. Marsh (1999) *Interim Report on Youth Offending Teams*. London: Home Office. http://www.homeoffice.gov.uk/yousys/sheff.htm.

Home Office (1994) *Criminal Statistics England and Wales 1993*. London: HMSO.

Home Office (1997a) *Tackling Youth Crime: A Consultation Paper*. London: Home Office.

Home Office (1997b) *No More Excuses – A New Approach to Tackling Youth Crime in England and Wales*, Cm 3809. London: Home Office.

Home Office (1999) 'Referral Orders – A Short Guide' at http://www. homeoffice.gov.uk/yousys/referral.htm.

Home Office (2000a) *Final Warning Scheme: Guidance for Police*. London: Home Office.

Home Office (2000b) *Final Warning Scheme: Guidance for Youth Offending Teams*. London: Home Office.

Home Office (2000c) *Implementation of Referral Orders – Draft Guidance for Youth Offending Teams*. London: Home Office.

Home Office (2001) *Implementation of Referral Orders – Guidance for Youth Offending Teams*. London: Home Office.

Hood, C. (1998) *The Art of the State*. Oxford: Clarendon Press.

Karp, D. and K. Walther (2001) 'Community Reparative Boards in Vermont', in G. Bazemore and M. Schiff (eds) *Restorative Community Justice*. Cincinnati: Anderson Publishing, 199–217.

Krauthammer, C. (1993) 'Defining Deviancy Up', *The New Republic*, 22 November, 20–5.

Marshall, T.F. (1996) 'The Evolution of Restorative Justice in Britain', *European Journal on Criminal Policy and Research* 4 (4), 21–43.

Marshall, T.F. (1999) *Restorative Justice: An Overview*. London: Home Office.

Marshall, T.F. and S. Merry (1990) *Crime and Accountability*. London: HMSO.

McConville, M., L. Hodgson, L. Bridges and A. Pavlovic (1994) *Standing Accused*. Oxford: Clarendon Press.

Merry, S.E. and N. Milner (1993) (eds) *The Possibility of Popular Justice*. Ann Arbor, MI: The University of Michigan Press.

Morris, A. and L. Gelsthorpe (2000) 'Something Old, Something Borrowed, Something Blue, but Something New?: A Comment on the Prospects for Restorative Justice Under the Crime and Disorder Act 1998', *Criminal Law Review*, 18–30.

Morris, A. and G. Maxwell (2000) 'The Practice of Family Group Conferences in New Zealand: Assessing the Place, Potential and Pitfalls of Restorative Justice', in A. Crawford and J.S. Goodey (eds) *Integrating a Victim Perspective Within Criminal Justice*. Aldershot: Ashgate, 207–25.

Morris, A. and G. Maxwell (2001) (eds) *Restorative Justice for Juveniles*. Oxford: Hart Publishing.

Morris, A., G. Maxwell and J. Robertson (1993) 'Giving Victims a Voice: A New Zealand Experiment', *Howard Journal* 32 (4), 304–21.

NACRO (1998) *A Guide to Diverting People from Crime, Northamptonshire Diversion Unit*. London: NACRO.

Newburn, T. (1998) 'Tackling Youth Crime and Reforming Youth Justice: The Origins and Nature of "New Labour" Policy', *Policy Studies* 19 (3/4), 199–212.

Newburn, T., A. Crawford, R. Earle, S. Goldie, C. Hale, G. Masters, A. Netten, R. Saunders, K. Sharpe and S. Uglow (2001a) *The Introduction of Referral Orders into the Youth Justice System*, First Interim Report, RDS Occasional Paper No. 70. London: Home Office.

Newburn, T., A. Crawford, R. Earle, S. Goldie, C. Hale, G. Masters, A. Netten, R. Saunders, K. Sharpe, S. Uglow and A. Campbell (2001b) *The Introduction of Referral Orders into the Youth Justice System: Second Interim Report*, RDS Occasional Paper No. 73. London: Home Office.

Newburn, T., A. Crawford, R. Earle, S. Goldie, C. Hale, G. Masters, A. Netten, R. Saunders, K. Sharpe and S. Uglow (2002) *The Introduction of Referral Orders into the Youth Justice System*, Home Office Research Study 242. London: Home Office.

Pollard, C. (2000) 'Victims and Criminal Justice System: A New Vision', *Criminal Law Review*, 5–17.

Pranis, K. (2001) 'Restorative Justice, Social Justice and the Empowerment of Marginalised Populations', in G. Bazemore and M. Schiff (eds) *Restorative Community Justice*. Cincinnati: Anderson Publications, 287–306.

Raine, J.W. (2001) 'Modernizing Courts or Courting Modernization?', *Criminal Justice* 1 (1), 105–28.

Sanders, A. and R. Young (2000) *Criminal Justice*, 2nd edn. London: Butterworths.

Silbey, S. and S. Merry (1986) 'Mediator Settlement Strategies', *Law and Policy* 8, 7–32.

Walgrave, L. (2000) 'Extending the Victim Perspective Towards a Systemic Restorative Justice Alternative', in A. Crawford and J.S. Goodey (eds) *Integrating a Victim Perspective within Criminal Justice*. Aldershot: Ashgate, 253–84.

Waterhouse, L., J. McGhee, N. Loucks, B. Whyte and H. Kay (1999) *The Evaluation of Children's Hearings in Scotland: Children in Focus*, Social Work Research Findings No. 31. Edinburgh: The Scottish Office Central Research Unit.

Whyte, B. (2000) 'Between Two Stools: Youth Justice in Scotland', *Probation Journal* 47 (2), 119–25.

Wonnacott, C. (1999) 'The Counterfeit Contract – Reform, Pretence and Muddled Principles in the New Referral Order', *Child and Family Law Quarterly* 11 (3), 271–87.

Wright, M. (1991) *Justice for Victims and Offenders*. Milton Keynes: Open University Press.

Yngvesson, B. (1993) 'Local People, Local Problems, and Neighborhood Justice: The Discourse of "Community" in San Francisco Community Boards', in S.E. Merry and N. Milner (eds) *The Possibility of Popular Justice*. Ann Arbor, MI: The University of Michigan Press, 379–400.

Young, R. (2000) 'Integrating a Multi-Victim Perspective into Criminal Justice Through Restorative Justice Conferences', in A. Crawford and J.S. Goodey (eds) *Integrating a Victim Perspective within Criminal Justice*. Aldershot: Ashgate, 227–51.

Young, R. and B. Goold (1999) 'Restorative Police Cautioning in Aylesbury from Degrading to Reintegrative Shaming Ceremonies', *Criminal Law Review*, 126–38.

Young, R. and C. Hoyle (2000) 'Examining the Guts of Restorative Justice', *Criminal Justice Matters* 40, 32–3.

9

'I can't name any names but what's-his-face up the road will sort it out': Communities and Conflict Resolution*

Sandra Walklate

Introduction

> The fear amongst people in this ward that you're pointing to now is that it could be the next door neighbour that burgles you, you're not sure who to trust. When there's no trust amongst a neighbourhood it perpetuates. They're looking over their shoulder and they're thinking there's a fear and perhaps its doesn't exist. ... these people in this ward have no trust of even their own sons.
>
> (Comment recorded in a police focus group in Bankhill: fictitious name)

> It's always been a self policing community, always has been. But I think that is also a weakness in the community. They still dislike vandalism and they dislike most of the crime that goes on, but they are unwilling to break from the community chapel. The community is strangling itself, because they have to break free from old traditions and the old 'I can't name any names but what's-his-face up the road will sort it out'.
>
> (Comment recorded in a police focus group in Oldtown: fictitious name)

The observations above were made during the course of a two-and-a-half-year comparative study of two similarly structured high-crime areas. That study was concerned to address how people who live in, got work in, go to school in, and generally manage their sense of well-being in those areas. The recognition of both the differences and similarities between those areas which this study uncovered, and which are reflected in the quotes above, informs this discussion of conflict resolution. This study began its life very much situated within the 'fear of crime' debate. However, during its course, it became apparent that the concept of fear was not as helpful as it was originally presumed. The social regularity and solidarity associated with one of the areas under investigation led to an appreciation of the ways in which the concept of trust might be more helpful in understanding the empirical findings. Misztal (1996:97) states that:

> Social regularities are obtained in an unreflective manner because we act in an habitual way for day-to-day purposes. Hence trust plays the role of a protective mechanism, which prevents chaos and disorder by helping us cope with the volume and complexity of information. It reduces the anxiety caused by ambiguity and the uncertainty of many social situations. It also tends to endow social order with meaning and neutralises its arbitrariness.

Understanding the importance of trust also informs the discussion that follows. At a practical level the quotes above highlight the central concern of this chapter which is what, if any, is the relationship between the nature of community dynamics and the way in which conflicts might be resolved at a community level? At a conceptual level, an understanding of such community dynamics raises a number of questions concerning how the notion of conflict resolution has been understood and whether there are alternative understandings. However, before addressing these issues in greater detail, it will be of value to make a number of observations about the notion of conflict resolution and its current saliency.

Conflict resolution: some observations

It is now over 20 years since the first appearance of the essay by Christie in *The British Journal of Criminology* entitled 'Conflicts as Property' (Christie, 1977). In that essay Christie was keen to make the case that the law, and the emergence of the professions associated with the practice of law, in taking disputes out of people's own hands, had not only denied them the right to manage their own disputes but had also, as a consequence, denied the development of more constructive and imaginative responses to such disputes. While arguably this was primarily a polemical essay, its influence has nevertheless been significant in lending weight to what Pepinksy and Quinney (1991) entitled 'Criminology as Peace-Making'. This version of criminology is concerned to look for ways in which it might be possible to marry knowledge about crime and offending with a more constructive approach to the use of penalties for such behaviour. One of the themes in this work places emphasis on 'reintegration'; of finding ways in which the offender is made aware of the consequences and impact of their offending behaviour yet simultaneously is reintegrated into (rather than ostracized from) the community.

At a theoretical level the work of Braithwaite (1989) has been influential in promulgating these ideas. His hypothesis is that in societies where there is a strong commitment to place collective interests over individual interests there are stronger incentives for people to conform and lower crime rates. His prime example of such a society is Japan. The practical implication of Braithwaite's hypothesis is concerned to establish mechanisms whereby offenders could be subjected to such collective processes, shamed by them, and subsequently reintegrated into the community with a stronger commitment to those community norms and values (that is, unlikely to reoffend).

To date many examples of such practices have emanated from Australia and New Zealand in the form of 'community conferences' or 'family conferences'. The relative success or failure of such practices is difficult to determine. What is less difficult to discern is the impact that such ideas have had on contemporary criminal justice policy thinking. In the UK faced by such criticism as the following:

> The current system for dealing with youth crime is inefficient and expensive, while little is done to deal effectively with juvenile nuisance. The present arrangements are failing young people – who are not being guided away from offending to constructive activities. They are also failing victims ...
>
> (Audit Commission, 1996:96)

It is little wonder that much has been made of the reparation scheme being run by the Thames Valley Police, following the Australian and New Zealand model. Chief Superintendent Perry is quoted as saying about the scheme: 'While young offenders feel ashamed of what they have done, this allows them to make good and to go back into their community' (*Crime Prevention News*, 1998:12).

As is discussed by Crawford in this volume, this theme of making good has been incorporated into the Crime and Disorder Act 1998. Such an emphasis rests on the hope that young people especially can be educated through the process of reparation on both the nature and the impact of their offending behaviour. It is hoped that as a consequence this will prevent reoffending and simultaneously repair some of the damage done to the victims of crime. In this way it is believed that both the victim and the offender can be reintegrated into the community, their conflict of interests resolved.

Such a policy commitment reflects the view that such strategies are not only workable but will have the desired effect; that is, reduce offending behaviour. It also reflects a presumption that such strategies constitute the preferred model of conflict resolution, and make sense, for both the individuals involved in the process and the communities of which they are a part. None of these presumptions are necessarily borne out by the evidence; neither do they necessarily follow from the policies themselves. Part of the reason for this lies in the tension between what might be expected from policy, what actually has been and can be delivered from such policy, and understanding what might already exist informally as ways of making amends between members of a community. In some respects, then, the questions raised by Christie (1977) still remain unanswered. In order to address some of these concerns this chapter will focus on two themes: what is known about the formal response to making amends, and what the empirical investigation referred to above has revealed about the informal responses to the same process.

Conflict resolution as making amends: the formal response

In the context of criminal justice policy, the Crime and Disorder Act 1998 is not the first occasion that the notion of 'making amends' has received policy support. In 1985 four pilot reparation projects were established as a result of an all-party penal affairs group report entitled 'A New Deal for Victims'. The underlying motivation for the establishment of these projects was, arguably, much more concerned with the overall benefits that such schemes might have for the (then) ailing criminal justice system than for the benefits to the victim or the offender; however, the effectiveness of these initiatives (alongside others) was examined and reported on. Such reports offer an initial insight into the workability of such schemes.

Early research into initiatives such as these suggests that what might be an attractive idea in theory is difficult to render meaningful in practice for all parties to the process (see, for example, Blagg, 1985; Launay, 1985; Walklate, 1986). As far as the Home Office pilot projects were concerned, Marshall and Merry (1990) report on the difficulty of securing victims willing to be involved, and Davis (1992) concludes that such schemes faced four key problems: marginalization by the courts; ambiguity of purpose, lack of clarity as to what might constitute making amends; and limited relevance to the participants. Arguably, problems such as these constitute the surface manifestation of deeper tensions between different styles of delivering justice presumed by the concept of reparation as compared with that contained within the criminal justice system. These tensions reflect a wider debate about the nature of punishment and society's right to punish, questions which are not of central concern here. They do suggest, however, that such processes of making amends, as *incorporations* to the current criminal justice process, are always likely to meet with difficulties.

So research suggests that making amends as a policy directive within the criminal justice system faces considerable practical difficulties. It raises philosophical tensions, and, as a consequence, does not appear to meet its desired objectives, for the victim or for the offender. Moreover it fails in its objectives for wider society either in the form of reintegration or conflict resolution, current legislative commitments notwithstanding. It would therefore be easy to conclude that reparation as a form of conflict resolution is doomed to failure as a systemic response to offending behaviour despite the much-lauded success of the Thames Valley Police initiative. Such a conclusion, however, would be short-sighted.

The idea of 'making amends' can take many forms, not all of which are expressed within the formal policy or legislative framework. As has been observed above, one of the dilemmas faced by initiatives informed by such a notion is how to render such a process meaningful to the participants. In other words, the idea in and of itself may be sound; what is required is a better understanding of how to make the idea work. Thus the question is raised concerning how, in what form, and in what circumstances does making amends work and for whom? It is at this point that it will be of value to return to the issue of community dynamics with which this chapter began.

Conflict resolution as making amends: informal responses

The notion of 'community' has been increasingly employed as a rhetorical device to invoke alternative policy responses to those of direct state intervention. This is nowhere more the case than in the context of criminal justice policy. The literature on 'making amends', in particular, is full of rather nostalgic references to the concept of community as an ideal form of social control (Cohen, 1985). Yet, when the possibility of alternative forms of conflict resolution is raised, such community images seem rather less than nostalgic. This statement requires fuller explanation.

The idea of a self-policing community, as highlighted in the comment from a police focus group at the beginning of this chapter, is problematic in contemporary terms, for more than just police officers. It is a notion which constitutes a fundamental challenge to the assumptions frequently made about high-crime areas in policy, political and academic debate. This has perhaps been made most explicit in the current embrace by the Labour Party of Etzioni's (1996) version of communitarianism. However, high crime-communities are not necessarily disordered, disorganized, fearful places as either current policy initiatives may assume or the more historically informed notion of social disorganization has led criminologists to believe. As alluded to in the quotation referred to above, high-crime areas can be experienced as highly ordered and safe places for the people who live there (see for example, Merry, 1981; Walklate, 1998). This was one of the key findings from this longitudinal comparative study of two similarly structured, predominantly white high-crime areas less than two miles apart.

During the course of a two-and-a-half-year research project in the two high-crime areas, the importance of understanding both the differences and the similarities between them as potentially 'self-policing communities became apparent. Indeed it was the different ways in which community dynamics around the routine daily management of crime and crime related issues which appeared to feed significantly into the sense of well-being possessed by the people who lived there' (Evans and Walklate, 1996). In the area referred to above as a self-policing community, part of the understanding of the dynamics underpinning this community was rooted in understanding the local processes of making amends. The following stories are illustrative of aspects of these processes. The first is presented here in the words of a retired police superintendent who spent some considerable time during his career working in this area. In referring to a warehouse incident of 1992, he says:

> Carpetworld came about as a response to the police and the community in the area, trying to solve a particular problem of stolen vehicles being used against property in the area. But again to raise their own profile, to inspire intimidation and to create the myth. They were then doing public displays of handbrake turns. There was a considerable amount of danger to resident kids in the area. In fact, there was one team who were doing it a lot and knocked three thirteen-year-old

girls down. They were not badly hurt, fortunately, but they could easily have been killed ...

The same people still live in that sort of area [———Road], those three girls, initially the incident was reported to us – this is one of the area which you mentioned at the beginning where an approach was made from Mr M and some of his friends to intercede and sort the business out. Eventually the people in the car had to pay £650 or make an offer, they didn't have to make an offer of £650 to the parents of the kids concerned. The other side of that offer is that if you don't take it you get done over for being a grass, so it's a bit like an offer you can't refuse.

The second is articulated in this quotation from a middle-aged female resident in this area:

There's also a positive side sometimes. It doesn't always work one way, sometimes it works another. I've heard of a case a few months ago where a lad had broken these pensioners' windows and he'd run off. Now a couple of people found out who he was, dragged him back to this house and asked if it was him. When they said it was, they made him apologise, gave him a thump and told him if he was anywhere near there again they would come back for him. Needless to say he's never been anywhere near. It has its own rules as well they sort things out there selves.

These stories allude to the importance in this local context a 'no-grassing' rule (Evans, Fraser and Walklate, 1996). They also allude to the belief in the powerful presence of a 'Mr Big': 'I can't name any names, but what's-his-face up the road will sort it out.' They are comments which acknowledge the presence of a local organized criminal gang commonly referred to as the 'Salford Firm'. The presence of this gang in the locality is widely acknowledged, both in official discourses about the area and in individual community members' articulations about their locality. The nature and extent of its presence and its influence can be disputed, but what is less in doubt are the aspirations towards some local political credibility associated with the gang's activities. This is worthy of further comment.

In reality this gang probably comprises 20 to 30 'full-time' members, involved in criminal activity at varying levels of seriousness. Understanding the political aspirations associated with these activities provides a different insight into understanding the phenomenon of 'grassing'. This is alluded to and then clarified in the following quotations taken from an interview with the spokesperson for the 'Salford Firm'.

> 'Cos a lot of people accuse us, saying 'That————, you know, encourages them to break the law', but I don't have to encourage them to break the law, people who make them break the law are those who are responsible for them breaking the law, you know the councillors, the politicians – *these* are the ones who are responsible, not me. I only advise them how *not* to get caught, you know, don't do this, don't go robbing off old ladies, mugging old ladies – it's not on – you know, don't go robbing and burgling ordinary people's houses of televisions, you know, if you want to go and rob, go to the Quays.

So:

> You've not got to be a grass, I mean, there's a code in that – when is it right to inform the police about a certain thing, and when is it not correct. You know, if someone rapes somebody or interferes with a kid, or mugs an old lady, as far as the correct-minded thing for people, you know what I mean, the concern – if somebody hands them in then they're not grassing, you know, but if somebody goes and says 'so and so has done a ram-raid' or 'so and so has done a post office', then it's grassing, it's not acceptable.

Moreover, when incidents occur which break this moral code:

> we try to find out who's done it and if they're really young people, then we'll given them a talking to, you know, to say 'it's out of order', you know what I mean, but if it's someone who's supposed to be, you know, responsible and knew what they was doing – knew that it was a woman on her own or a woman with three kids and no husband, you know what I mean, they get a smacking ... [this is] street politics, you know, 'It's not on – there's too many burglaries going on, we've got to put a stop to it', you know what I mean. We don't go and tell the police, you know, we've got to handle it ourselves, you know, there's got to be some kind of, you know, street justice, so when the lads find out who's going round breaking into people's houses, they get a smacking, you know what I mean, and it's called 'taxing', you know ...

The importance of this expressed 'moral code' lies not so much in what it does and does not deliver but in the fact that for local people it has a saliency in their routine daily lives: 'I can't name any names but what's-his-face up the road will sort it out'. This belief is given an added 'truth content' in two main ways: a clearly identifiable arena of 'public shaming' in the locality; and the viability of local stories of 'sorting things out'. Each of these will be commented on in turn.

In this locality there is an area in which nearly all the local amenities are located: a supermarket (now closed), a chemist, a betting shop, a job centre, a post office, a public house and a hardware store. This area provides the physical space for 'public shaming' ceremonies. In other words, if there is graffiti to be written, and written about a particular person who it is believed has 'grassed', then their name will appear here. It is here that people are named for the rest of the community to see: and since this is the only place where there are any local amenities it serves its purpose as a public arena of shame very well.

The use of this arena in this way serves a number of functions in the local community. It certainly provides a high-profile forum in which members of the local community are made aware of not only who has been accused of 'grassing' but also of the consequences of being so accused. The desire to avoid such 'public shaming' is one basis on which local choices are made concerning whom to inform about what. Moreover, the actual appearance of names in this arena serves a deeper function: it marks, potentially, those whose behaviour has been deemed outside the locally accepted norms and values. As such it serves to remind all members of this community of those norms and values. In this sense, there may be a similar functional relationship between the processes associated with public shaming and the further maintenance of social solidarity and cohesion found within this local community – processes not dissimilar, perhaps, to those identified in Puritan communities by Erikson (1966).

Of course, the naming of 'grasses' is not the only way that people can be made to pay for offending the community norms and values. As the quotations above have suggested, other informal mechanisms also exist for bringing offending behaviour into line. Those mechanisms might be monetary or physical but they nevertheless appear to exist as meaningful in the local stories of making amends. Such stories, of course, do not always highlight the ways in which recalcitrant young offenders are brought back into the community line; they can also highlight the ways in which 'grasses' can be reminded of the penalties for the more serious forms of this behaviour. For example:

> There is a sort of code, I think I touched on this briefly, that you do not victimise women. For instance, we persuaded a woman to go as a witness on two really serious assaults against a gang member. One was really an attempted murder and it took ages to get to court, it was

before we had the sophistication of witness-protection that we have got today, but we did our best but they kept intimidating this woman. They kept shouting at her and calling her names, making threats towards her, but when they eventually did something physical they didn't do it to her, they did it to her son. They caught him, he was in his late teens – nineteen – and they stuck a screwdriver up his bottom which caused all sorts of terrible internal injuries which is one of the traditional techniques of dealing with what they call a grass.

(Retired police superintendent)

Embedded in the processes described here is a recognition and acceptance that crime and the criminals are part of the community (not outside it), are often known by name, and that people can be made to make amends in a whole range of informal but none the less meaningful ways. The examples offered here are clearly suggestive of a hierarchy of local mechanisms of making amends, which in some respects mirror the conventional criminal justice process. Such a hierarchy may start with a warning (the use of graffiti for 'public shaming'), may then move to the requirement to pay compensation (as in the case of the car accident), may then take the form of an assault (if the offence has been to harass old people or engage in other behaviour which offends the local code of ethics), and finally may take the form of serious physical assault (if the 'no-grassing' rule has been broken in a way which is threatening to the local structures of control). The presence of this hierarchy of 'making amends' is well understood locally, reflects a sense of local justice which bears some similarities (and obviously some significant differences) to that of more conventional conceptions of justice, but nevertheless seems to have an effect. If, then, one of the principles of conflict resolution is that 'the community wants reassurance that what has happened was wrong, that something is being done about it, and that steps are being taken to discourage its recurrence' (Zehr, 1990:195), this certainly seems to be the case in this high-crime area.

Of course, not all high-crime areas share the same view of the crime problem. In the other area under investigation the problem looked somewhat different. In this area people did not feel protected by what they know to be going on in their locality, but threatened by it. As one female resident observed:

When I see blokes on bikes now, they might be innocent, but to me they're part of the gang and that's who they are and I do not like to see anyone on a bike.

(Established female resident)

Or as one elderly resident reported:

> There was a boy with a wheelbarrow full of tools, he broke into the park keeper's shed and walked out of the park with the wheelbarrow ... I'm sixty-three, I was frightened to stop him; it was a boy of about twelve. I know he'll come back with his pals.

Or, expressed more graphically:

> It's like terrorism really.
>
> (Male established resident)

As one of the quotations at the start of this chapter illustrated, the people in this area 'had no trust, not even of their own sons'. In an area like this it is the absence of the belief that 'what's-his-face up the road will sort it out' which is problematic; in other words, it seems to be the absence of the highly organized criminal gangs and the associated gang culture which is a salient factor here in contributing to a lack of sense of well-being in this locality especially for older people (Walklate, 1998). For people in this area, they knew about the nature of criminality there, but they did not know specifically who the criminals were (other than 'all young people') and, moreover, they knew that no one, including themselves, was likely to call such problematic young people to account. There were no working formal means, and no publicly articulated informal means for making amends. For people in this area the belief that 'This area is going downhill rapidly' arguably acted as a metaphor not only for what they saw going on in their locality, but also for what was not happening, along with their own sense of helplessness to intervene in what was going on around them.

To summarize: the preceding discussion has highlighted the importance of understanding community dynamics in order to offer a fuller picture of what 'making amends' might look like. It has clearly demonstrated that formal policy responses notwithstanding, the presence and absence of informal processes may also make a significant contribution to what might be considered to be locally meaningful processes of reparation. Understanding processes such as these leads to a more fundamental appreciation of what mechanisms might need to be in place to enable not only the informal processes to work, but also more formal processes. In some respects what is being articulated by the people in both of these communities is encapsulated in the quotation taken from Misztal (1996) offered at the beginning of this chapter. The presence of trust facilitates the management of daily uncertainty; its absence exacerbates it.

Conclusion: trust, making amends and conflict resolution

It has been argued elsewhere that the processes which underpin the surface manifestation of the community dynamics alluded to above reflect different kinds of trust relationships. They demonstrate, in this context, the salience of the questions of: whom you can trust; how you trust; how much you can trust; and when you can trust (Nelken, 1994). The sense of well-being that individuals construct for themselves in the two high-crime areas discussed above is mediated by their understanding of where they find themselves in relation to a 'square of trust' (Figure 9.1) (Evans, Fraser and Walklate, 1996; Walklate, 1998).

The manifestation of this 'square of trust' depends upon where individuals find themselves situated between the different corners of this square. In the two areas discussed above, these relationships were certainly differently constituted. In one, for example, it meant not trusting state officials to sort things out in favour of expecting the more locally organized criminal gangs to do something. Moreover, in the absence of the gang doing anything, other issues might be managed as a result of the presence of kinship and family networks: knowing someone's father or brother. Both processes, arguably, contributed towards local social

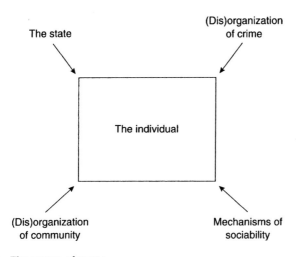

Figure 9.1 The square of trust

solidarity. In the second area, it meant offering a generalized trust to state officials to sort things out but with little expectation that this might happen and little to put in the place of an official response.

In other words, in one community the boundaries of what is acceptable and unacceptable are clearly known, adhered to and managed. Penalties for transgressing the boundaries seemed fairly swift and certain to follow, as demonstrated by the presence of a hierarchy of making amends. In the other community such processes, either formal or informal, appeared absent and the uncertainty thus generated seemed to have a deleterious effect on community relationships. In one community people trust that something will be done; in the other they do not. Moreover, this discussion, while emphasizing the importance of trust at this community level, is not intended to imply its lack of relevance in other settings. The importance of the presence and/or absence of trust is as relevant to the formal criminal justice policy response as it is to the informal processes discussed here.

For example, in discussing the problems of incorporating reparative approaches within a retributivist criminal justice system, Davis (1992:205) makes the following observation;

> The offender's action implies lack of concern for, perhaps even denial of, the victim's right to security in his or her person or possessions. So, reparation, if it is to be complete, must make some attempt to make amends for the victim's loss of the presumption of security ... Trust that the appropriate morals standards are shared by the offender cannot be restored by a court order requiring the offender to share those standards. If the victim is to be reassured, he or she must believe that the attitude in question is freely expressed.

This observation, arguably, encapsulates one of the key problems with the concept of reparation in particular, as formally interpreted, and arguably with peacemaking criminology in general. It raises the fundamental question: what constitutes a meaningful way of making amends for all the participants involved – the victim, the offender, the local community, the professional agencies, and wider society? It is not difficult to appreciate that a victim of burglary may be unwilling for an offender to engage in house repairs as a means of making amends for their offence; the trust that such a process requires may be too great an expectation to make of the victim even if benefits might accrue to all other participants to the process. How can all these interests be met in a manner that does a service to them all? The answer to this question may be that it is not possible to achieve all these objectives and, as the research reported here illustrates, it may not be possible to formulate a policy which would work in all localities (or at least a policy which can be shown works better than that already in place!), despite the enthusiasm of the proponents for 'making amends'.

To conclude: in the absence of transforming the nature of the criminal justice process as a whole, it is likely that a formal policy response in the form of making amends will continue to miss the mark for victims and offenders (though maybe not for the professionals involved). Moreover, in the absence of a genuine understanding of how people routinely manage their day-to-day lives (especially in high-crime areas), we may forever be formulating formal policy responses which will continue to miss the mark, especially for the people living in those areas. It may offend (some) current sensibilities to accept that in some high-crime areas alternative systems of control seem to work quite well in preventing reoffending behaviour for some kinds of crimes; and that urban life is not incompatible with trust and social cohesion, as Gellner (1989) assumes. Neither is the case made on the basis of some of the evidence here that it is necessary to 'restore communities' (Anderson and Davey, 1995), as the comunitarians would argue. The case may be made, however, that if it is desirable for policies rooted in the traditions of conflict resolution to work, they need to be more realistically informed about the mechanisms which sustain or threaten social regularity. One of those mechanisms lies in understanding the processes associated with the manifestation of trust at interpersonal, community and organizational levels. It is in the lacunae between these different levels that policies can be made to work or made to fail.

Note

* The research referred to in this chapter was funded under the ESRC's Crime and Social Order Initiative, grant number L210252036.

References

Anderson, P. and K. Davey (1995) 'Import Duties', *New Statesman and Society*, 3 March, 18–23.

Audit Commission (1996) *Misspent Youth*. London: The Audit Commission.

Blagg, H. (1985) 'Reparation and Justice for Juveniles', *British Journal of Criminology* 25, 267–79.

Braithwaite, J. (1989) *Crime, Shame and Reintegration*. Oxford: Oxford University Press.

Christie, N. (1977) 'Conflicts as Property', *British Journal of Criminology* 17, 11–15.

Cohen, S. (1985) *Visions of Social Control*. Cambridge: Polity Press.

Davis, G. (1992) *Making Amends: Mediation and Reparation in Criminal Justice*. London: Routledge.

Erikson, E. (1966) *Wayward Puritans*. New York: John Wiley.

Etzioni, A. (1996) *The New Golden Rule*. London: Profile Books.

Evans, K. and S. Walklate (1996) *Community Safety, Personal Safety, and the fear of Crime: End of Project Report*. London: ESRC.

Evans, K., P. Fraser and S. Walklate (1996) 'Whom do you trust? The Politics of Grassing on an Inner City Housing Estate', *Sociological Review* 44 (3), 361–80

Gellner, E. (1989) 'Trust, Cohesion, and The Social Order', in D. Gambetta (ed.) *Trust: Making and Breaking of Co-operative Relations*. London: Basil Blackwell.

Launay, G. (1985) 'Bringing Victims and Offenders Together', *Howard Journal of Criminal Justice* 24, 200–12.

Marshall, T. and S. Merry (1990) *Crime and Accountability*. London: HMSO.

Merry, S. (1981) *Urban Danger*. Philadelphia: Temple University Press.

Misztal, B. (1996) *Trust in Modern Societies*. Cambridge: Polity Press.

Nelken, D. (ed.) (1994) *The Futures of Criminology*. London: Sage.

Pepinsky, H. and R. Quinney (eds) (1991) *Criminology as Peace-Making*. Bloomington, IN: Indiana University Press.

Walklate, S. (1986) 'Reparation: A Merseyside View', *British Journal of Criminology* 26, 287–98.

Walklate, S. (1998) 'Crime and Community: Fear or Trust?', *British Journal of Sociology*, December.

Zehr, H. (1990) *Changing Lenses: A New Focus for Crime and Justice*. Scottsdale, PA: Herald Press.

Index

Africa, background 83–5; human rights/OAU approach 85–93; and non-governmental organizations (NGOs) 90, 92
African Charter on Human and Peoples' Rights 12, 85, 86, 87–8, 89, 91, 94n–5n
African Commission on Human and Peoples' Rights 12, 87, 89–92, 96n
Afrikaner nationalist criminology 22, 25, 37
Akers, R.L. 105, 108, 114
Alaska Native Justice Center (ANJC) 162
Alaska Native villages 13–14, 153; background 159–60; and boutique courts 166; and circle sentencing 164–5; community courts 162–4; languages 161, 168n; problems for 167–8; public safety issues in 166; and seeking a viable bush justice in 165–7; state government judicial options 161–5; teen courts in 156, 158–62; traditional conflict resolution in 161; traditional social control in 160–1; tribal courts 162, 168n; Village Public Safety Officers in 165
Alexander, J.C. 122
alternative dispute resolution (ADR) 8, 10
American Society of Criminology 106, 108, 113
Anderson, K. 120
Arikaner nationalist criminology, pure form of 22–3

Barak, G. 127
Bauman, Z. 16
Bazemore, G. 5
Beck, R.J. 155
Beirne, P. 46, 62
Bew, P. et al 53

Black Lawyers' Association (BLA) 26
Boheringer, G. 53
Bottoms, A.E. 34, 194
Bowling, B. 174
Braithwaite, J. 4–5, 8, 16, 111, 191, 210
Brewer, J. 71
British Crime Surveys 172
Brogden, M. 38
Brown, R.H. 129

Caulfield, S. 127
Centre for the Study of Violence and Reconciliation (South Africa) 27
Children, Young Persons and their Families Act (1989) (New Zealand) 172
Christie, N. 2–3, 171, 209
circle sentencing 164–5
Cohen, S. 41, 58, 59–60, 63–4
Commission of Inquiry Regarding the Prevention of Public Violence and Intimidation (South Africa) 26
community courts 162–4
community justice 15, 27–30, 32–4, 38–41, 57, 199–201; moral code of 214–17; and no-grassing rule 214–15, 216; and public shaming 216–17; and self-policing 213–14; and social control 212–13; and trust 218
Community Law Centre (South Africa) 27
Community Peace Foundation (South Africa) 27, 28
conflict, analogy to sex 2–3; appropriation of 2; change in nature of 6; conventional definitions 5; early warning/early action distinction 91, 97n; prevention of 6, 83, 93n–4n; relationship with crime 48–50, 70n

conflict resolution, and
    criminology/human rights discourse
    62–5; definition of 5, 17n;
    engagement with 1–2; and
    family/community conferences
    210; formal response 211–12;
    funding programmes for scholars
    62; informal responses 212–19;
    key features 6–8; large-scale 3–4;
    and making amends 210–21;
    management theory on 8–9; in
    Northern Ireland 57–65;
    observations on 209–11; origins
    5–6; relevance of literature 5–10;
    and restorative justice 171–2; and
    ripeness 7, 10; small-scale 2, 4;
    and state role/legitimacy 7–8, 10;
    and structural violence 6–7, 10;
    traditional Alaskan 161; and trust
    219–21
Correctional Services Act (1959)
    (South Africa) 32–3
Crime and Disorder Act (1998) 14,
    172, 175, 186, 194, 198, 210; and
    abolition of *doli incapax* 177, 198;
    key elements of 176–7, 203n;
    parenting order 177–8; reparation
    orders 179, 203n; reprimands/final
    warnings 178–80, 197, 203n; and
    YJB/YOTs 178
criminology, and conflict
    resolution/human rights discourse
    62–5; as dangerous discipline 16;
    explanatory/normative theory
    16–17; as important discipline
    1–2; as international/comparative
    project 57, 60–2, 72n; jobbing
    70n; as moral project 58, 59–60,
    71n; optimistic outlook 15–16; as
    political project 57, 58–9; role of
    59–60; transition/memory 72n–3n
criminology for a new democratic
    South Africa *see* progressive
    criminology
critical criminology, cooperative
    practices in 24–5, 27; institutional
    changes in 27; and Northern
    Ireland conflict 50–7; political
    aspects 24

Cullen, F. 136
Curle, A. 103

Davis, G. 211, 220
Del Olmo, R. 63
Diamond, S. 149
Downes, D. 175

Elias, R. 126
England/Wales, background to
    reforms in 172–6; legislation
    176–87; potentially confused
    roles/responsibilities in 192–4;
    principal dynamics/future questions
    194–201, *see also* referral orders;
    youth justice; youth offending
    panels (YOPs); youth offending
    teams (YOTs)
Erikson, E. 216

Farrell, M. 53–4
feminism 30–1
Ferndale, C. *et al* 29
Foundation for Inter-Ethnic Relations
    84
Fuller, J.R. 126, 128

Gelsthorpe, L. 177, 192
Gilbert, K. 136
Gilligan, J. 111
Gouldner, A. 1
Grachacha arbitration hearings 4
Graham, J. 174

Habermas, J. 126
Hall, S. 55
Hansson, D. 30
Hillyard, P. 55
human rights 11–12, 47, 55, 57, 59,
    68, 72n, 73n; advantages of
    engagement with 64–5; and
    criminology/conflict resolution
    discourse 62–5; law 83–4;
    monitoring 83, 94n; and OAU
    85–92; state/international
    difference 84–5, 94n; violations
    83, 94n
Human Rights Act (1998) 65, 192
humanitarian law 84

Independent Commission on Policing
(Northern Ireland) 61, 72n
Institute of Criminology and Criminal
Justice (Queen's University,
Belfast) 56
international criminal court 4
International Criminal Tribunal 85
IRA (Irish Republican Army) 47, 69n

Jamieson, R. 45
justice 2; alternative paradigm 3;
bush 165–7; and class
inequality/power relations 50;
juvenile 30, 32–3, 41n, 42n, 57;
rationalization of 196–7; social
148; state/popular 38–9, 147–8

Klerk, F.W. de 25
Knopp, F.H. 128

legal reformism 11, 22, 63; and
abolition of death penalty/corporal
punishment 32; development of
23–4, 27; prognoses for 37–8;
revival in 25–6
Lemert, E. 58

McEvoy, K. 47
Magee, K. 71
Marshall, T. 139, 211
Marx, K. 107, 109, 117, 119, 120, 121
Matza, D. 46
mediation 3, 6, 136
Merry, S. 211
Mika, H. 121
Miliband, R. 53
Misspent Youth report (Audit
Commission, 1996, 1998) 174–6
Misztal, B. 209, 218
Mncadi, M. 28
Morgan, R. 175
Morris, A. 177, 192

National Association of Democratic
Lawyers (NADEL) 26
National Crime Prevention Strategy
(1996) (South Africa) 34, 35, 38
National Deviancy Symposium
(1960s) 50, 51, 70n–1n

National Institute for Crime
Prevention and Reintegration
(NICRO) (South Africa) 27
Nelken, D. 62
'New Deal for Victims, A' (1985)
211
Nina, D. 28
No More Excuses (1997) White Paper
175, 181–2
Northern Ireland, background 45–6;
belief in official version of events in
51; as bleak/soulless place 52, 71n;
Bloody Sunday Inquiry in 73n;
Bolsheviks/republicans in 53, 71n;
civil rights issues in 53, 54;
conflict resolution in 57–65;
control/surveillance in 55; critical
criminology in 11, 50–7; end of
Stormont 52–4; government of
52–3; lack of cohesive
criminological/criminal justice
research in 52; law/conflict
relationship 55; legal reformism in
11; lessons learned from 57–65;
objectivity of research in 51;
ordinary crime in 48–50, 70n;
paramilitary violence in 48–50,
70n; peace process in 61–2;
positivism in 11, 46–50; post-
ceasefire period 56–7; radical
eclecticism in 55–6; responding to
criminalization in 54–6, 71n–2n;
terrorism in 46–8; tiered policing
in 53, 71n; transition/memory in
65–8; truth-finding investigations in
65, 66, 67, 73n

O'Dowd, L. *et al* 54
Omar, D. 21
Organization of African Unity (OAU)
12, 83; adoption of Cairo
Declaration 86; Conflict
Management Centre (Addis Ababa)
87; conflict mechanism 86–7;
Field Operations Section 87,
95n; and human rights within
context of conflicts 85–92; peace
fund 87, 95n; recent
developments 87–8

Organization for Security and
Co-operation in Europe (OSCE)
85, 88, 91

peacemaking   4–5, 6–7, 12–13, 17n,
210
peacemaking criminology (PMC),
background   101–2; chaotic
syndrome   110–14; conservative
syndrome   109–10; incredibility
syndrome   114–15, 123–5; as
criminal justice praxis   125–6;
critics of   106–7; definition of
103; described   103–6; diversity of
views on   105–6; Enlightenment
background   118; functionalist
syndrome   108–9, 122–3; and
human nature   119–20;
institutional/systemic action
126–7; international/global action
126; interpersonal/intrapersonal
action   128; Marxian/radical
syndrome   107–8, 117–18; origins
of   103–4; peacemaking as
metaphor   129–30; praxis   120–2;
responding to critics   115–17;
transcendent values   118–19
People Against Gangsterism and
Drugs (PAGAD) (South Africa)   35,
41
Pepinsky, H.   111, 113, 118, 210
Pepinsky, H.E.   104
political approach   7, 8, 24, 57, 58–9
positivism, features of   68n; and
Northern Ireland   46–50; and
ordinary crime   48–50, 70n; and
terrorism   46–8, 51, 68n–9n
progressive criminology   22, 24,
29–30, 41n

Quinney, 124
Quinney, R.   103, 104–5, 107, 110,
116, 118, 210

referral orders   181–2, 198; increased
use of custody   188;
increased/fewer 'not guilty' pleas
189; over-intensive contracts   189;
potential unintended consequences

of   187–8; victims' interests not
served by process   189–90; and
YOPs   190–2; YOT's workload   188
Reintegrative Shaming Experiments
(Australia)   158
responsive regulation   4
restorative justice   2, 3–4, 4–5, 9,
13–14, 38, 111–12; background
135–8; community involvement
145; critical components of   143–5;
definition of   138–41, 171; effect of
conventional justice on   137; as
global social movement   171;
healing/putting right wrongs
144–5; importance of   171; and
intermediate punishments   136;
key stakeholders   143; limitations/
qualifications   141–2; mediation/
reparation programmes   136; as
mode of conflict resolution   171–2;
normative/administrative tensions
194–7; obligations/liabilities
143–4; outcomes   136–8, 145;
principles   141–2; recognition of
needs/competencies of offender
145; and restitution   137; risks
147; signposts/road ahead   145–50;
social justice   148; stakeholder
notion   200, 202; starting points
144; state justice context   147–8;
and teen/youth courts   153, 157;
values/philosophy   147; vestiture
148–9; victim/offender exchanges
136–8, 144; and violation of
people/interpersonal relationships
143; vision of community   149–50;
worrisome features of   135–8
Rothman, D.   136
Royal Ulster Constabulary (RUC)   47,
49, 51, 53, 54
Rubinstein, R.   7
Rwanda   84, 85

Salim, S.A.   87
Shearing, C.   38
Shiff, A.   156
Singer, S.I.   155
Sitka Native Justice conference (1996)
164

Sollenberg, M. 6
South Africa 10–11; administrative
  difficulties in 34; background
  21–2; challenges facing 40–1;
  comunity social ordering in
  27–30, 32–4, 38–41; constraints on
  change in 34–6; control of public
  demonstrations in 26–7; and
  control of public demonstrations in
  39; criminological ideas in new state
  31–4; criminology in time of crisis
  22–5; fear of crime in 34–5;
  feminist discourse in 30–1; forms
  of intervention in 28–31, 38–9;
  future possibilities/prognoses
  36–40; and introduction of lay
  assessors in 33–4; move from
  resistance to proactive intervention
  25–31; people's courts in 28;
  policing in 32; transitional period
  25–31; treatment of juveniles in
  30, 32–3, 41n, 42n
South African Police Services Act
  (1995) 32
Special Rapporteurs 89, 96n–7n
square of trust 15
state punishment 2
Sullivan, D. 104, 105, 128
Sumner, C. 50

Takagi, P. 136
technocratic approach 7–8
teen courts *see* youth courts
Teitel, R. 9, 66
terrorism 2, 46–8, 55, 68n–9n
Tesha, T. 83
Tidwell, A. 8
Tifft, L. 128
Tifft, L.L. 104
transitional justice 65–8, 72n, 73n
trust 218; lack of/observations on
  208–9; and making amends
  219–21; understanding 209
truth commissions 4, 65, 66, 67, 73n
Truth and Reconciliation Commission
  (South Africa) 3, 36, 40

Ulster Special Constabulary (USC)
  53, 54

UN Charter on Human Rights 86,
  94n
UN Economic Commission for Africa
  87
UN Security Council 85
Unger, R. 16
Universal Declaration of Human
  Rights 86, 94n
University of Witwatersrand (South
  Africa) 27
urbuntu 3

Villa-Vincenzio, C. 3
Volpe, M.R. 127

Wallace, A.F.C. 135
Wallenstein, P. 6
Walton, P. 1
Wexler, D.B. 156
Wilkinson, P. 69n
Women's Committee on Peace and
  Development 87, 95n–6n
Wonnacott, C. 193, 196–7
Wozniak, J.F. 120

youth courts, background 153;
  origins/development 153–4; and
  recidivism 158;
  rehabilitation/community
  involvement 167–8; restorative
  justice in 153, 156, 157;
  state/federal promotion of 158–9,
  161–2; theoretical perspectives on
  154–6; and therapeutic
  jurisprudence 156; volunteers in
  157–8
youth justice 13–15; ambiguity/
  tensions in 192–4, 202–3; and
  appeal to community participation
  199–201; cautioning policy 173,
  178, 203n; and criminalization of
  disorder 198–9; developments
  in 172; earlier/more intensive
  intervention 197–8; Home
  Office research study 174–6;
  legislation 176–87; and making
  good 210–11; new vision for
  173–4; number of crimes 172–3;
  referral orders 187–92; reforms

youth justice – *continued*
in   202; shot-gun approach   172,
173, 201–2; welfarist civilizing
mission/moral scolding   201
Youth Justice Board (YJB)   177, 178,
180
Youth Justice and Criminal Evidence
Act (1999)   14, 172, 175–6, 180–1,
198; the contract   187; evaluation
of pilots   184; referral order
181–2; youth offender panels
182–4
youth offender panels (YOPs), cost
exceeds expectations   191–2;

evaluation of pilots   184; meetings
185–7; members of   183–4; model
of   183; origins/inspiration
182–3; over-run by lawyers   190–1;
potential conflict with court
192–3; reformalization of   191;
training panel members   184–5
youth offending teams (YOTs)   177,
178, 179, 186, 187, 188, 192, 193,
202

Zehr, H.   3, 136